GODLESS -- Living a Valuable Life Beyond Beliefs

Jeff Rasley

Published by Midsummer Books

http://www.jeffreyrasley.com

ISBN-13:
978-0692324813 (Midsummer Books)

ISBN-10:
069232481X

TABLE OF CONTENTS

Foreword

I'm a descendent of strict Puritan ministers who were prominent religious and political leaders of the early colonial period in American history. Richard and Increase Mather were both presidents of Harvard College, famous preachers, and leaders of the Massachusetts Bay Colony. In 1688 Cotton Mather began an investigation into the strange behavior of the children of a Boston mason, John Goodwin. Reverend Mather's investigation led him to declare that "an Army of Devils" had invaded Boston and an Irish washerwoman named Mary Glover was one of them. Thus began the Salem Witch Trials.

My Puritan ancestors would have tried me for heresy had this book fallen into their hands. Calvinist Presbyterianism and conservative Republicanism run deep in my ancestral veins, but I reject all religious doctrines and political ideologies. This book explains why. My religion has evolved into a worship of, and gratitude for, the awesomeness of nature and the universe we live in. My politics are moderate pragmatism.

I was a life-long member of the Presbyterian Church until just a few years ago. I served as Sunday school teacher, deacon, elder, liturgical leader, and held the highest lay office in the church, Clerk of the Session. But my profession was law.

Living the life of a trial lawyer with the expected back-scratching involvement in local politics left me feeling unclean after twenty-five years of it. So I prepared to make a career change into the "higher calling" of my ancestors. I applied to become a candidate for ministry with the Presbyterian Church. I already had a Masters of Divinity from Christian

Theological Seminary having graduated as co-valedictorian with academic awards in theology, Greek, and Hebrew. The evaluation of the counselor, who conducted the psychological and personality assessments required by the Presbytery, was that I was "highly recommended" for the ordained ministry.

When I met with the Presbytery Candidates Committee for a final review, an elderly lady on the Committee declared, "You seem more like a Buddhist than a Calvinist." The Committee members were not impressed with my bloodlines or academic performance. Their "examination" revealed that my faith was based on values rather than "Reformed Trinitarian Theology". They offered to send me through a "Calvinist re-education" class and then to reconsider my fitness for ministry. I declined.

The financial rewards of owning my own law firm allowed me the time and flexibility to pursue other ways to wash clean the dirt of litigation. One was Himalayan mountaineering. Another was planning and fundraising for development projects in remote villages in Nepal. Instead of the higher calling of ordained ministry, it was mountain climbing that led me to an unexpected alternative vocation -- combining Himalayan trekking with culturally sensitive development work in Nepal.

"Philanthro-trekking" is the term I coined to describe combining Himalayan trekking with supporting development projects in remote villages in Nepal. Philanthro-trekking connected me with the Rai people of Basa village. Basa villagers own and staff the expedition company I partner with to organize Himalayan expeditions and tours. I have worked with the village on creative development projects in the Basa area, involving education, health, sanitation, and energy efficiency.

By trekking with and doing development work with friends from Basa village I have learned much about their way of life. My Nepali friends showed me how to climb

Himalayan peaks and they guided me to villages where seeing a "white man" was a rarity. The most precious gift I have received from Basa is their welcome into the community as "Jeff Dhai" (respected elder brother).

My fundraising for development projects in Nepal also led me to a Quaker Meeting in Indianapolis. One of the donors to the "Basa Village Project" is a member of First Friends Indianapolis. He asked me to speak to the Meeting about our project work. I was warmly welcomed and First Friends became the sponsoring organization of the Basa Village Project.

Calvinists believe that before the universe was created God had already decided the fate of all living things, some of us to be condemned to Hell and some to be graced with eternal life in Heaven. Those living a pious life and believing in the correct Christian doctrines may be predestined for Heaven. But only God knows for sure.

What a contrast with the traditional religion of the Rai people of Nepal and with the Quakers! The Rai are animists. They think every thing has spirit and so all creatures and things, even inanimate rocks, have value. There is no heaven or hell; all of our spirits are recycled. My friends in Basa village have the most profound commitment to community and respect for the environment of anyone I've ever known. They helped to show me the way out of believing in religious doctrines and political ideologies by pointing the way toward a values-based life in community.

Quakers have no official doctrines and their founder, George Fox, claimed that all people have a "divine spark" within them. I was surprised and impressed by these and other similarities between Quakers and the Rai people of Basa. The Rai are much more into drinking and dancing; Quakers prefer to meditate. Both communities recognize and respect the spirit in others, they have no creeds, and both communities emphasize living by positive values. I became a member of First Friends Indianapolis and visit Basa just about every year.

Eventually I escaped the law after a thirty-year sentence. Release from the law allowed me time to transform the Basa Village Project into a thirty-member nonprofit corporation and to teach classes at Butler University about philanthropy and operating nonprofit organizations.

I would like to share with you what I've learned through my gradual awakening out of the traditional faith of my ancestors with the help of the Rai people of Basa and Indianapolis First Friends. The book is about learning to live life guided by positive values and unlearning religious and political beliefs. I hope you will find practical value in what's offered within these pages for your own life and inspiration to contribute valuably to your community.

~ ~ ~

This book is dedicated to my friends in Basa village who have taught me the Rai people's way of valuing everything, but especially human community. It is dedicated to 90-year old Howard Taylor, a courageous atheist and devoted member of First Friends Quaker Meeting in Indianapolis. It is also dedicated to Ray Schaefer, who sacrificed his life to end the suffering of his partner. Ray valued the education of Palestinian refugee children "more than living another ten or fifteen years," and so gave up his life so that his estate would fund the Sabra-Shatila Scholarship Program "before he dissipated it on his own care in old age."

~ ~ ~

Some names and factual details are changed to protect the privacy of the innocent and guilty.

Part I: Believe nothing. Value every thing.

Chapter 1: Beliefs Divide Us; Values Unite Us

By "Godless" I mean living life without being controlled by the gods of religious doctrines or political ideologies. "Living a valuable life beyond beliefs" means using positive values to guide your life decisions rather than making decisions based upon beliefs. Beliefs are supposed truths which cannot be proved. They are ideas in our minds, which do not necessarily have any basis in the objective reality outside of our heads. For example, "I believe God the Father, Jesus Christ, and the Holy Spirit are three different and the same entities," makes sense if you are a believing Trinitarian Christian. If not, it sounds a bit crazy. Values are what you care about. Positive values are the characteristics that you try to embrace and emulate in becoming the person you want to be. I would like to be a more generous person; so, Generosity is a positive value I will try to embrace in becoming the person I want to be.

Beliefs divide us, values unite us. An example: I was chairman of a committee for the local YMCA. One of our purposes was to figure out ways to make the "C" (Christianity) more meaningful in the daily operation of the Y. All members of the committee were self identifying Christians, but went to different churches and had different theological points of view. Before we began to consider how to fulfill our task, I led a discussion of the six committee members on what we each thought Christianity meant in the context of the YMCA. Five of us agreed that it meant welcoming people of all faiths and any background and promoting traditional Christian-cultural values, like respecting others, being honest, taking care of your own health through proper diet and exercise, and spending time in prayer or meditation. One member became upset with the rest of us. "Paul" argued that the "C" meant the Christian faith. He agreed it was important to promote the values we discussed, but he thought the Y should evangelize for Christian beliefs. Paul resigned from the committee after he failed to persuade the rest of us that he was right and we were wrong. Paul's beliefs divided him from us, even though we were united with him on values.

That example may seem relatively trivial. What is currently happening in Syria, Iraq, Afghanistan, and in many other regions wracked by religious-political divides is not. Millions of lives are at stake because of the militancy of Islamic and other extremists. And, as long as the US remains the world's chief police officer, the lives of American soldiers (my son James being one) and the health of the economy is at stake. Our military has lost thousands of lives and suffered tens of thousands of combat injuries, and trillions of dollars have been spent in Afghanistan and Iraq, in large part, because of conflicting religious-political beliefs among the local populations.

The way forward toward a more peaceful world and harmonious communities is letting go of divisive beliefs and ideologies. Instead of trying to live according to a prescribed set of beliefs, we should try to guide our lives with positive values. Beliefs divide us into believers, those with different beliefs, and unbelievers. Values unite us in shared aspirations to become better persons living in better communities.

Most people in most cultures and countries share a similar set of fundamental values. That's why people of differing backgrounds generally get along with each other. Notice how diverse people from all over the planet speaking different languages manage to negotiate the sidewalks in Manhattan, Paris, or Tokyo without pushing, shoving, or any significant violence. Most of us most of the time practice the value of respecting other people's physical space.

Divisions arise and trouble begins when religious doctrines or political ideologies are more important than valuing Tolerance and Consideration for others. Caring more about the abstract ideas and beliefs of religions and political parties than about people has caused much pain and suffering in the world.

It is horrifying HORRIFYING what the Islamic Jihadists have done with suicide belts and beheadings. (Typing these words while revising the manuscript of the book news is just breaking that a young man, Peter Kassig, who grew up near where I live, has been captured by ISIS and is going to be murdered by beheading. Shock! Appalling! Inconsolable grief. Fury!) We cannot fathom how humans can be so inhumane and can murder and terrorize in the name of their religion. But religions and political ideologies have been the inspiration or excuse for slaughter and terror down through the ages. It was just twenty years ago that Serbian Christians raped and murdered thousands of Bosnian Muslims after Yugoslavia broke apart. Catholics and Protestants had just quit knee-capping and blowing each other up in Northern Ireland when the Bosnian War broke out in the 1990s.

I have traveled through forty-eight states in the US and over forty other countries. I have studied and written about the customs and cultures of Himalayan villagers in Nepal, Palauan islanders in Oceania, and the Outlaws of Kalalau on Kauai. My experience is that almost everyone, regardless of race, ethnicity, or culture, agrees with the fundamental value of trying to live healthy decent lives as individuals and helping out members of our communities that need assistance. I can't remember ever meeting a mature psychologically stable adult that thought it was wrong to take good care of your self or to offer help to those in need when you are able to. It's when there is a clash of beliefs over religion or politics that swords get drawn.

So you might be thinking that this guy believes it's better to live by a system of values than a system of beliefs. Isn't that a belief? Close but no cigar. The book offers evidence that the claim is true. It's not just belief.

Religious beliefs can't be tested. My claim can be tried out and proved for yourself. Consider this; you are probably already living according to numerous positive values, such as Honesty, Courage, Kindness, etc. Do you feel good about yourself and the direction your life is going, when your actions are true to the values you cherish? Are you approximating your best self when you act consistently with those values? When you participate in a group or community in which all members respect each other and relate to everybody in the group with kindness and honesty isn't that preferable to being in a group with people who treat each other disrespectfully? You can actually experience how your life is better and a community functions better when guided by positive values.

Now, try to test out some commonly-held religious beliefs; like, if you are Christian, Jesus was born of a virgin or Heaven awaits those who have the right faith. We can't confirm these beliefs experientially nor any other way, can we? We're just supposed to accept them as true without any supporting evidence.

If you were diagnosed with Ebola, would you put your faith in the local shaman, priest, minister, rabbi, imam, or would you prefer to be treated at the Emory University Hospital, whish successfully treated and released in August 2014 the first two Americans to return from West Africa with the disease? I suspect your choice would be the hospital where medical staff put their faith in the scientific method rather than religion. Researchers working on experimental drugs and physicians treating patients value results. They do not rely on religion.

When there are important decisions to make, the people most of us rely on are those with the relevant professional certification, be it medical, legal, tax-financial, or whatever. We value education, training, and experience. We either don't particularly care what religious or political beliefs the surgeon has, or we might prefer that she shares our beliefs, but what's most importance is competence. We value

Competence and we value results.

Religious popes and political potentates tell us, "You just gotta believe!" But believing does not make something hoped for happen or the imagined real. In *Field of Dreams* it wasn't enough just to believe they would come. Ray (Kevin Costner) had to build the ball park to make his dream a reality.

~ ~ ~

Some readers might experience this book as a paean to agnosticism and a sermon (maybe even a rant) against religion and politics -- guilty on both counts. But, you'll also experience an intellectual adventure in the form of a nontechnical brief with logical proofs, data from scientific and sociological studies, historical evidence, references to art and literature, journalist accounts, and experiential anecdotes marshaled to support its claim. It even has a bit of (attempted/lame) humor mixed in with all the serious stuff.

Right up front, you need to be warned that, if you are expecting a defense of atheism, you'll not find it within these pages. Atheism requires us to believe that there is no God or gods. That's clearly another belief which isn't supported by the evidence. More on that later, but you'll discover that I'm advocating a middle way of preserving the valuable aspects of religion while dispensing with its superstition-based doctrines, creeds, and dogma. As to political ideologies, we'd be better off without them. Traditional American political pragmatism focuses on solving problems with practical solutions. Dividing into warring ideological camps makes it almost impossible to solve problems our communities and nation face. In the amended words of Larry the Cable Guy, "Set aside ideology and get 'er done."

Dear Reader, if you are a believer who harbors no doubts about your political ideology or religious doctrines, happily trust what religious and political leaders tell you is the truth, and do not want to consider an alternative to conventional ways of thinking; well, you might want to close the book and request a refund. If you are among the 42 percent of Americans (according to a December 16, 2013 Harris poll) that believe in ghosts, you might want to scream and run away before you finish. But, if you have an open and curious mind, please read on.

~ ~ ~

So here's one example of harm caused by using beliefs to guide life decisions: the ongoing "Jenny McCarthy on Oprah proclaiming that vaccines cause autism in children" controversy. Some parents have taken so seriously the authority of a proclamation by a celebrity on a popular television show that they have refused vaccinations for their children. Reports in the news media describe clusters of outbreaks of mumps, measles, and whooping cough in areas in the US where parents have refused vaccines.

Time Magazine reported in its June 21, 2014 issue that there were 334 documented cases of measles to that date in 2014; more than any other year of the last twenty. "Federal health officials attribute the rise to more people refusing vaccinations." The medical journal *Pediatrics* recently published a study which found that parents who had rejected vaccines on the basis of their beliefs did not change their beliefs when presented with scientific evidence showing the danger of failing to vaccinate their children. These parents were also provided with the information that no link has been found between vaccines and autism.

Media reports described it as "surprising" that antipathy of the parents toward vaccines hardened, rather than softened, after they were provided with information about the benefits to their children of vaccines and the dangers of failing to vaccinate. It should not be surprising that true believers refuse to be persuaded out of their beliefs by facts and evidence. That is the nature of firmly held beliefs. The belief is reality for the believer.

So why should we care about what somebody else has

inside their head? Like the Queen said in *Alice in Wonderland*, "Why, sometimes I've believed as many as six impossible things before breakfast." Regrettably, as Lewis Carroll's scary-crazy Queen of Hearts goes on to illustrate, people do act on their irrational beliefs. "Off with their heads!" ordered the Queen. Harm to others or one's own self is often the result, when beliefs conflict with reality. Those parents, who believe vaccines cause autism, because Jenny McCarthy or their pastor says so, are risking the health of their children and others.

Pathological beliefs can spread more quickly today than ever before due to the Internet. "This question is especially important today, when 85 percent of US adults regularly use the Internet, which can spread delusional beliefs with the rapidity and randomness of plagues. Delusion-inspired ideologies, such as those that sanction violence as a response to religious differences, proliferate on the Web. They harken back to pogroms, witch hunts, and other persecutions that targeted individuals and groups thought to be associated with devils and demons." Richard Restak, "Going Haywire – Delusions Can Occur in Perfectly 'Normal' People," *The American Scholar*, Autumn 2014.

~ ~ ~

The capacity to believe developed in the brains of our pre-human ancestors as a survival mechanism, according to Michael Shermer, science historian and publisher of *Skeptic Magazine*. During a June 19, 2014 TED Talk on NPR, Shermer offered this anecdote: "You are a hominid three million years ago walking on the plains of Africa. Your name is Lucy, okay? And you hear a rustle in the grass. Is it a dangerous predator, or is it just the wind? Your next decision could be the most important one of your life. Well, if you think that the rustle in the grass is a dangerous predator and it turns out it's just the wind, you've made an error in cognition ... But no harm. You just move away. You're more cautious. You're more vigilant. On the other hand, if you believe that the rustle in the grass is just the wind, and it turns out it's a dangerous predator, you're lunch. You've just won a Darwin award. You've been taken out of the gene pool ... So the default position is just: Believe all patterns are real -- All rustles in the grass are dangerous predators and not just the wind. And so I think that we evolved ... there was a natural selection for the propensity for our belief engines, our pattern-seeking brain processes, to always find meaningful patterns and infuse them with these sort of predatory or intentional agencies ..."

A modern Homo sapien who believes everything seen or heard is a meaningful pattern is probably schizophrenic. We have evolved and learned to become more skeptical and discriminating than our ancient ancestors. Yes, of course, it's impossible to navigate through modern life without any beliefs. As an experiment, take note of the number of times during an ordinary day that you use the phrase, "I believe". I've done the experiment, and, despite the thesis of this book, I find myself saying "I believe" this or that numerous times in ordinary conversations.

The book is not a screed against thinking, expecting, believing some things are more likely true than others. I think/expect/believe that the stock market will go up in 2014. My belief is based on past experience and some degree of analysis of economic trends and current events. In my case the analysis is pretty superficial, but, if asked, I'd say, "Yeah, I believe the market is gonna keep going up this year." But I also know I may be wrong. That's the nature of ordinary-conversational sorts of beliefs. We hold them, but we also change them as we receive additional information. "I think" is interchangeable with "I believe", when talking about these sorts of beliefs. We are not wedded to beliefs we hold about such things as the weather, sports teams, and even other people. These beliefs are opinions.

We also use the term "belief" interchangeably with self-confidence. Performance in athletics, business, or any competitive endeavor improves if you believe in yourself, believe you will succeed, believe you will win. Sports and life coaches understand that a positive mental attitude is helpful for getting in the flow whether the effort is to produce art, score touchdowns, or make a sale. "You gotta believe!"

Religion and politics are of a different order of beliefs. Shermer describes in his TED Talk how belief as a survival mechanism branched off into superstition. Believing that divine agencies can take care of us and evil spirits are what cause us harm is a root source of religion. Believing the strong and charismatic leader will take care of us, and when things go wrong it's his/her fault, is the source of politics. On the upside, beliefs which have a basis in actual experience (like snakes do rustle the grass and when fundamental economic factors are positive the stock market trends upward) do help us navigate through daily life. The downside is when they become irrational, superstitious, and a way to avoid responsibility. Rather than praising or blaming the gods when things go right or wrong, progress is made when we figure out what works and what doesn't.

Religious beliefs tend to be the most irrational and the most difficult type of beliefs to live without for many people. Next in line is political ideology. This book is more concerned with religion than politics, but both come under scrutiny and attack in the following pages.

~ ~ ~

Belief in a god or gods is cross-cultural and satisfies universal needs for us humans. We want to be cared for and we want to feel that our lives have meaning beyond ordinary existence. Believing in God or gods that have some concern about our lives and destiny during and after life is the most common way to satisfy the ego's desire to transcend the ordinary. So we have created god(s) in our own images.

When people who are not scholarly theologians talk about their god(s), it sounds to nonbelievers like nonsense. (So does the talk of scholarly theologians, it just sounds like more sophisticated nonsense.) God talk is mostly about beliefs, not facts or knowledge. The reality of this type of belief is completely subjective. It exists only in the mind of believers.

Knowledge can be demonstrated to others. You don't say, I believe the floor will be there when I roll out of bed. You know the floor is there, because it has always been there when you got out of bed and you can show the person sharing your bed, "Yup, there's the floor; still there." But, "I believe in God;" or, "If I receive the rites of the Sacred Mysteries of Confession and Holy Communion before I die, I'll go to Heaven;" these are merely statements of belief. You can't show God to anyone else and you can't prove that you will, or anyone else has, gone to Heaven after receiving Extreme Unction. You can believe it with all your heart, mind, and soul, but you can't prove it to anyone else. You do not actually know it to be true. Yet, "believers" are expected to live their lives as if such religious dogmas are statements of fact. Unlike what are described above as ordinary beliefs, which we modify as we learn additional facts, religious beliefs are supposed to be absolute and as unchanging as the laws of physics. (Never mind that the religious establishment does change official doctrine from time to time. Hey Catholics, what happened to Limbo?)

Most religious doctrine has little or no connection with our own personal experience. We are told by the religious authorities what we are supposed to believe. Unless you can testify under oath that your god communicates directly with you, you are relying on what others have told you, or what others have written, as to the supposed truths about God. What religious people believe is what the prophets, preachers, priests, and popes of their religion tell them. Yet the truth claims of religions, for the most part, contradict how we actually experience reality.

If you encounter someone on the street who tells you

that she heard a burning bush talking to her, and the bush was the almighty and eternal ruler of the universe, you would think the woman was psychotic or on an acid trip. But Jews and Christians are expected to believe that God informed Moses through the medium of a burning bush that, "I am what I am". We would think a person crazy who claims to have experienced many of the things depicted in the Bible, but we are expected to believe these crazy things actually occurred because they're in the Bible! Why would educated, rational, people living in the 21st Century choose to believe the wacky and weird events in the Bhagavad-Gita, the Quran, the Book of Mormon, or any of the other sacred books of religion actually happened? Religious leaders expect their followers to accept lunacy as reality!

Religious beliefs might start with simple, superficial, and harmless statements like, "I believe God exists, and I believe God created the world, and I believe God loves me and all creatures;" but it never stops there. Religions go on to make claims like: Krishna created the Hindu caste system, which puts Brahmin priests on top and poor folk so far down they are untouchable; Jehovah parted the Red Sea to let the Israelites escape Pharaoh and then smashed and drowned the Egyptian soldiers; demons hurled a fiery disc at Buddha which turned into flowers as he became enlightened; Jesus walked on water; an angel gave Abraham and Ishmael the sacred Black Stone which is now inside the holy Kaaba in Mecca.

Rational-thinking people tend to assume that the stories in the sacred literature of other religions were made up -- concocted by very imaginative story-tellers. Or, that most of the stories about Vishnu, Shiva, Abraham, Moses, Buddha, Jesus, Mohammed, the angel Maroni, etc., if you are not a believer, were based upon some actual event but greatly exaggerated in the telling, retelling, eventual writing, and rewriting. Yet, we hesitate to apply rational scrutiny to the stories and beliefs of our own religion.

Religious scholars, folklorists, and anthropologists explain that many religious beliefs come from stories turned into oral traditions, which were eventually written down. The priestly class of religious professionals then developed doctrines and rules of conduct based on the sacred writings.

To take just one example, the Apostles' Creed began to evolve out of particular verses in the Gospel of Matthew in the Second Century after Jesus's death. There is no surviving original text of *Matthew* or any of the Gospels. *Matthew* as a written text reflects some of the legends and oral traditions about the life and teachings of Jesus. But written texts were irrelevant to many early Christians, because they were illiterate. So, simple statements summarizing the teachings of leaders of the Christian movement began to circulate among early Christian communities. There were various versions of these easy-to-remember summaries of the Christian faith. The final version of the Apostles' Creed approved by the Roman Church wasn't developed until the Eighth Century. Church leaders and scholars spent hundreds of years arguing over the proper wording. So this Creed, a product of centuries of battles, both theological and military, recited by Christians round the world, is supposed to tell you what you believe?!

Do you find it a bit peculiar that Christians are expected to accept as true a series of statements which took eight hundred years of bloody in-fighting during the Middle Ages to finalize? Christians only a few generations removed from Jesus couldn't agree on the fundamental tenets of the faith. But Christians in 2014 are supposed to accept as The Truth the particular words and phrases those argumentative Church leaders were eventually able to compromise on.

A long and tenuous line of hearsay connects the modern believer with the ancient stories on which her faith is based. Religious instructions telling us how to live our lives rest upon the infirm foundation of oral traditions transmogrified into beliefs from which rules of conduct were derived by the priestly class. Those with the vested interest of requiring obedience and the tithes and taxes of the rest of us to support them financially make the rules in both religion and government.

The thoughtful person must ask herself; do I really get the life I want when the beliefs I am supposed to hold and the rules I am supposed to follow have such an unsupportable foundation? Wouldn't it make better sense to let go of religious doctrines but not necessarily abandon your religious organization (if you belong to one), and to put aside political ideologies but not give up on the political process?

~ ~ ~

Beliefs are the source of, or rationale for, bias and prejudice. If I believe the "mark of Ham" means dark-skinned people are unclean or inferior and I'm an employer, I will discriminate against African-Americans in hiring. If my interpretation of Shinto is that Japanese are innately superior to all other racial-ethnic groups, I will have contempt for the people of other nations.

Walking around New Delhi, India I chanced upon a mosque. The building was open and I was curious to see what it looked like on the inside. I didn't see anyone as I walked into a spacious area that I assumed was the prayer hall. It had not occurred to me to remove my sandals as there were no worshippers or anyone present. All of a sudden I heard a shriek and I noticed out of the corner of my eye an elderly man hobbling toward me wielding a broom. He gave chase yelling and scolding after I eluded his attempt to whack me. I dashed out of the building and loped off down the street. At a safe distance, I turned to see him shaking his fist and chattering at me like an enraged squirrel.

I guessed that I had violated a rule against wearing footwear into the prayer hall. I had not intended to break a rule or to offend the caretaker. It should have been obvious by my clothing (t-shirt and trekker shorts) and physical appearance that I was not a local and may not have been familiar with Muslim customs.

Reflecting on that experience with a Muslim friend a few years later, I was assured that Welcome of the stranger/foreigner is a value promoted by Islam. Rather than guiding his behavior by that value, the caretaker responded with anger that I had violated Muslim purification rules. I had entered the prayer hall without removing my sandals, hadn't washed my feet, was there for purposes other than prayer, and I was an unbeliever. The old man's hostile and violent behavior was directed by his belief in these dogmatic rules rather than the value of welcoming a visitor. Instead of Compassion for the ignorant, the man treated me as an infidel. I was not one of us; I was one of them.

~ ~ ~

Because religious doctrines are not founded on hard reality, but on the imaginations of those who told the original stories from which the oral traditions developed, a believer's understanding of reality is distorted. Many people will tell you and truly believe that women have one more rib than men. The provenance of this belief is the Adam and Eve story in *Genesis* 2:21-22 in which God made the first woman out of the first man's rib. This belief continues into the 21st Century despite that x-rays have been around since 1895 and they indisputably show that men and women have the same number of ribs. Not to mention that anatomists and physicians have been cutting open cadavers for hundreds of years. Many somewhat educated people continue to hold this belief based on the *Genesis* story. This belief survives despite the availability of clear and convincing evidence that men and women have the same number of ribs!

It's easy to laugh at the ridiculous beliefs of other people, cultures, and religions. It's not so easy to be objective about, or find the humor in, our own.

When ardent believers in opposing religious doctrines or political ideologies encounter each other civil discourse is not usually the norm. Why get pissed off because someone you meet has a different take on religion or politics? Yet, the advice often given by well-meaning elders is not to bring up religion or politics at the dinner table. The ire it raises is evidence of the insidious power of buying into a belief system. It ought to be interesting to encounter people with different perspectives, shouldn't it? Among curious, liberal-minded folks it is. But hard core believers react the way rabid racists do when forced to engage with people of other colors.

I'm afraid this book is likely to piss you off and turn you off if you are an orthodox believer in a religion or political ideology. Cynical nihilists who find no value in anything and think reality is random meaninglessness will probably not find much to agree with in these pages either.

There is a middle way between nihilism and a belief-driven life. It even allows for the belief, in the sense of thinking it is more likely, that there is a creative and sustaining force affecting our universe, which we can call God or the gods. If your understanding of reality leads you to the opinion that there is a Creator-Sustainer, and you recognize you could be wrong, your belief may have value for you and it is not harmful to others. The same concession is made to political ideology. If you think, based on evidence and your thoughtful analysis, that Capitalism, Socialism, or any other political-economic-social system is the best model, but you are willing to compromise on specific issues in order to make progress at solving problems, then your belief in that system may have value for you and doesn't harm others.

A pragmatic values-based approach to religion and politics is the way forward into a future in which we are not killing each other over religious or political beliefs. It is a way to build up rather than tear down community.

Chapter 2: Fight Violence with Values!

"Politics is the art of looking for trouble, finding it everywhere, diagnosing it incorrectly and applying the wrong remedies." - Groucho Marx

When two people of opposing ideologies argue, they are ships passing in the night. They can't resolve disputes about what to do and how to solve problems, because they are in fundamental disagreement about how the world works. Channel surfers can watch a report on MSNBC about the economic impact of the Affordable Care Act ("ACA" or "Obamacare") and then switch to Fox News. You'll get completely different forecasts of how the Act will affect job growth and medical care costs. Not because objective experts disagree about the economic impacts of the ACA, but because the editorial staffs of the two networks promote opposing political ideologies. Instead of facts leading to conclusions, "facts" are selectively reported and interpreted to support conclusions consistent with the Left's and the Right's ideologies.

Many other examples would suit, but a fundamental rift in American politics is the argument between rightwing Republicans and leftwing Democrats over reducing the national debt.

"Liberals" believe that spending more tax dollars will stimulate the economy and that's what is needed to create more jobs and better lives for Americans. "Conservatives" believe reducing taxes will put more money into the private economy and thereby create more jobs and a better life for Americans. Nonideological expert economists tell us that both are right and both are wrong. Sometimes economic stimulus from the government is needed to goose a recessive economy. Other times, public debt becomes a drag on the economy and pushes it toward recession. Nonideological economists recommend a nimble-flexible approach, dependent on the current situation.

It doesn't require a PhD in Economics to understand basic principles of economic reality. When the economy is booming and tax dollars are rolling in -- time for the government to save. When private enterprise is not producing jobs, it's time for government to spend money on infrastructure to create jobs. If the budget is managed properly, funds will be available to support the government's additional spending and the extra spending will boost the national economy and not be a drag. Carefully following this basic economic principle would relieve the need for countries with developed economies from incurring massive debt.

There are legitimate arguments over how much spending and when to increase and decrease spending. But the catastrophic mistake made by many governments is to disregard basic laws of economics in order to blindly follow laissez faire or socialist policies. True believers in either ideology are unable to adjust their thinking to changing circumstances. They are more interested in pushing their political agenda than actually solving problems. Disregarding economic reality for political reasons helped push us into the worldwide recession of 2008.

~ ~ ~

Away from the cameras after the famous "Kitchen Debate" between Soviet Premier Nikita Khrushchev and Vice-President Richard Nixon in 1959, Khrushchev supposedly shared his actual view of Soviet-style politics this way: "If the people believe there's an imaginary river out there, you don't tell them there's no river there. You build an imaginary bridge over the imaginary river." Khrushchev postured for The People as the legitimate heir to Lenin and Stalin -- a true believing Marxist. He actually thought "Communism" was an "imaginary river".

Soviet dictators from Lenin until Mikhail Gorbachev manipulated the masses to build a system which consolidated power in their party cronies. Many people believed in the ideals of communism. And many believed they'd be shot or sent to the Gulag, if they didn't pretend to believe in Soviet Socialism. The system finally fell apart when the reality of the superiority of democratic capitalism to deliver a higher standard of living along with real political participation and protection of basic civil rights had become too obvious to continue to deny. President Gorbachev let it be known that the emperor had no clothes. Soviet Socialism collapsed after seventy years of lies, cruel repression of dissent, the Cold War, and a nuclear arms race which cost both sides trillions of dollars.

Not since we were in competition with Neanderthals, was the human race in as much danger of extinction as during the Cuban Missile Crisis. Thankfully, Kennedy and Khrushchev negotiated an uneasy but peaceful resolution. These two leaders were more pragmatic than ideological when the US and USSR were on the brink of nuclear war for thirteen days in October of 1961. Many of their advisors and many in the populations of the two countries saw the crisis as a contest of political-economic ideologies and wanted to go to war to settle it once and for all.

What is the likelihood they would be used, if ideological true believers, rather than pragmatic politicians, had control of nuclear weapons? The fear that the risk is too great is the foundation of the policy of Western governments opposing the development of nuclear energy by Iran. We just don't trust the Ayatollahs not to press the button if they get the chance. Likewise, it's the reason the possibility of organizations like Al Qaeda or ISIS getting their hands on a dirty bomb scares the shit out of most anyone who's not a radical Islamist.

Yes, yes, I know the US is the only government that has used a nuclear weapon. We can argue 'til the cows come home about the ethical and strategic wisdom of President Truman's decision to drop The Bomb. (It's difficult for me to be objective, because my dad was a paratrooper in the US invasion force. Chances are I would not be if the US airborne troops were dropped on the Japanese mainland as planned.) There was an ideological element to World War II -- fascism vs. democracy -- but the decision to use the atomic bomb was based on the expectation that it would end the war with fewer lives lost than a massive land invasion. That is not the sort of calculation fanatical ideologues make.

Ideologically fanatic leaders like Hitler, Lenin, Mao, and Osama Bin Laden do not give a damn about the loss of human life. The sacrifice of human lives on a massive scale is just collateral damage in the pursuit of their political goals.

~ ~ ~

Ideologues believe they have the right answer for all situations. Laissez faire should always be our guiding principle and the less government the better! Or, government is there to solve problems; if there's a problem with the economy or society, the government should step in to solve it. Ideological opponents will never agree. They are unable to look at the problem of national debt or deficit spending and see the same realities.

It would make for better government if executive officers and legislators operated like engineers, scientists, and philosophers. Political, economic, and social issues could be handled as problems to be solved. Issues would be defined, relevant facts determined, various solutions considered, and the ones with the highest probability of success implemented. Political ideologies serve no purpose other than to gum up the works in the process.

"Hell, there are no rules here - we're trying to accomplish something," Thomas Edison said describing his pragmatic approach to inventing new, and adapting old, technologies. The *Stanford Encyclopedia of Philosophy* describes Pragmatism as "a philosophical tradition that originated in the United States." I was taught in my college freshman survey course in philosophy that Pragmatism is the only school of philosophy which truly originated in the US. Pragmatism is exemplified by American figures like inventor Thomas Edison, Melvil Dewey, who created the Dewey Decimal System, and Franklin Delano Roosevelt, a President willing to experiment with policies until he found ones that worked. (There's more on American Pragmatism in Part III, so, if it turns you on, hang in there; there's more to come.)

What actually works best? If our elected representatives and civil servants followed Edison's pragmatic approach to governance instead of posturing and pushing ideologies think how much more effectively our state and federal governments would work.

We need to counter the damage done by fanatical ideologues with pragmatic problem solving guided by positive values. On the personal level, if we discard our beliefs in political ideologies and religious doctrines, we will be free to decide who we really want to be. If governments pragmatically pursue value-based policies and religious institutions focus on nurturing positive values, the world could be rid of the scourge of fanatical beliefs. Fight violence with values!

Chapter 3: Agnosticism, Santa Claus, Awe and Gratitude

The father of Philosophy in Western Civilization, Socrates, claimed that he knew nothing. He encouraged his students to start with the humble confession of ignorance, and then seek wisdom. Socrates devoted his life to debunking the mistaken beliefs and conventional wisdom of his fellow Athenians. He died a martyr to the cause of skeptical inquiry. The Socratic Method lives on as a tool law professors use to relentlessly question (and often humiliate) their students, pressing them to keep thinking about what they really know and what they believe they know, and to recognize the difference. Law professors hector and harass their first year students seemingly without mercy. It's like being turned upside down, held by the ankles, and shaken until all the ignorant assumptions drain out your mouth and ears.

Patient reader that you are, if you already feel like your beliefs have been shaken but not stirred, please hang on. This is not just a hectoring critique of religion and political ideologies. The second part of the book is mostly about values, where they come from and what does it mean to live a valuable life. Part III is a series of specific examples and applications of positive values. Casting away all belief systems does not mean having no values. On the contrary, values serve as guides to show us a pathway forward on the road of life.

Belief systems also light a way forward. But every religion and political ideology claims to lead its followers down the right path. They each claim that theirs is the only really true path. But they conflict with each other! How can Christianity be the one true religion when some of its primary claims are in direct and irreconcilable conflict with Judaism, Islam, Hinduism, and Buddhism? And vice versa for each religion. If one is the truth and the right way, then the others are untrue and lead their believers astray.

You'll often hear it said that "all religions are basically

the same" or their "core beliefs are essentially the same." Not true. There are similarities among denominations and sects within the same religion. For outsiders it's difficult to discern the differences between Shia and Sunni, Anglicans and Roman Catholics, or Nyingma and Vajrayana Buddhism; although tens of thousands have died fighting over those minor differences. But the belief systems of Hinduism, Judaism, Buddhism, Christianity, Islam, and other major religions are very different. Take for instance, animal sacrifice -- Hindus have festivals of animal slaughter, the others condemn it; an after-life -- Jews, not so much; Christian Heaven has some similarity to Paradise for Muslims, but Buddhist and Hindu reincarnation have nothing in common with Heaven or Paradise other than they follow death; Messiah -- The Jews are still waiting; for Christians it's Jesus, with which the others absolutely disagree.

The diversity in beliefs among the religions and within their many sects and divisions is wide and varied. However, there is commonality in the most fundamental values promoted by the major religions. They all advocate taking good care of yourself and giving aid and succor to those in need.

~ ~ ~

There are occasional fits and starts toward interfaith collaborations. Humanistic and ecumenical-oriented Christians like to "celebrate" commonalities shared by different denominations and religions. Ecumenists are willing and actively campaign to make doctrinal compromises to achieve greater unity across religious lines. Strict orthodox believers look with jaundiced eyes on these proposals. They view doctrinal compromises as attempts to water down the Truth into wishy-washy ecumenical indistinctness. The hardliners recognize something the liberal ecumenists might be uncomfortable to admit; liberals have lost many of their traditional beliefs. They want to hang on to comforting symbols and practices, but many thoughtful, well educated folks would like to dispense with the silly-ass dogmas which they don't believe anymore. Fundamentalists scorn these folks as back-sliders and faux Christians, Muslims, Jews, Hindus, Buddhists, or whatever.

Be that as it may, what the new-agey squishy liberal ecumentalists have come to realize is that the beliefs of their traditional religions do not hold water. The "faith" can't withstand analytical scrutiny. Sure these folks want to hang on and stay within the fold of their "faith community" for good reasons. They enjoy the community; they want to raise their kids in the traditions they grew up with; it would upset grandparents if the next generation left the church, temple, or mosque; the organization does good works and supports the right principles; it's comfortable.

Okay, so let's stay within our traditional faith community, political party, or whatever group which has stated doctrines we don't truly believe. Let's also have the balls to tell the truth respectfully. We can do that without being offensive. Those of us who have let go of the orthodox beliefs of our heritage need not be evangelical about pushing unbelief as if it were a sacred doctrine. Just be honest with yourself and others when asked.

I was once asked by a fellow Presbyterian what I would say when asked about The Resurrection. The context was that I was a candidate for the ordained ministry, and this respected Elder of the church knew I was going to be examined by "The Candidates Committee" about my beliefs in Presbyterian doctrines. "Bill" sidled up beside me during coffee klatch after services, darted suspicious looks in all directions, and then popped the question about The Resurrection. Bill admitted that he didn't believe in The Resurrection and wondered how an educated and rational fellow like me was going to be able to duck The Question. He presumed that I did not believe in Christian superstitions like the Virgin Birth and Resurrection. He also assumed that we both had to pretend to believe in these superstitions in order to hold leadership positions within the Presbyterian denomination. It was sad, silly, and hypocritical.

Because I went to seminary I came to know quite a few Christian ministers, and I represented several churches and Christian ministers in legal matters. Several ministers of Protestant denominations and two Catholic priests came clean with me about their personal beliefs. What I discovered was that, when they were not "on", many leaders of Christian churches admitted to being plagued by the same doubts about the dogmas of their Church and Christian superstitions as me and any other thoughtful-analytical person.

As a candidate for the Presbyterian ministry, I was counseled by other ordained ministers to "tell them what they want to hear" rather than what I really thought and believed, in order to pass the required examinations about my beliefs. I was co-valedictorian of my seminary class, won awards for accomplishments in ancient Greek and Hebrew, and was "highly recommended" by the psychologist who performed personality tests for our presbytery. I was rejected for ordination because, as one committee member put it, "You seem more like a Buddhist than a Calvinist." I made "the mistake" of trying to be honest about my beliefs, or lack thereof. So that door closed because I valued truthfulness. (In retrospect I realized the Committee was right to reject me. I had become more like a Buddhist than an orthodox Calvinist. What horrors would have ensued if, instead of the Lord's Prayer, I would have given in to the temptation to lead the congregation in chanting "Om mani padme hum".)

~ ~ ~

I am picking on Christianity more than other religions because, as my own religious tradition, I know it best. (Btw, I still follow it in a way. I'm an active member of a Quaker meeting.) But the book is not an attack just on Christian doctrine; it is an attack on all religious cant. Have you had the experience of becoming disillusioned with what the hierarchy of your religion held up as what good _____ (fill in the blank with Christians, Jews, Moslems, Hindus, Buddhists, or whatever group you belong to) were supposed to believe in. Every religious organization expects followers to accept a set of beliefs for which there is no more proof than the existence of Santa Claus.

Children eventually come to realize that Santa is not real, despite all the stories and talk about him, pictures of him, and even movies and TV shows starring Santa. And many thoughtful kids come to realize that most of the doctrinal claims of their religion are, like Santa, based on mythology.

Santa is real in a way. At his best, he exemplifies the value of generous giving. And our culture promotes this value by telling Santa Claus stories. Telling stories, books, movies, television shows, YouTube, etc. are the media through which values, positive and negative, are now passed down through generations. We should take the old stories seriously, but not as literally true. Religious leaders are treating us all like gullible children when they preach at us adults about Bible stories as if they are reporting established facts. The stories may be sacred, but that does not make them true.

In her book, *The Battle for God*, Karen Armstrong describes the difference between "mythos" and "logos". Logos is "the rational, pragmatic and scientific thought that enabled men and women to function well in the world." Mythos, on the other hand, "was not concerned with practical matters, but with meaning. ... Moreover, mythos is not just a logos with a different focus ... it's something experienced and made real in an entirely different way. ... Myth only became a reality when it was embodied in cult, rituals and ceremonies, which worked aesthetically upon worshipers, evoking within them a sense of sacred significance and enabling them to apprehend the deeper currents of existence."

Too many religious leaders confuse mythos and logos. They fail to grasp that the myths are allegorical tales, rather than literal truths. Mythologies are the traditional medium of transmitting values and meaning from one generation to the next. Instead of using them in this delightful way, religious myths have been perverted for the nefarious purposes of dumbing down and keeping followers in line. That doesn't work on independent thinkers (like you thoughtful and intelligent reader who bought this book).

Either with a cynical friend or the skeptic in your own head, at some point didn't you have a conversation like this about the religious claims you were taught as a child: Come on man, you don't really believe that Jesus was born of a virgin, was crucified, died and went down into Hell and three days later was in Heaven, but also hung out with Thomas and the gang on the Road to Emmaus, yet sits by the right hand of God, who is his father, but the Father and Son are also the same entity along with the Holy Spirit, because these three beings are separate but the same. Come on, man!

When skeptical Thomas demanded to see proof that Jesus had come back to life after being crucified, Jesus showed Thomas the nail marks on his hands. Despite his repeated demands that his disciples believe in Him and his Father, when push came to shove, Jesus accepted Thomas's request for "autopsis", Greek for "seeing with one's own eyes". Jesus understood that for the thoughtful skeptic evidentiary proof is more important than a charismatic leader's demand that followers "take it on faith". Right on!

Educated thoughtful people rely on the scientific method combined with rational thought and interpreted through our own experience as the best way to go about trying to understand the world in which we live. We cannot accept in our heart of hearts ridiculously irrational claims by religion as factually true. We can pretend to believe such claims or we can spend a lifetime, like highly educated theology professors, bobbing and weaving and wiggling around trying to explain the unexplainable as metaphor, paradox, or things just to be taken on faith.

Theology and religious studies can be fun intellectual games. They have occupied many brilliant minds and filled millions of volumes, and they provide employment for Humanities majors (like me). Each generation of theologians comes up with a new and compelling interpretation of the traditional beliefs of their faith. The game never ends, because the irrational cannot be finally and satisfactorily twisted into the rational and provable.

I am not saying that all reality can be comprehended by rational empiricism. Neither do I think that only what is observable by human perception is real. A tree falling in the forest really is falling whether observed or not. Science and spirituality agree that there are dimensions of reality that are not penetrable by human perception or intellectual comprehension, at least at our present stage of development.

No one has actually seen, heard, smelled, tasted, or touched the Higgs-Boson particle, but there is compelling circumstantial evidence to prove its existence. String theorists posit that there are many other dimensions outside the scope of our ability to perceive them. The Terasem movement is beaming digitized diaries into outer space in the hope that conscious beings from some other planet will eventually receive them and want to make contact with us. The statistical evidence of the number of planets that might support life is compelling that there must be aliens out there, although most sane astronomers will tell you that we have not yet made contact. Mystics experience the ineffable and call it God or nirvana or enlightenment or Sahaja. They beautifully describe a state of being beyond normal consciousness.

It's quite clear that there is reality beyond our ability to perceive with our senses and understand in normal consciousness. I had an experience I call mystical, when I was alone, lost, and dead-tired solo-kayaking under a starless sky at night on the Pacific Ocean. I began singing the *Gloria Patri*, and, although I had been paddling the better part of twelve hours, my body was suddenly filled with an unnatural strength and all the fear, which had consumed my mind, leaked away. How could singing that ancient hymn replace the calories of energy my body had burned and release my mind from the fear of being lost and alone at night at sea? It's inexplicable, but it happened.

Creating a belief system and claiming it was inspired by a mystical state is making a huge leap beyond the experience of a rationally unexplainable event. I think it's fair to say that most of those who have made that leap are charlatans out to gain followers, power, and money from the gullible. If the mystery is beyond the ability of human consciousness to comprehend it, then it cannot be explained through a set of belief statements. Stories, poetry, and art are the best media to try to express the ineffable.

The ancient stories which gave rise to the oral traditions which transmogrified into religious doctrines should have been left alone. They expressed authentic experiences of awe and mystery. The stories conveyed the values and wisdom of their ancient cultures.

As to doctrinal beliefs, what good does it do for anyone to claim or believe that Jesus actually is God and God is Jesus and they are both the Holy Spirit and the Trinity is truly three separate but the same beings? Holding that sort of belief does no harm in itself; but, a few hundred years ago people were killing each other because of disagreements about whether Jesus was really God. Just as Sunnis and Shia are doing now over their disagreement about Mohammed's rightful heir.

Doctrinal beliefs like the Trinity provide no value to anyone except anally fixated scholastics. Life is neither enhanced nor diminished by walking around with that belief in your head. On the other hand, telling the stories of the amazing affect Jesus had on people's lives, singing the Gloria Patri, or gazing around the Sistine Chapel requires no commitment to Trinitarian Dogma. These are beautiful experiences which remind us of the wondrousness of the reality in which we live. And that is valuable.

To participate in practices and traditions which express the awe we feel when contemplating the mystery of the amazing fact of the existence of our world and our selves within it does not require ceding our rational intellect to superstition. We should be able to live and enjoy the gathering of a worshipping community without getting hooked on surrealistic superstitions.

~ ~ ~

Human consciousness is miraculous. What greater wonder is there that you are alive and conscious to touch the cheek of the one you love lying beside you, or looking out your window to see a little chipmunk skitter across the porch with a tiny berry in its mouth, or seeing rays of the rising Sun sparkle across a glacier with Himalayan peaks glowing through your open tent flap, or hear and feel your mewling baby nuzzling against your shoulder? What is more divine than any of the quotidian experiences of everyday life or the ecstatic once-in-a-lifetime event? It's awe inspiring to contemplate the miracle of our own being in this world, what we have experienced, and the possibilities of all that we might yet experience. What value is there in believing in some hard-to-define omnipotent or omniscient Being?

Maybe there is value for you. If so, let's do it without demanding that others accept our particular definition or version of that transcendent reality. Because, once we begin to assert the righteousness of our beliefs people are divided into us and them and separated into believers and unbelievers.

If Jack fervently believes that Lot's wife was turned into a pillar of salt, because it says so in *Genesis* 19.26, and Diane doesn't believe that, then one of them must be right and the other wrong. But both are sure that they are right and the other wrong. Their disagreement is over the unprovable and so they won't be able to convince the other, try as they might. If believers accept that others have different beliefs or don't have any belief about God, or whether laissez-faire capitalism or communism is the ideal state, or whatever one's particular religious or political faith -- if we can just agree to disagree -- believing in unprovable things wouldn't really matter. Beliefs would matter to those who hold them, but they wouldn't destroy community or be the excuse to harm other people. Too often, believers are unwilling to tolerate dissent or opposition.

People have killed each other and started wars over beliefs about some pretty absurd things. If space aliens are watching us, they must be shaking their heads (if they have heads) over us silly humans fighting and dying over the differences in beliefs between Protestants and Catholics, Sunni and Shia, capitalists and communists. Why do we think these differences in beliefs are worth fighting and dying for?

How can someone look into the eyes of another human being while burning him with hot irons and stretching his body on the rack to the point of tearing his tendons and ligaments apart in the name of Jesus under authority of the Holy Catholic Church, as Christian inquisitors did? How can someone cut off the head of another person with a knife and claim it is done in the name of Allah and his true prophet Mohamed? We humans have done that and worse under the auspices of religion and political ideologies.

Chapter 4: Sheep, Wolves, and Shepherds

Some "believers" follow a religious tradition, or leaders of their "faith", like sheep. They don't question. They just keep their heads down and their noses tight to the tail of the sheep in front. (He said with a sheepish grin.) These folks are harmless to others if herded in a way that doesn't cross paths with more determined sheep. And harmless to themselves so long as they are not led over a cliff by a charismatic leader who is a wolf in sheep's clothing. Remember what happened to the members of the Peoples Temple. They were led by Reverend Jim Jones (an alumnus of my seminary alma mater, Christian Theological Seminary) out of God's country, Indianapolis, Indiana, to the Babel of the West Coast, San Francisco, and then to mass suicide in Guyana.

The personality type I have had irksome experiences with is not sheepish. She is the believer who is fired with the passion of her faith and can't stop talking about it. This is the true believer that can't be reasoned with and gets upset when challenged or questioned sharply. Try examining (can't help it; I was a trial lawyer for twenty years) a True Believer about why he believes and what evidence he has to support the truth of his beliefs. A friendly discussion about religion it will probably not be.

The most fanatical believers become violent persecutors of unbelievers. Some become crusaders, inquisitors, or jihadists. Others are just the boors you try to avoid at a party.

A young man who is a friend of our family sunk into depression after loss of a job and girlfriend in his mid-twenties. "Joby" became involved with a Muslim group, and for a time his new found faith seemed to help lift him out of depression. Joby had grown up Mormon, but was not devoutly religious as a teenager. After joining the mosque, Joby's voice changed. His speech pattern slowed and he enunciated words very carefully, as if English was his second language rather than his native tongue. He insisted on talking about religion, specifically his new one, and he did so VERY

CALMLY. Joby had been an amusing kid with a ready laugh. He was now very serious. He was not the same person. It was pretty clear that Joby's religious fanaticism was just one symptom of a deteriorating mental condition. Joby was briefly committed to a psychiatric ward and then had to be taken under the care of an older sibling. His commitment to Islam seems to have fallen away in his climb out of the hole of depression and back to mental health.

In some religious fanatics the passion eventually cools and the former zealot adopts the vacant "thousand yard stare" as meaning slips away. She might hang on to a vestige of her faith, but will probably join the line of sheep or drop out. Others will not have an easy time of it. "Religious Trauma Syndrome (RTS) is a new term, coined by Marlene Winell to name a recognizable set of symptoms experienced as a result of prolonged exposure to a toxic religious environment and/or the trauma of leaving the religion. It is akin to Complex PTSD, which is defined as 'a psychological injury that results from protracted exposure to prolonged social and/or interpersonal trauma with lack or loss of control, disempowerment, and in the context of either captivity or entrapment, i.e. the lack of a viable escape route for the victim'." ("The sad, twisted truth about conservative Christianity's effect on the mind," Salon, Saturday, Nov 1, 2014, Marlene Winell and Valerie Tarico, AlterNet.) It is safer and healthier to find meaning on more solid ground.

~ ~ ~

We less passionate and less emotionally needy believers hang on to our traditional religion, because there is much we like about it. We appreciate its moving liturgies, the society of friendship it offers, inclusion in a community, and the good and charitable works that it sponsors. Perhaps most importantly, we agree with the values that our traditional religion promotes, especially the fundamental value of caring for self and others.

It's perfectly justifiable and unhypocritical to remain within a religious community which promotes values with which you agree while knowing the truth claims of the religion are largely superstitious nonsense. Wouldn't it be refreshing though to be honest about what we really believe and don't believe about God within our churches, mosques, and temples? We are able to think and openly discuss the irrational beliefs of other religions, why not our own?

Sharing a meal with a Jewish friend, his teenage son, my teenage son Andrew, and I were having a conversation about religion. I made the point that all religions look sort of ridiculous from the outside. To followers on the inside, who have been brought up within the religion, it is not so easy to view the beliefs critically. The other three were nodding their heads in agreement until I said that point applied to Judaism as well. I mentioned a couple peculiar aspects of Judaism. The face of my friend's son assumed a thoughtful look. But the father's brow furrowed and his jaw worked with agitation. He began arguing vehemently that Judaism is quite rational and really makes perfect sense if correctly understood. My friend is extremely bright, sophisticated, and quite secular. He was not, however, ready for his son to begin seriously questioning the faith of his fathers.

Wouldn't we all be better off if we could be honest about our doubts and unbelief? If the understanding rippled out through religious and political organizations that many members do not really believe in the platforms and creeds, the organizations would actually be better off. They could concentrate on being supportive communities which accept people for who they are. Organizations could focus on solving problems the community or individuals face through sympathetic, but rational-objective, inquiry. Members would no longer need to feel hypocritical, guilty, or ashamed for not being sufficiently orthodox about the beliefs mandated by the organization.

You've heard the argument about how many hospitals

and schools could be built instead of spending the $8.5 billion on another aircraft carrier. What if the resources devoted to religious and political evangelism were reallocated to education and healthcare? All the time and energy spent on political campaigns and religious evangelism, creating tracts, knocking on doors, TV and radio ads, televangelism programs, missions to the unconverted, etc. could be devoted instead to caring for neighbors in need.

Time reported in its August 4, 2014 issue that six percent of Americans identify themselves as atheists or agnostics. In 2009, according to the *Time* article, that percentage of the population was only four percent. That's a two percent increase of "unbelievers" in a population pool of over 350 million in five years, which means about seven million more Americans opted out of any religious faith in the last five years. A study published in 2005 in *The Journal for the Scientific Study of Religion* by sociologists C. Kirk Hadaway and Penny Long Marler revealed that only 17.7% of the US population attended a Christian church on any given weekend. Polls, politicians, and Church leaders have long claimed that the US is one of, if not the most, Christian of nations and that at least forty percent of the population regularly attends church services. Recent polling has exposed the forty percent claim to be a rural myth (a/k/a an urban legend).

ChurchLeadership.Org has been tracking declining church attendance in the US. Its most recent report put it, a tad snarky, thusly: "20.5% of Americans 'frequently' attended church in 1995; 19% of Americans 'frequently' attended church in 1999; 18.0% of Americans 'frequently' attended in church in 2002. Now, by extrapolating the data and doing some statistical evaluation and adding some hope for revival, we can see the figures drop to 15% of Americans in attendance at a church by 2025, and a further drop to 11% or 12 % in 2050. Soon, we can catch up with Europe, which is currently 'enjoying' two to four percent of its population in regular Church attendance. By the time these predictions come to pass, Europe may have no significant Church presence at all."

"Nearly three-quarters of the public (72%) now thinks (sic) religion is losing influence in American life, up 5 percentage points from 2010 to the highest level in Pew Research polling over the past decade," according to the Pew Research Religion & Public Life Project report of September 22, 2014.

While institutional religion is losing influence in American life, there are indications that, to some extent, it's being superseded by (the dreaded) secular humanism. University of Southern California appointed a "humanist chaplain" at the commencement of the 2014 school year. Bart Campolo is a reformed Baptist minister, now an agnostic, who intends to use his position as Humanist Chaplain to "create a hopeful humanist community … a church for people who don't believe in God," according to The Wired Word, October 26, 2014 issue.

Institutional religion would be more successful at retaining influence and members if those of us who have doubts were not required to recite that which we do not believe during worship services. We'd also have more respect for religion if it didn't make such obviously untrue truth claims.   Many of us who grew up in a religion feel comfortable within the communal bond of church, temple, or mosque, but are uncomfortable being expected to accept superstitious dogma. We'd like to stay within the bosom of mother church despite our unbelief. But, the Church needs to save itself from itself in the coming age of unbelief. It can do so by deemphasizing beliefs and reemphasizing values.

~ ~ ~

The claim of this book is not that the only meaning in life is found through objective intellectual analysis. Of course not. Humans are far more than just rational intellect. Yes we have minds, but we also have feelings (heart) and the will to do things and desires for experiences which are not necessarily rational. Feelings and desires may be a-rational or irrational, but they are essential aspects of our human being.

It would be a poor desiccated life lived without the feelings invested in and inspired by art, literature, and music. Athletics offer joy, enthusiasm, and glory to participants and fans alike. To push beyond normal limits is inspiring to witness and triumphant to experience. Military service, social service, and volunteerism bring out the best in us; not because the will to sacrifice and perform is necessarily rational, but because it makes us better people. Religious expression has also been a source of the greatest beauty and glory known to humankind. All of these other-than-rational aspects of human being are valuable. They express an appreciation of being alive that goes beyond just getting through daily life.

This book would itself be ridiculous and a failure, if it claimed that there was no worth, meaning, or value to what is at the root of religious expression. We can create and express spiritually-inspired beauty and promote living valuable lives without believing in God, the gods, or religious doctrines. But we must do that within communities. Because, we don't just value ourselves, we value other people and express those values through communal activities.

Chartres Cathedral, Michelangelo's Pieta, the sacred thanka paintings and architecture of the Dalai Lama's Potala Palace are just a few of the exquisite and moving examples of religious art. These are among the highest and best expressions of human creation. Some of these great artistic and architectural works were probably influenced by orthodox religious beliefs. But the inspiration to express beauty, even when representing religious themes, is just that -- striving to express and share our value of the beautiful, to reach above and beyond the normal experience and consciousness of quotidian life.

To sculpt a figure of Buddha does not require the

sculptor to believe in reincarnation or the four (or more) manifestations of Buddha. Carving the Pieta out of quarried marble did not require Michelangelo to believe that Mary, wife of Joseph, was a virgin when she gave birth to Jesus. Religious art is a vessel into which much beauty has been poured. But creativity need not, and should not, be constrained by the bounds of what is religiously permissible.

When a particular political ideology has the authority of law, freedom and artistic expression suffer. Nazism banned the product of, and punished the creators of, "degenerate art". The Soviets did the same to "bourgeoisie art". Some Muslim nations ban "representative art" on religious grounds, and woe to the artist, filmmaker, or journalist who would dare to "insult the Prophet". (From a September 29, 2014 article in *The Guardian*: "Mohsen Amir-Aslani who was executed in Iran last week for heresy. A 37-year-old man has been executed in Iran after being found guilty of heresy and insulting prophet Jonah, according to human rights activists." For god's sake, it was just fish-bait Jonah, not The Prophet!)

The incomparable Russian writer Fyodor Dostoyevsky supposedly recorded in his private journal that even if it was proved that Jesus had never existed, Dostoyevsky would still be a Christian. Perhaps Dostoyevsky believed so strongly in Christianity that he would continue believing even though Christ was a myth. Or, perhaps he meant that the values promoted by the Jesus character of the Bible are so fundamentally right that he would continue to live by those values no matter the historical truth of the Gospels. What inspired Dostoyevsky as a writer and human being to follow the way of Jesus was not a belief in the literal accuracy of the Bible or the creeds of his Russian Orthodox Church. It was an understanding that the values Jesus taught, as expressed in the Christian Gospels and the traditions of the Church, provided a guide to live a good and valuable life. Dostoyevsky's literature depicted the dangers inherent in the restrictiveness of religious doctrines and political ideologies.

He challenged his fellow Russians, and all readers, to go beyond beliefs and find value in life itself and the human spirit.

~ ~ ~

We love and cherish, perhaps even worship, Shakespeare. Great truths about human being and all reality are found within the Shakespeare canon. But, we don't consider William Shakespeare a divinity. Nor do we read his plays as Holy Scripture for which there can be only one correct interpretation. Shakespeare devotees may engage in life-long disagreements about the best interpretation of *Hamlet* or *Macbeth*. Just like Shia and Sunni Muslims have disputed the succession to Muhammad for over a millennium. The difference is that lovers of Shakespeare do not claim that there is only one absolutely true understanding worthy of killing and dying for.

Disagreements are interesting and educational when arguments are made in good faith and with respect for differing views. They become upsetting and sometimes violent when the disputants make claims of Absolute Truth. You might think you've found a wonderful truth in James Joyce's *Ulysses* or Van Gogh's *Starry Night*. Aren't you even more delighted when someone exposes you to an even deeper truth or understanding? Of course you are, if you value learning and you are not an irrational fanatic.

There are no absolute truths - where knowledge ends - for the true seeker of truth. Truth seeking is a life-long journey. It's best to travel light. Better to lessen the burden by dropping the baggage of belief in divinely given absolutes.

~ ~ ~

Is it your experience that people who claim to have found The Truth and the answers to all life's problems are a pain in the ass? Isn't there usually the reek of self-righteousness permeating the air around such folk? The odor should warn us off, because these people are dangerous.

Have you seen super-orthodox Jews bobbing their heads and mumbling their Talmudic prayers, students at Islamic madrassas shouting out their memorized Koranic verses, or Buddhist monks mindlessly chanting mantras from the Sanskrit? In some cases these folks are earnestly engaged in the ancient traditions of their faith and culture. In others it is the unthinking repetition of fanatics. There is nothing wrong with learning or memorizing sacred texts. The danger is following sheep-like the commands of those who would use mind-numbing tactics to gain control over their followers.

The religious zealot who has lost touch with the world as the rest of us experience it in normal consciousness is a danger to himself and others. At the very least, she is like a blind person in traffic without a cane or guide dog. At worst, he takes control of an airplane and crashes it killing all aboard. The fanatic is unable to see reality, because he is blinded by the bright light of orthodoxy. She will not understand in ordinary human terms what she is doing when she straps on the suicide belt.

The 20th Century has a record list of leaders who ordered their followers unto death for The Truth, from Hitler and Mao to Jim Jones and David Koresh. Dictators and prophets leave a trail of death and destruction. Their followers believe in the infallibility of the Great Leader right up to the bloody end.

Werner Erhard (né Jack Rosenberg) has taken advantage of followers as "highly evolved" and diverse as Yippie Jerry Rubin and Apollo astronaut Buzz Aldrin with the quasi-religious scam called Est. Sophisticated investors trusted their retirement savings to Ponzi schemer Bernie Madoff. If people quit putting their "faith" in charismatic frauds, we would be closer to retiring the old saws, "There's a sucker born every minute" and "If it's too good to be true, it's probably not." We need to learn to stop following false prophets, whether they are promising paradise on earth or in the hereafter.

It's our responsibility to take good care of ourselves and our world. We must avoid pie-in-the-sky answers offered by charlatans and snake oil salesmen. There is no end to learning how we can improve our communities and be a true shepherd of the Earth. That is the closest to everlasting life actually offered in this reality.

We need to find, but not blindly follow, religious and political leaders that value Community. There are community leaders trying to better the world rather than lining their own pockets with the hard-earned cash of followers. These are the authentic religious and political leaders who find ways to bring people together rather than dividing us into different ideological camps. The wolves in shepherds clothing can be defeated. There is hope for a new awakening in religion and politics. But it won't happen by just believing; we have to act and support politicians and preachers that are working to promote the positive values we want to live by.

Chapter 5: Living without Religious and Political Beliefs

"Imagine there is no heaven
It's easy if you try
No hell below us
Above us only sky

Imagine all the people
Living for today

Imagine there's no countries
It isn't hard to do
Nothing to kill or die for
And no religion, too

Imagine all the people
Living life in peace

You may say I'm a dreamer
But I'm not the only one
I hope someday you will join us
And the world will be as one

Imagine no possessions
I wonder if you can
No need for greed or hunger
A brotherhood of man

Imagine all the people
Sharing all the world

You, you may say I'm a dreamer
But I'm not the only one
I hope someday you will join us
And the world will live as one"
John Lennon - *Imagine*

John Lennon's utopian dream of all people living in peace, if only we would rid the world of religious beliefs and national identities, is, indeed, only a dream. It is only to be imagined, because there is no likelihood of its reality within the lifetimes of the living or any foreseeable future. But for those who see and rue the destruction wrought by religious prejudice and nationalistic imperialism, Lennon's imagined world is worth striving toward. Letting go of divisive religious beliefs and jingoistic nationalism would be big steps down that path toward a more peaceful world.

Religions and nations, which claim they are superior to all others, are stumbling blocks on the pathway to world peace. As I write this book, Russian troops have invaded and occupy Crimea and are threatening to cross the eastern border of Ukraine. The European Union and the United States have issued sanctions against Russian officials and the old tensions of the Cold War are ratcheting up.

Why has Russia invaded Ukraine? Many complicated answers are offered about history, culture, ethnic solidarity, natural resources, access to sea ports, etc. All of these excuses may be boiled down to Putin's/Russia's desire to be greater than it is at present. Think of most any war which began with aggressive action by one country against another. The aggressor wanted to take something from the country it attacked. The aggressor always claims a superior right to what it wants.

The US should have all the Southwest territory north of the Rio Grande -- The Mexican-American War. Japan should control the Pacific -- the attack on Pearl Harbor instigated the US's entry into World War II. Saddam wanted the oil fields of Kuwait -- the US and its allies responded with "Dessert Storm". The Islamic State of Iraq and Syria wants to establish "the Caliphate" and has taken over portions of Syria and Iraq -- the US and others (as I write this) are preparing to go to war against ISIS. And so it goes.

Religious wars of an earlier age were much the same as nationalistic-territorial wars. The Crusades by Christian armies and counter-offensives by Muslim armies followed by clashes between Catholic and Protestant forces drenched the Middle East and Europe in blood for centuries. Each side wanted to control the so-called Holy Land and have the upper hand in claiming the Truths which supposedly originated in those lands. How bizarre is it that our species turns on itself and kills its own members to control little chunks of the planet and to control which god is prayed to?

Religion, nationalism, and ethnicity tend to be intertwined in many territorial conflicts; Israel/Palestine, Northern Ireland, Rwanda, and Syria are examples which received much media attention during my lifetime. Perhaps not quite as extensively covered, but there has been as much pain and suffering in Kosovo/Serbia, Kashmir, Burma/Myanmar, Sudan/South Sudan, Nigeria, and now, Ukraine.

International news is a litany of roiling ethnic disturbances, religious strife, and nationalistic aggression. Watching any TV channel reporting international news on almost any day leaves the viewer ready to accept John Lennon's idealistic prescription for world peace.

On the other hand, we may remind ourselves of the beauty and good works inspired by religion mentioned in the last chapter. Nations bind people together and create systems of law and order, which provide security of person and property. Ethnicity is a source of pride and cultural diversity which makes the world a more interesting place. A small and personal example: When I attended the University of Chicago, one of the most enjoyable off-campus activities was to visit the many different ethnic neighborhoods and to sample cuisine from all over the world but right there in Chicago. It was delightful!

At their best, ethnic identification, nation states, and religions bring vast numbers of people together. But, they also divide. No matter how large the tent, there are always those outside of it. When we divide the world into us and them, there will probably be, at the least, suspicion of them.

Race riots and mayhem broke out in Los Angeles in 1992 after the cops who beat Rodney King were exonerated by jury trial in Simi Valley. The white jurors found the white police officers not guilty, even though a nationwide TV audience judged the policemen guilty by virtue of the video showing them beating the crap out of an unresisting large African-American man. As the riots turned deadly, Rodney King appeared on TV again to ask plaintively, "Can't we all just get along?"

The cops, the jury, and the rioters did not get along. Because, they judged the other by the color of skin instead of the content of character, contrary to the admonition of Rev. Martin Luther King, Jr.

~ ~ ~

This book castigates organized religion as one of the prime offenders against peaceful unity. But what about racism and nationalism? The case against race, ethnicity, and nationality as obstacles to peace is different than religion. We do not choose our race, ethnicity, and nationality. Those characteristics are determined by genetics and place of birth. Religion might be initially enforced and later encouraged by parents and family, but eventually we choose to stay, leave, choose a different religion, or choose none at all.

Sure, you can move to another nation and try to ignore your ethnicity -- just about impossible to change your race (Michael Jackson notwithstanding). There are similar problems with gender and sexual preference. But religion is qualitatively different than the other characteristics, because it is a personal commitment as opposed to determination by birth. The same is true of political ideology.

I cast my lot with Dr. King that we will have a better world when we look past race and ethnic origin, as well as gender and sexual preference, to judge by quality of character. Then, we will more likely be able to "just get along". To judge not by color but by character, we must give up the belief that our race, ethnicity, nation, gender, and sexual preference are superior to all others. Ridding oneself of the belief in superiority of a given status we possess, and "the other" does not have, is the essential step the individual must take to end racism, sexism, homophobia, and imperialistic nationalism. What is required beyond that is acceptance of others and respect for differences.

The last few paragraphs might seem like the typical cant of politically correct liberalism. But moving past all of the "isms" is more complex than simply valuing diversity. Pride in one's own origin, race, ethnicity, gender, and sexual identity is a worthy value. Finding the balance between the value of pride in national-racial-ethnic-gender-sexual preference and the value of diversity requires sensitive consciousness. Part II of this book delves into the challenges of finding the balance between apparently competing values.

Extreme religious and political beliefs pose a different challenge than the "isms". Ideological extremism is constructed out of a system of beliefs rather than a status determined by birth. Rules of proper conduct are based on those beliefs. Letting go of religious-political beliefs, whether you grew up with it or converted to it, requires a conscious process of deprogramming and reevaluation. It means abandoning a whole system of beliefs which help to direct the believer's life.

Richard Restak, an eminent neurologist, neuropsychiatrist, and prolific author, quoted earlier, describes the therapeutic process of recovering from delusional beliefs: "Recovery most often begins with a 'double-awareness phase,' during which the deluded person starts to question the validity of the delusional belief while continuing to maintain it. Only gradually does the patient decide to consider alternative possibilities by encouraging and affirming the first stirrings of the patient's doubts about the delusion. But the process cannot be rushed. Since delusion is an affliction of belief, reasoning can go only so far in combating it. What proves most effective is a calm acceptance on the part of the listener to the existence, but not the content, of the delusion." *The American Scholar*, Autumn 2014.

Few of us will participate in a deprogramming intervention with a delusional believer. (Although, in the 1970s three were regular "yellow journalism" features about parents snatching their adult-children from cults to deprogram them back to normalcy.) Our primary task is to live a valuable life. We do that by consciously choosing the values we will use to guide our lives, rather than somnolently accepting the dictates of religious or political authorities. Replacing delusional religious and political beliefs by mindfully guiding our lives with values we have chosen might not necessarily require leaving your religious organization (unless you're kicked out).

One of my closest friends is a devout Roman Catholic. "John" is a sensitive, thoughtful, and intelligent person, despite the fact that he is an attorney. He has allowed me to examine him in long conversations about why he remains an active and committed member of the Roman Catholic Church. I've hit hard on the conflicts between his values, such as equality of opportunity for women, and the rules of his Church. I've ranted about the ridiculousness of the Church hierarchy issuing orders on family life. The men making the rules have never been (at least legitimately) fathers, and certainly not mothers. How inane is it to put celibate men, who wear funny costumes, in charge of determining fundamental questions about family, like birth control practices, child care, and appropriate sex education!

John chooses to remain within the Church, despite his private agreement with most of my criticisms of Roman Catholic policies. He values the traditions, the community of his parish, the feeling of fulfillment he receives through participating in Mass, and the values the Church promotes with which he does agree, such as compassion for the poor and those experiencing suffering.

John tolerates the failings of his Church, because his connection with it fulfills his needs for community and to continue a family and ethnic tradition of which he is proud. It also affords him a venue for expressing the values he cherishes. The worship experience of the Mass is meaningful to him, because he loses himself in the liturgy, he participates in a tradition he values, and it is an emotionally and intellectually satisfying experience shared with folks he cares about and who care about him.

Participating in the community of a church, temple, or mosque, enjoying the beauty of worship, and promoting the traditional values that accord with the values you have chosen, all may be part of living a valuable life. There is certainly value in engaging in worship which gets you outside of yourself. It's good therapy for the rampant narcissism of contemporary urban culture to recognize that we are not the center of the universe. It's not the community or the practice of worship in itself that must be left behind, just the belief systems prescribed by religions. You might even discover that the values promulgated by your religious community largely match those you consciously choose to be guided by.

In Christianity there are many references to Jesus being the "good shepherd" and his followers being "like sheep". (My favorite line in Handel's *Messiah* is "we like sheep". Being from Indiana farm country the punning possibilities of that line were not lost on my teenage cohorts at church; he said with a wolfish grin.) It's a desirable state to be sheep-like?! Domesticated sheep are useful but not very bright animals.

As a follower of Christ, John is certainly not entirely sheep-like nor is he the black sheep of his parish. He's a popular lay leader. John is conscious about what he accepts and what he rejects in the Church. Two of his three children have left the Roman Catholic faith. Straying from the path has not weakened the family bond. Millennials, in even greater numbers than Baby Boomers, are likely to break from religious and political traditions to find their own way.

Let's think intentionally through whether we really want to follow where the religious and ideological shepherds want to lead us. To do that, we need to let go of the structures religion and/or political ideologies have built within us as "cradle believers" or converts. We must free our minds of superstitious beliefs. And, we have to release ourselves from the psychologies of guilt and shame for not being "good" Christians, Jews, Mormons, Muslims, Marxists, Libertarians, or whatever "faith" that has a hold on us. Then, we can begin to see clearly where we want to go and how we can guide ourselves through life's journey.

The journey may take us straight back to the pew we've shared with our family in the church of our ancestors. It might lead us into the polling booth to vote straight ticket for the same political party as our parents. The purpose of the journey is to discover what we truly value and then express those values through participation with family, friends, and in our communities, including a religious one, if we belong to a religious organization, and a political one, if we participate in a political party. Or, we might leave the old behind and discover new and different communities. The journey should not lead to hermetic isolation, but to a more engaged life in community.

Chapter 6: Should We Worship Him, Her, or It?

As to there being a Creator of our universe outside or beyond the material reality of the universe, agnosticism is the most reasonable position. It is not now possible, and I doubt it will ever be within the human capacity, to prove or disprove that our universe was created by a Being. Whether the universe is being directed by conscious forces beyond our human comprehension, well, we just can't know one way or another for certain, can we?

Agnosticism is an intellectually safe landing place. Yet, relatively few (although increasing in numbers) people have landed there. Is that because most of us have given the issue of a Creator-God deep and sustained thought and have become convinced of the existence of God? Or, is it because the pressure to commit to a religious position is such a powerful cultural force?

Indeed, reasonable people might think it is more likely than not that a force or forces were and are involved with the initiation and operation, in some sense, of our universe. It is convenient to call such a force or forces God or gods. Those who have that intuition, or think a creative force seems likely, may want to express their appreciation or gratitude in worshipful ways. I am thankful that our world exists! Aren't you?

Alternatively, one might just as reasonably think that it seems most likely that the universe just is. It exists and it operates through a combination of random events and relativistic laws of physics. There is no need to assume a creator or a force or forces giving purpose or meaning to the universe. That is our job. If that's what you think, aren't you still grateful that the universe exists and you are alive within it? I am!

Whatever one thinks about creation or the lack thereof, feeling gratitude that the universe exists is a worthy response to being alive as a human being. Whatever it is that has created the conditions for life and our particular lives, are we not grateful? Even if reality is ultimately sheer randomness, isn't it good to be alive and that your world exists?

Some folks feel a connection with whatever is the creative energy that is moving our universe into the future. Such a feeling of connection is rightly called spiritual or mystical in relation to the unknowable but awesome force holding the universe together. Expressing appreciation of the awesomeness of our universe through meditation, prayer, song, story, dance, art, liturgy, and other forms we call "worship" is a reasonable response and it feels good.

Albert Einstein, the greatest scientific mind of the 20th Century, said, "The most beautiful thing we can experience is the mysterious." Behind all the laws physical science has discovered "there remains something subtle, intangible and inexplicable. Veneration for this force beyond anything that we can comprehend is my religion. To that extent I am, in fact, religious."

A religious response, in the sense of a worshipful attitude, is not illogical. Reality is and it continues to exist and evolve, so there is a sustaining force holding it together and pushing/pulling it forward into a future. To feel and act worshipfully out of a sense of awe and gratitude is wholesome and appropriate. Participating in this fundamental aspect of religion has value.

~ ~ ~

That attitude of gratitude ought to be the guiding light of religious communities and worship services. Those imbued with it ought to be welcome in the communal worship of their traditional religion. We should not have to hide our lights of doubt and unbelief under a bushel.

But, in my experience many members of mainline Protestant, Roman Catholic, and reformed Jewish congregations are "stealth worshippers". They do not believe in the truth of their denomination's doctrinal statements. But we continue to find meaning through membership in a "faith community" and in participating in services and practices that express our awe and gratitude for the existence of our world.

I have had cloak and dagger conversations with stealth worshippers who attend Christian and Jewish services. There may be many attending Hindu, Buddhist, Muslim, etc., services as well. None of my friends worshipping in those traditions have yet to confess their unbelief to me. (Although, one of my Nepali friends, Ganesh Rai, attends, Hindu, Buddhist, and animist services, and tells me he believes in whichever religion he is practicing at that moment.)

Some stealth worshippers are like my 90 year-old friend Howard, who is an unashamed and open atheist and pillar of our Quaker Meeting, Indianapolis First Friends. He makes no bones about his disbelief or about his commitment to Christian ethics and devotion to his Quaker meeting. Others remain in the closet and let it appear that they accept the doctrines of their denomination, but will privately admit their doubts and unbelief. Open and closeted stealth worshippers reject the orthodoxies of their denominations but value participating in the community.

It would be better for all concerned if we could all come out and have the courage of our non-convictions and to stand up for unbelief. Our ambivalent feelings about the worship experience would subside, if we weren't required to mouth words we don't really believe. Services which contain the elements of traditional Christian worship, the hymns, chants, incense, candles, prayers, sermons, meditative silences, confessions, or whatever, but which do not contain any "declarations of faith" would create a more authentic experience for those of us who value the essential religious response of awe and gratitude but not the doctrines and dogma.

If religious services were stripped of doctrinal claims, doubters and skeptics could participate without having to be stealth worshippers. We could participate without reservation in our traditional (or different) faith communities and enjoy all that we love about religion, the music, prayer and meditation, hearing a good message, supporting social justice causes, and drinking coffee after worship services.

The Quaker services I have regularly attended for the last five years come close to this model. The Society of Friends (official name for Quakers) does not have any official creeds or doctrines. There are published brochures of "Queries" by different Quaker organizations. The Queries are questions that it is suggested Quakers consider, such as: "What, if any, is an appropriate amount of alcohol to consume?" Answers are not provided. The Presbyterian Church (USA) -- the denomination in which I grew up -- has an entire book full of creeds Presbyterians are supposed to believe.

Worship services at Indianapolis First Friends are not very different from the services of the Presbyterian churches I attended throughout most of my life. We have announcements, sing hymns, have prayers, and pass the collection plate; the pastor gives a sermon. The major differences are that the Presbyterians recited the Apostles' Creed and the Lord's Prayer at each service. There is always ten to fifteen minutes of silence at First Friends during which participants may speak "if they feel led" to do so. Presbyterians can barely tolerate a "moment of silence".

Easter occurred while I was writing this book which emphasized a couple other differences between my experience with Quakers and other mainline Protestants. At a Presbyterian church people are likely to greet one another in the parking lot and hallway on Easter Sunday with "He has risen!" The expected response is "He has risen indeed!" At First Friends folks simply said, "Happy Easter." Instead of discussing the Resurrection, the topic for our adult discussion group was the triple homicides of three Christians at a Jewish Community Center by a KKK member who meant to kill Jews.

Our minister's Easter sermon was about the

Resurrection, and she made it clear that she believes that Jesus was corporeally resurrected. Many, possibly most, of the members of First Friends share that belief. Many do not, and feel comfortable expressing their doubts or unbelief to each other.

Since Quakers do not stand and recite any creeds or sit and mumble the Lord's Prayer, the level of discomfort with a particular Quaker pastor's theology is minimized. She's just another Quake expressing her beliefs. She doesn't wear a robe or have any sign of authority other than she leads the worship service. For me, it's a relief no longer to feel guilty or conflicted about reciting the Apostles' Creed and Lord's Prayer. Every service in the Presbyterian Church I had to decide, do I say or not say what I'm not sure I believe?

The Lord's Prayer is not as offensive to doubters and unbelievers as formal Christian creeds. Creeds are declarations of required beliefs of the particular Christian denomination. The Lord's Prayer just attributes amorphous characteristics to "our Father" and requests that He give us food and forgiveness and we humans will in turn forgive others of their trespasses or debts, depending on whether the prayer is spoken by Catholics, Anglicans and Lutherans, or by Calvinists. The prayer begins with a typical statement of confusing religious nonsense, "Our Father, who art in Heaven ..." Why "Father"? Does the Christian God have male sex organs? What and where is "Heaven"? He's in Heaven, but isn't He supposed to be everywhere, even inside our heads knowing our private thoughts, or is He just wired to know what's going on in all places and at all times?

A worship service that emphasizes an attitude of gratitude and would be welcoming to believers, searchers, doubters, and nonbelievers, would not advocate for specific theological beliefs. It would not require the worshippers to recite statements which some would be uncomfortable affirming. It would not declare that God has a penis and not a vagina, or vice versa.

~ ~ ~

Some Unitarian services and Buddhist chanting ceremonies I have attended fit the description of a worship service devoid of belief statements. A friend in South Dakota, who participates in Lakota Sioux pow-wows, tells me that they sing, dance, and drum, but do not make any doctrinal declarations.

I'm told that followers of Confucius engage in ritualistic practices, but, because Confucius held that ultimate reality is beyond human comprehension, Confucian practices do not represent any particular theological position. If true, of world religions with a significant number of adherents, Confucianism might be the most authentic expression of communal engagement expressing awe and gratitude without making any truth claims about ultimate reality. But it's debated, even among its adherents, whether Confucianism is actually a religion. I've not attended a service, so I can say no more about it, but I'm intrigued.

If the superstitious, unprovable, and divisive claims of Truth were stripped out of Christian worship services, most of the typical worship service would still be there. By dispensing with those claims, churches could focus more effectively on their function of bringing people together to care for each other and our world. And more people would feel welcome and comfortable, because we would not feel pressured to state or accept beliefs about which we are unsure or which we reject. "Faith" would be seen as living faithfully to the positive values advocated by the church, temple, or mosque, rather than believing in creeds and doctrines.

~ ~ ~

So, there is no problem in worshipping whatever is that is the creative and sustaining force of our universe, or just engaging in worship practices. If worshipers took it no further, and recognized that the universe might just be a self-contained reality which came to be on its own -- that would make religion more honest, wouldn't it?

Now, I realize that belief in God and the other secondary beliefs of most religions offer believers more than just an intellectual answer to the question of whether the universe was created or not. Believing in heaven, reincarnation, or any other form of an after-life is comforting to the bereaved and satisfying to the aggrieved. An extreme example -- your child is murdered. That your child's murderer will go to Hell or be reincarnated as a cockroach helps assuage the pain. Expecting to see your child in heaven helps the anguished parent live through what must seem like unbearable grief. There is no denying the comfort offered by belief in an after-life under such terrible circumstances.

But what is at the root of this form of comfort? Isn't it the feeling and sense of being cared for, being loved? I want God to care enough for me that the murderer of my child would be justly punished in Hell and I will be reunited with my child in Heaven. That's perfectly understandable.

But doesn't the care, concern, and love of actual, living human beings feel better and comfort more satisfactorily than the imagined love of an unseen god? Being actually touched, hugged, held, kissed, and fed by family, friends, and members of our congregation -- that's real. It's not imagined or abstract like the love of an incorporeal god.

While writing this book, I learned that a friend had suffered a devastating injury and another friend's son came down with what could be a fatal illness. Their families sent out messages asking friends to pray for the ailing loved ones. These friends of mine are "believing Christians", and do think that God can heal injuries and illnesses. But as important -- I think more important -- was the need to connect with others who care enough to put busy lives on hold and pray for, and to return messages of love and support for, the injured husband and ailing child.

Jan Morris, writing for *The American Scholar* (Summer 2014) in her article, "Keep Smiling -- an Agnostic Sermon on

Getting Old," offers this advice from the age of eighty-seven: "We can never know the truth about the afterlife, so I see no point in worrying about it ... sincere adherence to just one essential rule of conduct should be enough to earn us redemption ... St. Peter called that ultimate essence Love, pure and fervent. I prefer to think of it as Kindness, an all-embracing, omnipotent virtue, encompassing love, compassion, unselfishness, mercy, and all the other values that almost every religion respects ... I myself require no holy mumbo-jumbos, miracles and exorcisms, angels and ascensions... if there is any ultimate judge out there beyond the Milky Way, we can hardly be faulted if we have done our kindly best." What a keen, courageous, and delightful insight by one, presumably, closer to the end of her life than most of her readers. Wow!

If we have lived and loved and actively participated in a church, temple, mosque, club, or any community of caring people, we will be valued. Because we have given Kindness to others, others will give it to us. That is the way good people are -- they value each other and they are kind to each other. Knowing that friends will be there for us in our times of need, as we have been there for others in our community, is a much more genuine comfort than any abstract belief in a loving or justice-dispensing god. We can see, touch, smell, taste, hear, and feel the care and concern of our family and friends. We can only imagine it from a divinity. Instead, let's imagine a Church (or any religious organization in any religion) that welcomes any beliefs or lack of beliefs, but is primarily concerned with promoting positive values through a caring community.

Besides, we know God doesn't really love us, nor does God do justice within our world. Otherwise, God would not have let our child be murdered.

Chapter 7: Comforting Traditions; Lies We Tell Our Children

For many years I practiced the discipline of a twice-daily silent prayer. I tried to make my final conscious thought before sleep and my first conscious expression when I awoke, "Thank you, God." I would repeat the phrase in my mind until a sense of peace and gratitude settled in. For the last few years I have practiced the same discipline, but my mantra is just "thank you". Using controlled breathing, inhale "thank", exhale "you" a few times, then exhale "thank", inhale "you", until there is nothing, just breathing. (This might remind Garrison Keillor fans of his joke about Unitarians praying "to whom it may concern.")

I do miss talking to God. I was taught that God was always there to listen. But eventually I had to admit that I was just talking to myself. My "faith" was not really belief in the sense that I was as convinced of the reality of the Christian God as I was of this chair I'm sitting on. I had hoped that God was there and took an interest in me; still do at times. But hope falls short of belief, and eventually I think I spiritually matured enough to find the courage to let go of what had been drummed into me through years of Sunday school and church attendance. If God exists, I have no knowledge of Him, Her, It, or them.

But yeah, at times I still miss God, being able to talk to God. It was comforting, although delusional.

We humans are comforted by many illusions, until harsh reality disillusions us. As a child, I was comforted and fired up by patriotic devotion to my government and country. I looked forward to serving in the US Army as my father had in both World War II and Korea. As a teenager I came to understand that Presidents and generals had repeatedly lied to the American public to justify the unjust war in Viet Nam, which killed a million Vietnamese and sixty thousand Americans. I could not volunteer to fight in that war. I was disillusioned and ceased valuing Patriotism. Eventually I reevaluated it in a more enlightened and nuanced way.

During the period of my devaluation of Patriotism I learned that even good old Uncle Ike Eisenhower had lied to the American public about our U-2 spy planes not flying over Soviet air space. He got caught in the lie when Francis Gary Powers was shot down over Sverdlovsk, USSR. Nixon's Watergate and Dick Cheney's phantom WMDs in Iraq were lies that disillusioned two generations of Americans. Edward Snowden's leaks of classified National Security Administration documents reveal that our government continues to lie and spy on foreigners as well as citizens.

These periodic revelations of governmental deceit and deception push citizens toward a deepening cynicism about our leaders. We've reached a point where it's hard to believe anything the Authorities tell us. Better to be skeptical of all claims intended to inspire us common folk to give our votes, time, treasure, and lives to support those who inhabit the palaces of power.

Preachers and religious leaders also regularly lie to their followers. The most egregious liars are the televangelists and gurus promising remission from sin and the keys to salvation in exchange for financial contributions. They bilk millions from the lonely elderly and naive young.

Unlike political leaders, preachers, imams, lamas, and gurus are rarely put to the test about their beliefs. They can exhort and demand that believers stay on the path of righteous piety, but it's the rare religious leader who has to demonstrate his beliefs much beyond being nice. Political leaders, on the other hand, are forced to reveal whether they are actually committed to their stated principles and platforms by the decisions they make and the policies they implement. And guess what? Surprise, surprise; many do not stick to their campaign promises. They lied to us! They didn't really believe what they said during the campaign. They just told us suckers what we wanted to hear, so we would believe in them and vote for them.

The pulpit holds as many hypocrites as the political podium. The cover up by the Roman Catholic hierarchy of serial child abuse by priests is one of many disturbing examples of religious hypocrisy, deceit, and attempted damage control. But, buttoned-down middle-American mainline ministers are also perpetrators of lies by perpetuating superstitions of the faith. Because I got to know some of them quite well, I know that preachers I heard in churches I attended did not actually believe the Christian superstitions they professed from the pulpit. Even in my undogmatic Quaker meeting we tell our children the stories of Noah's Ark, Jonah being swallowed by the whale, the Virgin Birth, walking on water, Christ's resurrection, etc., as if we adults believe the stories to be accurate historical representations of what happened long ago and far away.

We might convince children to continue to believe in these myths several years longer than they will hang on to Santa Claus. But a day of reckoning for these deceits will eventually come; probably during adolescent rebellion or when the kids are out of reach away at college. Maybe it will be a long-delayed reaction which finally erupts during a mid-life crisis; or, when we are finally too old to give a damn about what others think.

~ ~ ~

The lie we Christians tell the most often, which is so desirable, and the most wrenching to leave behind, is that God loves and is particularly interested in each of us. Children in Christian congregations are reminded ad nausea about how God loves them and God wants them to do this and not do that. The Christian God is described by liberals, conservatives, and moderates as a dual-personality schizophrenic. "He" (and on Mothers' Day in liberal congregations, "She") is both a loving parent and benevolent dictator. God loves each one of us deeply and personally, but

He also has a whole lot of rules we better follow, or else. Most importantly, we have to believe in Him, or we will not be saved (whatever the hell that means).

The center piece of Protestant worship is the preaching of the sermon. Which is what? The answer given in seminary is that it is exhorting the faithful by proclaiming The Word and providing religious instruction to the congregation. To what end? On the surface a sermon appears to take the form of a lecture, but it's really more an appeal to the emotions than the intellect. It bears similarities to a lawyer's opening and closing argument to a jury. Perhaps that's because John Calvin, the founder of the great preaching branch of Protestantism, studied law. Whatever its origin the sermon in Christian worship is like medication. It must be given and taken on a regular schedule.

But why do those who are already saved believers need to be re-converted to the faith each week by being preached at? We need to be intellectually convinced and emotionally uplifted on Sunday, because all that we experience Monday through Saturday flies in the face of the fundamental claim of the Gospel -- that each of us is loved by God and we are saved by faith in God. If events of our own lives do not convince us that the world is not directed by a loving parent, then the daily reports of horrors in the news media should. If they could, preachers would simply provide proofs to their congregations -- like a Geometry professor -- that believers are "saved". But they can't, so they just keep repeating it every Sunday drilling it into the heads of their congregations. Believe and you will be saved!

Preachers follow the Hitler/Goebbels maxim for effective propaganda; repeat a lie often enough and it will eventually sound believable. Propaganda which confirms our own prejudices and emotional needs is especially compelling.

Salvation and forgiveness of sins -- we long to be purified and cleansed of the dirt we've picked up in living our lives. Heaven -- where we'll be reunited with our loved ones and blessed by God for all eternity. These beliefs are so compelling, because they fulfill deep desires. They comfort us in times of trouble. Wish they were true. But there ain't no proof, just repeated emotionally appealing belief statements. Preaching that God loves each and every one of us is propaganda as wish fulfillment.

~ ~ ~

"Nowhere is the contrast of viewpoints more stark than in the secular and religious understandings of childhood. In the biblical view, a child is not a being that is born with amazing capabilities that will emerge with the right conditions like a beautiful flower in a well-attended garden. Rather, a child is born in sin, weak, ignorant, and rebellious, needing discipline to learn obedience. Independent thinking is dangerous pride. ... When assaulted with such images and ideas at a young age, a child has no chance of emotional self-defense. Christian teachings that sound true when they are embedded in the child's mind at this tender age can feel true for a lifetime. Even decades later former believers who intellectually reject these ideas can feel intense fear or shame when their unconscious mind is triggered." (From *Salon* article cited above by psychologists Drs. Marlene Winell and Valerie Tarico, "The sad, twisted truth about conservative Christianity's effect on the mind".)

We send our children to school five days, where they learn critical thinking and science. But on Sunday we feed them crazy-ass stories about Lot's wife being turned into a pillar of salt, Samson killing a thousand Philistines with the jaw bone of an ass, the sea opening for the Israelites, Jesus turning five loaves and two fishes into food for five thousand, walking on water, etc., etc. And we don't say, "Kids, these are wonderful tales, just like the Greek myths you learned about in school." Instead, the Bible stories are told to children as if they are nonfiction.

It was embarrassing. Sunday after Sunday I sat in our

family pew watching the youth pastor deliver "the children's message". The kids are cute and the young pastor is doing her best to sound earnest as she tells the story of Jonah being swallowed by the whale. I squirm in the pew knowing that the intellectually-inclined kids will eventually reject the nonsense they are being fed. My fellow worshippers crane their necks and perk up their ears, not to hear what the youth pastor is saying, but because they want to witness the adorable reactions of the kids. I feel for the youth pastor doing her job as best she can for little or no pay.

Why not be honest and tell our children the truth? Kids love Greek, Roman, and Norse mythology, and they learn from it. We can teach the wisdom and values of Judeo-Christianity through the traditional Bible stories. The stories are fun and interesting and worth telling for sheer enjoyment. There is value in maintaining the tradition of telling the stories. They are great stories! Samson is as great a hero as any of Marvel's X-Men. So why not take a more enlightened approach to religious instruction? Is it because that's how we were taught and it's comfortable and easier to keep doing the same thing?

There is comfort in tradition. My parents taught me that America was the best and closest to perfect country in the history of civilization. "My country right or wrong!" It was us against them. Other countries were either allies or enemies. We could be critical of the other political party ("the god damn Democrats") and argue about domestic and foreign policy. But America was always in the right vis-a-vis other countries. Those who opposed us were worse than just wrong; they were evil communists and our enemies.

Despite their nationalistic jingoism, my parents also taught me to be respectful of differing points of view and to think for myself. So, like many teenagers awakening to political consciousness in the late 60s and early 70s, I was not impressed with the conventional wisdom offered by the cultural authorities. A hurtful generation gap developed between the well-meaning World War II generation and their children of the post-war baby boom. The generational animosity was unfortunate and it was unnecessary.

My sons think critically and are just as critical of American foreign policy as their father. My children did not become as disillusioned with their government as I did. My wife and I were honest with them about the greatness and the flaws of our government and the history of our country. Both boys grew up with a healthy skepticism about their government, or at least the politicians who run it. My eldest son is an officer in the military. He loves his country, is loyal to its government, and will do his duty. James doesn't blindly support foreign adventurism, but three of his most cherished values are Duty, Loyalty, and Honor.

If we are honest with our children, isn't it likely that they will respect the values we would like to pass on to the next generation? It is likely that they will not become disillusioned with their parents and the traditions of previous generations, if parents explain the traditions in ways that make sense to curious minds. If we admit our ignorance about God, the creation of the universe, and all the other edicts and proclamations of "faith" that flow out of those primary beliefs, the next generation will probably not begin to wonder whether their parents, Sunday school teachers, and pastors are nitwits.

Whether we are told by a stern-faced Calvinist preacher or a sweetly beatifically-smiling New Age guru that God loves every one of us -- well, how should we reply? That it is a most peculiar form of love that a loving parent would devastate us with tsunamis, earthquakes, volcano eruptions, not to mention HIV/AIDS, Ebola, Black Plague, flu, sooner or later a killer asteroid, and eventually our Sun burning out. We are selling our children snake oil telling them over and over how much God loves them and all the children in the world. They see pictures of abused children and videos of orphaned children in war-torn Syria and radio reports of starving children in Sub-Sahara Africa. If they watch the news on TV or get it through the Net, they experience second hand death, destruction, and injustice wreaked upon innocent people. Only a perverse and abusive parent would allow, or cause, planes and trains to crash and burn His children or ferries to sink and drown Her children.

I still engage in my daily and nightly devotions. And I go to church every Sunday -- the Quakers call it a "meeting" -- and lead an adult discussion class at the Meeting. I value participation in a community devoted to caring for each other and the world, and it feels good to engage in rituals and practices which express gratitude and awe for that which we cannot comprehend. I enjoy the community, it's meaningful, and it's fun; so long as I am not guilted into mouthing words I do not believe.

~ ~ ~

There is value in maintaining the traditions of our culture and communities. But each generation, like it or not, is free to pick and choose what they will accept and what to reject of the traditions, beliefs, culture, and values of preceding generations. Reflective and creative people will not replicate the previous generations. They will contemplate, challenge, and reject, and, we hope, improve upon what they received from prior generations.

So consider that it is our real parents who have loved us, not an imaginary, holy, and abstracted "Father". It is our family, community, and culture which have taught and nurtured us. The love and instruction of my parents, my schools, my church, my community, and American culture gave me the courage to question the irrational beliefs of my Church, suspect the government of lying, and reject some of the values of our consumer culture. I was told to respect authority, but I was also taught to think independently.

I say the Pledge of Allegiance to the Flag at the weekly

meetings of a club I belong to. I sing the National Anthem when I attend an Indianapolis Colts or Indiana Pacers game. I value my country as a national community and support its fundamental civic values of personal freedom and equality of opportunity. And I participate whole heartedly in Sunday worship services at the Quaker meeting, which does not require me to swear to any catechism or dogma.

There is great value to being in community. I am not an island unto myself, and neither are you. While it takes personal commitment and effort to discern the values we may choose to guide our lives, we did not discover them on our own. They were there in the living examples and ethical instruction of our parents, grandparents, extended family, teachers, preachers, coaches, Boy and Girl Scout leaders, and the wider culture.

We owe it to those from whom we have learned valuable life lessons to be discerning and avoid the temptation to follow the preceding generation like sheep. We owe it to the succeeding generation to keep our churches, temples, and mosques alive and our polity vital, so they can reshape those communities to express the positive values that turn on their generation.

Chapter 8: Religion's Awe Full Temptation

It seems to be very difficult to avoid the temptation of moving beyond the simple and humble attitude of gratefulness for the conditions of life to starting a religion. We like to make up explanations for cosmic mysteries, but we don't seem to be content just telling the stories. Eventually somebody starts calling the stories sacred and true. From the imagination of some ancient and talented storyteller evolve the gods which his descendants begin to worship.

Religious imagination is kind of like the Beatlemania of the 1960s or the more recent Beliebers. Passionate fans imagine they have a personal relationship with their celebrity-idols. But the beloved Bieber doesn't even know the moony-eyed girl dreaming of him in her bedroom or shrieking at his concert exists.

It is charmingly sweet to see tween girls worship their teen idols. From the vantage point of maturity, it is also silly and embarrassing. Some of those teenagers probably look at their parents with jaded eyes, while the old fuddy-duddies mutter their stale prayers in worship of an imagined God. At least Bieber can be seen and heard, if not touched.

The Bible includes an extended letter from an adoring fan to the beloved. Biblical scholars are divided on whether the *Song of Solomon* is addressed to God or an imagined or real lover. The passionate imagination of the author is akin to the passionate longing of the celeb-fan. Perhaps a bit more sophisticated than the imagination of a tween girl (parents hope); here's an R-rated passage from *Song of Solomon*: "O loved one, delectable maiden! You are stately as a palm tree, and your breasts are like its clusters. I say I will climb the palm tree and lay hold of its branches. Oh, may your breasts be like clusters of the vine, and the scent of your breath like apples, and your kisses like the best wine that goes down smoothly ... There I will give you my love."

An imagined love relationship is much easier to handle than a real one, like with your spouse, or between parents and children, or with your siblings. Those relationships are rocky and require work. At times they are an utter pain in the ass. But they're real.

The imagined relationship with a teen idol or a god is perfect; because the loved one is perfect. When Justin gets arrested or behaves churlishly, his adoring fans discount or disbelieve it. He can do no wrong. If a tree falls on the passing car of a pastor and his family in southern Indiana, while they are driving home from worship, and all seven in the car are killed -- God is still good, right? Everything happens for a purpose, it's in God's hands, blah, blah, blah. God is always excused; because God is perfect, right?

In Dostoyevski's *The Brothers Karamazov*, Ivan has had enough of the excuses. He rails at his younger brother, Alyosha, who is studying for the priesthood as a novice monk. Why would a loving God let suffer "a child's tears to her 'dear and kind God'!" Ivan tells the story of a Russian General whose pack of hounds has gathered for a hunt. "One day, a serf-boy, a little boy of eight, threw a stone in play and hurt the paw of the General's favorite hound." When the General found out what happened, he ordered the boy stripped naked, forced him to run, and then released the pack of dogs on him. The little boy was ripped to shreds. Ivan declares that the God who would allow that to happen doesn't deserve to be worshipped.

Religious imagination is a beautiful thing, when it is the inspiration for creativity and caring community. It takes a dangerous turn when it transmogrifies into theological claims about God and "His" relationship to human beings. Once people have bought into the fantastical claims about the all-powerful, ever present, all-knowing, and loving God, their minds are ripe for picking. If the masses can be convinced of stuff that absurd, they will believe anything. And then, the religious professionals can lead their sheep wherever the "good shepherds" want them to go.

Alyosha's faith was shaken by Ivan's rant against God. But he was afraid to let go. He accused Ivan of being in "rebellion" against God and the Church.

~ ~ ~

We are not a humble species and we became less humble as our religions became more "developed". Many ancient cultures, which still exist in smaller and smaller pockets, understood that all things, whether animate or inanimate, had spirit. Their "primitive" religions recognized spirits in animals, trees, and mountains. More (self-proclaimed) sophisticated religions developed pantheons of gods which behaved like aristocratically privileged humans. The ancient Greeks and Romans, Hinduism, and Tibetan Buddhism are of this ilk. The monotheistic religions, Judaism-Christianity-Islam, began to describe God as a wrathful and disgruntled, but loving father. Down through the centuries He has revealed different aspects of the human personality, sometimes destructive and sometimes constructive, sort of like entropy and synergy but with a staff and white beard. (Sir Ian McKellen as Gandalf might come to mind.) For intellectually inclined believers God has become more abstract, fading from a person into an idea. E.g., God is Love. Mystics sexualize God; they like to enter into an ecstatic union with Him. Yikes! In all of these efforts to describe God(s), we humans have created Him, Her, It, Them, into the images that fulfilled our own needs and wishes.

Religious practices reflect a bargain made with that religion's God(s). The bargain is that we'll be taken care of, if we do what our God(s) expect of us. How's that worked out for Jews during the Holocaust, Christians persecuted by the Roman Empire, "untouchables" in Hindu countries, or the thousands who have died as collateral damage in the wars of Crusade and Jihad? Doesn't look good, but we're supposed to believe that they are in Heaven or Paradise, or at the very least they made it to Limbo (Oops! The Vatican abolished Limbo in 2007) or Purgatory. Just believe! Yeah, right.

It makes sense to imagine that everything in the world has spirit. In some sense, even rocks are alive. They are composed of subatomic particles which have motion and change over time. We should respond with gladness to be alive ourselves in this awesome universe. But we just can't seem to resist the temptation of moving from the primal response of awe and gratitude to creating surrealistic, weird, and absurd versions of God(s).

Some Christian and Jewish friends that have trekked with me in Nepal find it amusing that local Hindus actually believe paying homage to Ganesh will bring success in business or on a test in school. Ganesh's father, Shiva, cut off his son's head and replaced it with that of an elephant; and Ganesh's usual mode of transportation is to ride a mouse. How successful is that guy with the big ears and trunk riding a mouse? Yet, believing the walls of Jericho fell down because the Ark of the Covenant was paraded around for seven days is expected of a good Jew? Christians are to accept that Saul and his companions were blinded by a light on the Damascus Road but only Saul heard the voice of Jesus telling him where to go. Auditory hallucinations are a typical symptom of schizophrenia. It's not so easy to laugh at the peculiarities of our own religion.

~ ~ ~

We want to have more control over our lives and fates than what we actually have. Through religion we try to harness powers that will help get us what we want. We try to capture in a name, Ra or Zeus, or a concept, all-powerful all-knowing all-loving God, the awesome forces that direct the events outside of our control. If we can propitiate those forces with sacrifices, confessions, rituals, or liturgies, we will be blessed and not cursed. We want to have power over the powers that rule over us and our world.

Different cultures and peoples have developed

different ways to express this will to power over the mysterious forces. To foreign eyes different religious beliefs and practices might appear quite bizarre indeed. Yet the impulse is the same. Somber Lutherans with heads downcast in prayer asking that God bless this or that are basically doing the same thing as Hindus who slice open the throat of a goat. We really don't want to leave it up to random fate. We want to have an influence over whether our friend Chuck recovers from cancer or Margaret passes the Bar exam.

Prayers and rites of propitiation are pretty harmless (except to the goat). But things turn dangerous when strong personalities step in and offer to show the rest of us how we can bend divine powers to our will and receive the blessing of the Almighty.

Alongside beliefs about God(s), the authority of the priestly class arose. Those who claim to know more about God or the gods than the rest of us, whether they are priests, prophets, popes, shamans, or seers, assert power over us. It is a power grab based on emotionally charged, but bogus, claims.

Religious leaders, like political leaders, make unprovable, but viscerally appealing claims. They then turn those claims into doctrines, creeds, platforms, or edicts. Those who do not accept these truths are outcasts, heretics, blasphemers, and enemies. Ostracism, inquisitions, and religious wars follow. Rid first the community and then the world of the unbelievers! (Then no one will be left to question our authority.)

To avoid being taken advantage of by the prophets and priests, we need to learn to accept that we only have as much control as we really have, and no more. Praising and praying to God(s) very well may give us more control over ourselves for the moment. It helps to slow down and contemplate what life means and what we want out of it and what we should give to it. And it especially feels good to do this with other caring folks. But we should resist the temptation to think that through rites of sacrifice or prayers of supplication we can harness supernatural forces to do our bidding and bend the future to our will.

What is to happen in the future is created by all the myriad actions of past and present over which we have little control. Cancer, diabetes, and water shortages do not answer to our prayers. Not to say that we are powerless, but better to use the powers we actually control like following a healthy diet, exercising regularly, handling our financial resources wisely, funding beneficial research, and preserving food and water resources. Better to live conservatively and give liberally than to expect miracles.

Religious leaders who claim special knowledge and connection with the supernatural and tell us that, if we follow their lead, God will bless us -- watch out! Asking us to mail in our checks or put our money in their collection plate is just the beginning. Some will lead their followers down dark and dangerous paths, like the Westboro Baptists disrupting funerals of deceased military veterans or Jihadists buckling on suicide vests.

Religious leaders may know more about their holy books, rites, and rituals than the rest of us. But anyone who appreciates that she is alive and living in an amazingly wonderful reality knows as much about God as can actually be known. All the rest of it is just imagination, speculation, and belief.

~ ~ ~

The cosmogony of current astrophysics is that once upon a time, or, when time began, there was a massive explosion of super condensed matter. Physicists call this a "singularity". After the singularity of the Big Bang our universe began to evolve and came to be how it is. What caused the singularity, why it occurred, was there a creative force other than the energy stored within the matter itself; these questions are unanswerable. Scientists can theorize, philosophers can speculate, poets can emote, and mystics can evoke an oceanic feeling. But we don't really know why it happened.

The agnostic position is the most humbly honest. And it poses the least danger of hardening into creeds which will become weapons of alienation and division. The atheist stands on no firmer foundation than the theist. Neither can prove the other wrong or their own belief right.

The response of wonder to existence and the desire to shape that response into some coherent system of beliefs seems to be a common human need down through the ages. But history reveals that, when that common feeling of awe is shaped into a system of claimed but unverifiable truths, bad things happen. It matters not whether the claims are a religion or an atheistic philosophy, like Marxism or Fascism, bad things happen.

If we can discipline ourselves to respond to the great and fundamental questions of philosophy and theology with a sense of awe and gratitude, and take it no further in terms of claiming to know the answers, good things would happen. That response of awe and gratitude is the creative source of beautiful art, literature, temple and cathedral architecture, the worshipful attitude of St. Francis, and the mindfulness of Thich Nhat Hanh. The world is richer for these creative expressions.

If one supposes that there must be God(s) to explain the existence of the universe and its evolution, and that supposition gives rise to beautiful art, respect for others and the environment, then, no problem, man. If belief is channeled into community building through worshipful practices like prayerful meditation or composing hymns and chants, stories and art, cool! Any religious organization which promotes the pursuit of truth, beauty, and goodness without making false claims of Truth and using coercion to enforce conformity to the party line is probably a force for peace on earth good will toward men and women.

The challenge for religious and political organizations is to overcome the temptation to make claims that cannot be supported and which divide people into us and them, believers and unbelievers. All of the major religions have given in to this temptation more often than they've resisted it. They are like the courageous man who stared temptation in the face one thousand times; and gave in nine hundred and ninety nine.

Chapter 9: Bumpy Progress toward a Better World

The looking glass of history reveals a pretty ugly picture of what follows after peace-promoting founders of religion, like Siddhartha Buddha and Jesus of Nazareth, depart the scene. Religious organizations tend to be very good at promoting positive values and building communal connections among members. The historical attitude toward those who do not believe is not such a pretty picture.

During my lifetime there has been an increasing emphasis among mainline Christians to be compassionate, welcoming, and inclusive. Extraordinary efforts have been made by some Christians, like the Sanctuary Movement which began in the 1980s to provide shelter for undocumented immigrants. Most denominations are now willing to ordain women and to allow them to hold leadership positions within the denominational hierarchy. The fights over ordination of gays and lesbians, and to what extent those with "different" sexual orientation are to embraced by Christian churches, continue. But it's undeniable that progress is occurring in the acceptance of difference and compassion for "outsiders".

In the last twenty years I have consulted with five Protestant churches about best practices. Each one was in the process of initiating "more welcoming" policies and strategies. These congregations each had a genuine desire to broaden and diversify the demographics of their membership.

In the 1980s there was a theological backlash against the liberal social gospel movement and liberation theology of the 60s and 70s. Mainline denominations began losing members in the 1970s as Baby Boomers reached maturity (at least in the sense of years since birth). The popularity of Christian evangelicalism in the 1980s did not reverse the losing trend of mainline churches, but it did increase the numbers attending independent churches. Mega churches with charismatic preachers started popping up and TV evangelism added to their geometric growth.

The Evangelical movement was good for numbers, but there was an uncomfortable aspect to it for many cradle Christians. There was an aggressively pushy attitude among many evangelicals. They did not consider you a real Christian unless you'd been "born again" by accepting Jesus Christ as your personal savior. The coercive aspect of the evangelical movement has largely subsided. I can cite numerous evangelical friends as some of the kindest and most compassionate folks I know.

Evangelicalism is being superseded by a millennial movement bearing the rainbow symbol promoting diversity. Within mainline Protestant churches women are increasingly taking over leadership positions. The New York Times declared in an article on August 24, 2006 that 51% of seminary students in the US were women. The Church of England in July of 2014 finally allowed the ordination of women as bishops, lagging just a few hundred years behind the other major Protestant denominations. The mainliners are all in the process of debating, changing, or bending their rules against gay ordination and same-sex marriage. The General Assembly of the Presbyterian Church (USA) in June 2014 overwhelmingly voted in favor of changing the Book of Order to describe marriage as being between "two people."

An increasing attitude of tolerance of differences is not limited to Christianity. And, there are certainly so-called Christian churches and organizations that are racist, sexist, homophobic, and down right hostile to difference. But violence toward "the other" has generally diminished in societies which have paired developed economies and universal access to education. There is a lot of evidence that our species is currently moving in a bumpy but progressively tolerant and less violent direction.

Harvard psychologist Steven Pinker analyzed statistics of graveyards, population surveys, and historical records for his book, *The Better Angels of Our Nature: Why Violence Has*

Declined. His and other historical-statistical analyses show that, despite the two World Wars in the first half of the 20th Century, there's actually been a reduction in war deaths, family violence, racism, rape, murder, and violent crimes world-wide during the modern era. The FBI's statistics of reported violent crimes in the US show a dramatic reduction in the last two decades. It's down over sixty percent since the 1990s. According to Pinker, "The decline of violence may be the most significant and least appreciated development in the history of our species."

Before we become too self-congratulatory and complacent we need remember that history has not been a steady and ever upward trajectory toward a more enlightened and peaceful planet. There have been eras of progressive advancement followed by decline. In Europe the Dark Ages followed the Golden Age of Greece and Rome. Germany was considered one of the most cosmopolitan and advanced countries in the history of the world before starting the two World Wars. Cultural advancement has flourished and withered in cycles for millennia in the Middle East. It flourished in ancient Babylon and Egypt, then in Persia and later under the Ottoman Turks. Decline followed each of those cultural golden ages.

The current trend of increasing cultural compassion could begin a downward trajectory any moment. Currently the most religious-oriented violence, if frequency of disturbing reports in the news media is the best evidence, must be in the Islamic-dominated Middle East followed by Central Africa. Palestinian/Israeli clashes were relegated to the back pages the first half of 2014, but then open warfare broke out again in June. Daily reports of slaughter and atrocities in Syria and Iraq have dominated the news throughout the year. Christians have abandoned their homes and fled Egypt and neighboring countries due to harassment and church bombings. Sudan has been wracked by civil war.

Division of the country into North and South did not end the ethno-religious violence. Boko Haram has made front page news with abductions of school children and massacres of Christian church-goers and civil servants in Nigeria. In the US we tend to think of Buddhists as gentle folk, but in Myanmar (Burma) mobs of the Buddhist majority have killed and ransacked homes of Muslims in recent years as Buddhism is increasingly linked with a nationalistic movement advocating ethnic cleansing.

Our world still has a long way to travel before we reach the outskirts of John Lennon's imagined utopia. The dark forces of religious intolerance and racial-ethnic hatred continue to rear their ugly heads. Progress is, indeed, bumpy.

Using religion to divide and conquer is not a causally necessary development. It can be curbed by holding onto the attitude of gratitude, that most basic and heart-felt religious response. Being grateful that you are alive in this awesome world should be inspiration for affirming the fundamental value of all other human beings and the rest of the natural world. Our innate religious inclination ought to be the source of union rather than division.

Our world is full of wonders. When a child looks in a microscope the first time and sees a new universe of microbes, the look on that child's face is the equivalent of a religious response. The first time I saw the Himalayas, my response was: Awesome! Consider the monarch butterfly; that fragile-beautiful little creature migrates from Canada to Mexico every year. How amazing is that! Those of us who have witnessed the birth of a child -- can we even express what that experience was like? We need not ascribe our response of wonder at the world to a God or gods defined and circumscribed by the dictates of a religion. We can just be in awe of all of it.

Rather than constructing a fortress of beliefs which let some in and exclude others, the sense of religious awe ought to be a source of reconciliation, of recognizing our common humanity within this shared world. Because, whatever our differences, we do come from a common genetic source and we do share the resources of this finite planet. If more attention was paid to our commonalities, and differences were seen as interesting or even amusing, there would be so much less violent ethno-religious hatred in the world.

~ ~ ~

Living without (beyond) belief does not exclude the possibility of holding and expressing a worshipful attitude toward whatever the creative and sustaining force of our universal reality may be. I have hiked many days on mountain trails in the Nepal and India Himalayas chanting the sacred Buddhist mantra of "Om mani padme hum". Singing the Christian praise hymn to the Trinity, The Gloria Patri, has given me strength and joy on solo sea-kayaking adventures. The literal statements of the words of the mantra and hymn were not important or meaningful to me. It was the feeling they evoked and the state of mind they induced.

Living beyond beliefs does not exclude participating in religious community or engaging in religious practices. I can't prove the paradoxical reality of The Trinity or that Buddha's compassion is manifest in the world through the lotus flower. But, I can feel the awe and compassion that sacred hymns, mantras, dances, paintings, sculptures, and cathedral architecture represent and evoke. Living beyond beliefs allows me to focus on the beauty and emotional essence of religious practices. Not being burdened with belief actually helps to open the heart and mind to the primal quality of reality. The joyful experience of worship and willingness to share is beyond beliefs.

When you are not looking through the rose-colored glasses of doctrine or ideology, the actual beauty of the world is more vivid. The practice of mindful attentiveness to other people and nature is enhanced when assumptions based on beliefs are not made. "Assumptions make asses of you/me."

So said a weathered old carpenter I worked with on a road and bridge crew when I was nineteen. That old bloke was right.

Trouble begins when we start making claims about transcendent reality by separating it from our experience of awe. God(s) begin to be described and then assumptions develop about what God(s) expect of us. The process really takes off when Holy Books or golden tablets are discovered.

Prophets, priests, and popes use the holy books to erect increasingly elaborate belief systems which privilege them at the expense of the rest of us. Religious potentates claim authority and power over us commoners, because the rules derived from the sacred scriptures always give special privileges to the priestly class. Historically, religious leaders demanded that secular rulers submit to the higher authority of religion. But without an army to support its sovereignty, religion has had to accept lesser privileges, like tax exemptions and making fans wait through a prayer for the start of NASCAR races.

~ ~ ~

The original charismatic founder/leader of most religions is quite revolutionary vis-a-vis "the establishment". As the religion becomes part of the established order it tends to support the status quo of society's power structure. Yet, it's not necessarily an easy relationship between government and religion, because each demands priority from The People.

The Hindu caste system puts the Brahmin-priests on top followed by the Kshatriya caste of military rulers. Tibetan Buddhism evolved a theocracy with the Dalai Lama as supreme religious and civil ruler. Christianity and Islam have both struggled with the tension between church or mosque and the state. In Muslim and Christian dominated countries there have been periods when religion dominated government and periods in different countries when the state controlled religion. Turkey and Egypt are currently embroiled in political turmoil as parties and factions clash over the evolving relationship between government and religion. In the US legal actions are filed every year which wend their way up to the Supreme Court for rulings on the US Constitution's "Separation Clause". Several countries in the European Union are finally beginning to dissolve the constitutionally based relationship between government and a state church.

On the international level, almost every year since 1999 Pakistan, with the backing of the Organization of the Islamic Conference ("OIC"), has offered resolutions at the United Nations which would prohibit "defamation" of Islam within non-Islamic countries. The resolutions have been opposed by "Western democracies" (really republics, which are not limited to the Western Hemisphere, e.g., Australia, Japan, and South Korea). Opposition of the constitutional democracies with developed economies is based on the view that the "religious anti-defamation" bills are a guise for Islamic countries to discriminate against non-Muslims and to empower Muslim movements within the more pluralistic societies of non-Muslim countries.

In 2009 the UN General Assembly did approve a resolution deploring the defamation of religions by a vote of eighty nations in favor and sixty-one against with forty-two abstentions. The votes for passage came from the OIC nations, most African nations, and other "third world" countries. Speaking against another bill backed by the OIC in 2011, Eileen Donahoe, the US Ambassador to the United Nations Human Rights Council, said, "We cannot agree that prohibiting speech is the way to promote tolerance, because we continue to see the 'defamation of religions' concept used to justify censorship, criminalization, and in some cases violent assaults and deaths of political, racial, and religious minorities around the world." Given that all countries with majority Muslim populations supported the resolution, Ambassador Donahoe's statement, as representative of the opposition of the "Western democracies", exposes a gaping rift between "the West" and Islamic and African nations. "We" see "them" as using religion to suppress human rights. "They" see "us" as trying to suppress Islam.

Nevertheless, a sea change within the UN has begun in recent years. Revulsion at the barbarities of violently radical Islamists has raised consciousnesses. There's a growing consensus that religion should not be used as a tool of repression. Conversely, governments should allow all people the freedom to practice their religions.

In 2011 the UN Human Rights Committee issued a statement that "... it would be impermissible for any such laws to discriminate in favor of or against one or certain religions or belief systems, or their adherents over another, or religious believers over non-believers." After fifteen years of debates and politicking, the UN has changed course from promoting and protecting beliefs to being concerned with protecting believers and nonbelievers alike from both civil and religious oppression.

From the Office of the High Commissioner for Human Rights at the UN: "The international human rights movement was strengthened when the United Nations General Assembly adopted the *Universal Declaration of Human Rights* on 10 December 1948. Drafted as 'a common standard of achievement for all peoples and nations', the *Declaration* for the first time in human history spells out basic civil, political, economic, social and cultural rights that all human beings should enjoy." Article I of *The International Bill of Human Rights* states: "All human beings are born free and equal in dignity and rights. They are endowed with reason and conscience and should act towards one another in a spirit of brotherhood."

The UN's concern for human rights had its historical antecedent in what was the clearest expression of concern for human rights emanating from the political Age of Enlightenment: "We hold these truths to be self-evident, that all men are created equal, that they are endowed by their

Creator with certain unalienable Rights, that among these are Life, Liberty and the pursuit of Happiness." *Declaration of Independence, July 4, 1776, The unanimous Declaration of the thirteen united States of America.*

These Declarations may be interpreted to express a *belief* in universal human rights, and we often talk about the human rights and civil rights movements being founded upon beliefs in such and such. But it is not a set of beliefs or religious commandments that are the guiding lights of the centuries of struggle for human rights. The fundamental concern of the human rights movement has been to persuade all people of the value of other human beings. The fight has been to reform institutional structures to recognize the value of individual liberties and right of assembly in communities and to create economic systems which allow all members of society to live a decent life. These are values, freedom and equality of opportunity, not beliefs. Rather than supporting that struggle, divisive religious belief systems and repressive political ideologies have been obstacles in the path of human progress.

~ ~ ~

Institutional religions have been historical forces of repression as have political ideologies like monarchy, oligarchy, fascism, and Marxist-Leninism. It's not just in the history books; it continues. Religious authorities control and repress conduct through force of law in theocracies like Iran. Christian denominations as diverse as the Roman Church and the Amish use the socio-economic force of excommunication and ostracism to repress dissent. The tool of choice by mainline Protestants and liberal Jews is "guilting" or shaming members when they fail to conform their conduct to church or temple expectations. It's less painful than torture, but it still has the effect of coercing conformism and separating out dissenters.

The sins of religious persecution, crusades, inquisitions,

and ethnic cleansing are not historical anomalies. Horror stories of beheadings and severely cruel punishments, like stoning to death women accused of adultery, regularly appear in news accounts from Arab countries and the tribal areas of Pakistan. Religious persecution has adapted and significantly moderated in most constitutional democracies, for sure. It has not disappeared from our world.

A recent incident of religious repression in the US involved two Mormon activists. Kate Kelly the founder of Ordain Women, an organization advocating ordination for Mormon women, was notified in June 2014 by a bishop of the Church of Latter-Day Saints (LDS) that she is facing "excommunication on the grounds of apostasy". John Dehlin, a psychologist who directs a podcast series which has advocated for the rights of gay and lesbian Mormons, received a similar notice threatening excommunication. The LDS leadership wants to silence these two activist Mormons because their "actions contradict church doctrine and lead others astray," according to an official statement from the LDS Church reported by *The Daily Beast*.

The Beast's report of June 13, 2014 went on: "The church's intent to silence discussion is clear in Kelly's notification regarding her informal probation (as it) states: 'It is important that you understand that you are not required to change your thinking or the question you may have in your own mind regarding the ordination of women, but you need to make it a private matter.' The letter also orders her to 'take down www.ordainwomen.org and disassociate yourself from Ordain Women.' In other words, Kelly said, 'I don't have to change my mind. I just have to shut my mouth.'"

The LDS is not alone in its efforts to suppress dissent against doctrines which discriminate against women and gays. A quick Google search of "gay ordination refused" turned up articles on a Methodist minister defrocked for performing his gay son's wedding; a New Zealand Anglican Bishop's refusal to ordain a gay man; an article by the Catholic

News Agency fear-mongering that "the Obama administration might revoke the tax exempt status of religious organizations which refuse to perform gay marriages"; "African Christians will be killed if the Church of England accepts gay marriage, the archbishop of Canterbury has suggested," reported *The Guardian*, April 4, 2014; and many more.

It's bumpy progress, indeed, toward an imagined future of peace on earth good will toward all men and women.

10: Bad Men and Their Good Books

Most religions have holy book(s). Customs, traditions, organizational policies, creeds, doctrines, and all the other ways religions try to direct the behavior of adherents is usually justified through reference to sacred scriptures. "Sola Scriptura!" thundered Martin Luther and the Protestant reformers. Luther, Calvin, Knox, and other Reformation leaders were enraged by the Roman Church's drift away from justifying all matters of faith through authority of Scripture.

The Reformers protested that man-made policies and practices did not necessarily bear the stamp of divine approval. Look how often the Israelites got into trouble by trying to think for themselves. In the prophetic narratives of the Old Testament, whenever the Israelites strayed from following the rules delivered by God to Moses as set down in the Torah, the Jews would pay dearly. The Protestant reformers declared that faithful Christians must rely strictly on God's Word and not on rules conceived by mere mortals, which popes and bishops surely are.

This righteous critique of the Protestant reformers side steps the niggling little issue that the Holy Bible was written by mere mortals and what got in and what got left out was decided by other mere mortals.

So what is the basis for claiming that your holy book is The One True Book and that it answers questions that the arts and sciences, common sense, and all the other holy books cannot? It was given to us by God! But so were the sacred scriptures of all the other religions. Yet, they contradict each other. How can that be? There are even contradictions within the holy books of the same religions. Contradictory tales of gods and heroes within Hindu and Buddhist traditions are legion as are contradictions within the Old and New Testament. One little example: Who went to The Tomb to discover The Resurrection? In the Gospel of Matthew it's "Mary Magdalene and the other Mary"; in *Mark* it is "Mary

Magdalene and Mary the mother of James, and Salome"; *Luke* reports that it was "Mary Magdalene and Joanna and Mary the mother of James and the other women", and in *John* it's only Mary Magdalene.

My New Testament professor in seminary recommended that all Fundamentalists read *Gospel Parallels, a Synopsis of the First Three Gospels*. It places side-by-side corresponding passages from *Matthew*, *Mark*, and *Luke*. Passage after passage reflect differences, many small, but some significant, in the accounts of the events covered by, what Christian biblical scholars call, the three Synoptic Gospels. ("Synoptic" means seeing with or personally witnessing.) So, the three "eye witnesses" provide conflicting versions of the "facts". The fourth gospel, John, provides yet a different report. Being trained in the law I might be a bit anal about this, but no jurist would enter summary judgment on the dogmatic claims of Christianity with so much contradictory testimony.

~ ~ ~

The power of a holy book rests entirely on belief in its power, not on reason, logic, consistency, or literary craft. The Bible might be respected by a Hindu, but it has no more power to compel his behavior than the Bhagavad-Gita has over a Christian. Objectively, no holy book has a greater claim to be The One; but each one is proclaimed as the one and only holy book by the followers of each particular religion. Claiming that your holy book is the right one, and all the other sacred scriptures are wrong, is exactly the arrogance that compels religious divisiveness and oppression.

This is not to deny that there is much wisdom worth studying and learning within the holy books of different religions. We just need to recognize that their descriptions of creation, supernatural events, and the powers of their super-hero-prophets are wonderful stories of myth and legend. Stories move us and myths offer ancient wisdom about how the world works. They are not to be taken as accurate journalistic reports of actual occurrences.

Maybe Jesus did somehow come back to life. I don't know; I wasn't there. But when the so-called eye witnesses can't get their stories straight, how are we to judge the truth of the claim, and why would we choose to believe it? Because the religious authorities tell us to be like sheep.

Supernatural events aside, we also need to be skeptical about accepting the power relations and socio-economic-political structures advocated in the sacred scriptures. Although supposedly ordained by God(s), they are not necessarily just. The Vedas describe a caste system which privileges some members of Hindu society over others due to the vagaries of birth. Christian slaveholders justified slavery because Ephesians 6:5 states, "Slaves, obey your earthly masters with respect and fear, and with sincerity of heart, just as you would obey Christ." Consider the damage that passage has done. Frederick Douglass called slavery "the great sin and shame of America". Others have called it America's "original sin". Slavery still exists in some societies, and in the US we are still coming to terms with its legacy.

Passively following religious or political leaders who proclaim their way is The Way is dangerous. When you are asked to just believe, or accept it on faith, you are giving up the most valuable gift given you by Nature or Creation -- your freedom to choose how to construct your life.

All of those otherwise decent folk who supported the institution of slavery would not have approved the treatment of human beings as chattel, if they had not been convinced by religious and secular authorities that God approved it. John Henry Newton, author of the hymn *Amazing Grace* and captain of slave trading ships, was a practicing Christian while he was engaged in the slave trade. Eventually his eyes were opened and he became an active abolitionist. He explained in an abolitionist pamphlet circulated widely in England in 1788, *Thoughts upon the Slave Trade*, that he had earlier misunderstood Christianity but eventually realized it applied to all people. Despite approval of slavery by Church and State, Newton eventually exercised his own judgment and learned to value Africans as people and let go of the beliefs he had held as a Christian slave trader.

Those who claim they have all the answers, because they have studied the holy book more deeply than you have are simply wrong. They might know The Book better, but that doesn't mean they understand reality better. Knowledge of what is contained in any particular book is not wisdom. Being able to apply the wisdom offered through sacred scriptures to real life in the here and now so it has actual benefit demonstrates real wisdom.

Professional religious types might very well have good advice. The ministers of the churches to which I've belonged have been well intentioned for the most part. Some were influential in helping me to figure out who I want to be and how to live a good life. Those pastors had drawn from the Bible relevant intelligence about how to live according to humane-communal values. They taught what they had learned with a generous heart.

I have had several audiences with the highest lama of the Sherpa people, Tengboche Rinpoche aka Lama Tenzin, who is abbot of Tengboche Monastery high in the Nepal Himalayas. I have interviewed Lama Tenzin twice for articles and books I've written. In 2003, when sharing tea and conversation, I told Lama Tenzin that I was concerned about the desecration of Mt. Everest and that Sherpas were participating in trashing the holy mountain. (To Tibetan and Sherpa Buddhists it is "Chomolungma", which means "Mother Goddess".) He explained that there were conflicting values in play. Yes, the mountain is sacred, but Sherpas were the poorest people in Nepal, until they developed a tourist industry from trekkers and mountaineers coming to Chomolungma.

Before tourism, Sherpas were dependent on potato farming and yak herding to make a living. Mountaineers, like Sir Edmund Hillary, have created foundations to help develop infrastructure in the Khumbu, where the Sherpas live. The government paid little attention to the Khumbu in the past, but has become interested in policing and preserving the mountains which draw trekkers. The mountains have become revenue producers and a source of tax collection. Lama Tenzin explained, "The Mountain has given us food, schools, electricity, and running water. Each of us must decide what we value most."

Lama Tenzin told me that he hoped climbers and Sherpas would take better care of the Mountain, so its natural beauty would be protected. He said that he also hoped the climbers and trekkers would continue to come to Tengboche to hire his people as guides and porters, to spend money, and to make donations to the Monastery. Then, he laughed.

Less enlightened religious leaders have preached at me that I must live my life based on beliefs and rules they find embedded in the Bible. These sorts of preachers admonish us to follow rules that were not necessarily designed to help us create good and valuable lives in the twenty-first century world we inhabit. Those sorts of preachers don't laugh much.

Lama Tenzin realizes his Sherpa people must find a way to mediate and balance the spiritual and the worldly. There is no specific Commandment contained in the sacred Buddhist texts created a few thousand years ago that sensitively and sensibly answers the issues we discussed. But, Lama Tenzin's practical knowledge of the economics of farming, yak herding, and tourism, as well as high altitude ecology and government regulations combined with a deft touch in interpreting the ancient texts have served his people well.

~ ~ ~

My experience with committed believers in the Good Book has been a mixed bag of the best and worst of my fellow

Homo sapiens. Some years ago I visited a Holiness Church in a small town in Alabama. The congregation was warm and welcoming. I was treated with the finest of Southern hospitality, hugs and lots of food. They didn't have a choir but the music made by that small congregation was delightful, as good as the Soggy Bottom Boys in the movie, *Oh Brother, Where Art Thou?* When the pastor started preaching the warmth I felt began to turn into icy discomfort. The message of the sermon was that everyone had to vote for George W. Bush, because John Kerry was a communist in disguise. The preacher ranted about "homosexuals and communists taking over America!" He roared and bellowed that these homosexuals and communists were going to hell and taking everyone with them who supports the homosexual-communist agenda!

We must be consciously discerning. If we follow preachers of The Word like lemmings, we might be led over a cliff. Living in thrall to a system of beliefs based on the authority of one of many holy books according to one leader of one of the many different religions, all of which claim to own The Truth, is dangerous.

Ask yourself, why would God or the gods choose to reveal himself, herself, or themselves only through one particular sacred book? If God rules over the whole world, why would one particular ethnic group be chosen for special blessings? What difference could it possibly make to the Lord of the universe whether a puny human being believes in Her, Him, or It? It's a ridiculous projection of human ego to claim to know and speak for God.

Humble agnostics and people guided by humane-inclusive values do not claim any special-secret-magical knowledge. They generally support basic human rights for all people. These folks do not condemn to hell those with whom they disagree. Zealous believers claiming authority through The Book or their ideology are the ones who cast out heretics and start wars.

Chapter 11: Don't Get Fooled by Religious Tricksters

"... And the morals that they worship will be gone
And the men who spurred us on
Sit in judgment of all wrong
...
And the slogans are replaced, by-the-bye
And the parting on the left
Are now parting on the right
And the beards have all grown longer overnight
...
Then I'll get on my knees and pray
We don't get fooled again
Don't get fooled again
No, no!"
The Who, *Won't Get Fooled Again*

Biblical scholars tell us that the ancient Hebrew people were so in awe of their God that they dared not speak or write down its name. That kind of humble awe and worshipful attitude was a wise response to the mysteries of their universe. Over time that wise and humble attitude of the ancient Hebrews was replaced with something not so wise. They began to anthropomorphize their god into a vengeful protector against Egyptians, Assyrians, Babylonians, and other powerful, threatening neighbors. Yahweh eventually transmogrified into a business broker with whom the Israelites could make a deal. God was transitioned from "that whose name cannot be spoken" to a useful partner in getting what we want from the world.

The major deal with God was called a covenant, which is a legal term meaning promise. A mutual covenant is a contractual relationship between two parties making reciprocal promises to each other. The covenant between God and Israel was: You protect us and we'll worship you as our only God. Both sides broke their promises.

The Jewish kingdom was split by civil war into the separate countries of Judea and Israel, each of which was overwhelmed by more powerful invaders. The Babylonian king Nebuchadnezzar destroyed Jerusalem and exiled the wealthy and learned classes of the Jewish State into captivity and slavery in 587 BCE. That catastrophe is called The Diaspora by Jewish historians. Later, Israel was ruled by the Persians until Alexander conquered the Persian Empire. The Jews then came under the jurisdiction of Alexander's Egyptian heirs until the conquest of the Middle East by Rome. In 70 CE Jerusalem and the temple were sacked and burned by the Romans in the brutal suppression of a failed revolt. Another Diaspora occurred and the Jews were a scattered people suffering pogroms and the Holocaust until the State of Israel was reestablished in 1947. The Jewish State has been at war and suffered repeated attacks since the Nakba (forcible exile of Palestinians) in 1948.

Has the deal the Jews made with God worked out well for either party? Perhaps the heirs of the ancient Hebrews and the God of Abraham, Isaac, and Jacob would have both suffered less if God was not transformed from an unknowable source of awe into a character with whom the Israelites could do deals.

~ ~ ~

"Living beyond beliefs" means living with the humble acceptance that we do not know what created and propels the reality of our universe. Imagining God(s) to be characters like people we know, or wish we knew, is fun. Myths and morality tales are instructive about how to behave or not to behave. Who doesn't enjoy the tales of gods and heroes in Greek, Roman, and Norse mythology? The Mahabharata and Ramayana are filled with wonderful stories about Krishna, Arjun, Rama, Hanuman, Laxmi, and myriad others among the fantastic pantheon of Hindu gods and heroes.

The Norse myth of the death of Balder impressed me as

a child. It was fascinating to imagine the most beautiful man-god with golden hair standing and smiling while all the other gods threw deadly weapons at him for sport. He was invulnerable, except to mistletoe. The evil trickster Loki put a branch of mistletoe into the hand of the blind god of the night, Hod. Loki then directed Hod's arm for a fatal throw of the mistletoe branch into Balder's chest. In some versions of the tale Hod is killed by other gods for his unintended murder of Balder.

What impresses me now is the wisdom the myth reveals about how tricksters will lead the less discerning to harm themselves and others. The ancient Norse were forewarning us against blindly following the trickster charlatans of our own times. The choice to follow evil tricksters, like Charles Manson, Jim Jones, and Bernie Madoff has caused much pain and suffering. We were warned.

~ ~ ~

Creative writers, musicians, and artists of every generation have added to the body of work about the awesomeness of reality, about God, if you will. Many post-biblical and contemporary works are just as worthy expressions of the response of awe to the wonders of our world as the formal canons of the major religions and the ancient myths of each culture.

Think about it! Why should sacred scripture be closed to additions? Any literary critic and free-thinking Christian theologian would surely agree that the works of Dante, John Donne, and Tolstoy offer more valuable and deeper theological insights than Numbers and John's Third Epistle. Why restrict the sacred works of Christianity to the books voted on by the men who attended a series of councils of Church insiders several centuries after the death of Christ? Why accept as sacred only literature produced in the ancient Near East and Roman Empire, when so much beauty and wisdom has been created since those ancient times?

If religions were open to sacred texts and art being added to the canon every generation, religion would be less rigid. It would be more flexible as it flowed and changed with the times and the cares and concerns of each generation. If sacred scripture was not fixed, religion would not be so fixated on the rules created out of the concerns of people hundreds and thousands of years ago. It could preserve what the ancients learned by retaining the old, but blended and harmonized with the new.

Holy scriptures were composed by fallible human beings. Which works got into the canon and which were rejected were decisions made by other fallible humans. Christians to this day do not agree on the content of the Bible. One man, Jerome, largely, but not entirely, determined what would be included in the Christian Bible when he brought out his Latin-Vulgate version in 450 CE. The Roman Church debated and disputed the details of exactly what's in and what's out for the next eleven hundred years. The Council of Trent in 1563 finally put an end to the debate, sort of.

Roman Catholics, Greek Orthodox, Coptic, and Nestorian Churches include some or all of a bunch of books in a special section of their Bibles referred to as the "Apocrypha" or the "Deuterocanonical" books. Most Protestant denominations exclude all of these books. But to add to the confusion, the original Anglican King James Bible of 1611 included in its Apocrypha three books the Roman Catholics excluded; 1 and 2 *Esdras* and the *Prayer of Manasseh*. Some ancient versions of the Bible included up to eight books that most Christian denominations are not even aware of. There are now hundreds of different versions of the Bible each of which is a favorite of one of the hundreds of different Protestant denominations.

I'm not pointing out the historical messiness of the creation of the Bible to argue for its illegitimacy as a sacred book. On the contrary, spending centuries working out what's in and what's out is a process I'd recommend continue. But when a fundamentalist Christian supports an argument "because it's in the Bible", an appropriate rejoinder would be, "Whose Bible and which version?" The creation of any particular edition of the Bible is a human project of committee work involving negotiation and compromise. The product is not a magical book of Absolute Truth. It's just the best efforts of a particular group of scholars and editors to achieve their own agenda.

Within a particular religious community there is value in maintaining a tradition of reverence for a particular book. Bonds within families and among the community are strengthened by reading and rereading for successive generations the pieces within The Book which contain comforting notions, intriguing stories, and challenging insights.

I treasure memories of my great grandmother reading Bible stories to my brother and me at bedtime. I hope my children still regard their song and story time with sentiment and that they will pass on the tradition to the next generation.

Sentimentality and nostalgia are sweet and bitter. There is sweetness in the return to the comforting arms of loving parents and grandparents in memory, or to wherever we felt warm and safe as children. There is also a bitter taste, because those moments of safety are now so temporary and ephemeral in memory. We are inevitably and too quickly forced back into the harshness of reality, where all is not warm and fuzzy. This is the way the world is. We can create temporary shelters of loving safety within family and communities. But we are fools if we expect the world always to offer care and kindness because we hold the correct beliefs in our heads or follow the true faith.

It behooves us to be "wise as serpents", like Jesus advised his disciples, according to *Matthew* (chapter 10, verse 16). We should not shy away from critically evaluating the sacred books of our own religious traditions. We may feel sentimentally connected with the sacred books, rituals, and other traditions of the religion of our heritage, but we need to understand what The Book actually says and what the traditions mean.

The Book in each religion, denomination, or sect became canonically sacred because those in power during a particular time declared it the sacred book. We can certainly give great deference to the decisions made by our ancestors, but we need not be shackled by their judgments. We have the right and duty to critically evaluate the content of the literature which is supposed to serve as the foundation for our religious understanding of reality. When we find art and literature that better expresses the sacred to people in our own time, we ought to recognize it.

Blindly accepting "every jot and tittle" within a holy book as The Truth is like Hod letting Loki guide his arm. We've been warned.

Chapter 12: Democracy and Apologies to Galileo

Despots will use religion and political ideologies to justify their rule. Fanatics that believe their religion or their political ideology has the answers to all questions want to impose their beliefs on everyone else. If power is seized, or won through election, by an ego-maniac who believes he is entitled to rule over others, personal freedoms will suffer. When basic civil rights, like freedom of expression, the press, assembly, religion, and privacy are curtailed or lost, respect for government and law erodes. Disorder is bred and spreads. A repressive regime responds by passing harsher laws. And that breeds greater distrust and dislike of the government. Eventually society descends into chaos (Somalia, Syria, and Libya are current examples) or violent revolution (the US's revolution, the French Revolution, and Russian Revolution are earlier examples; Egypt and Nepal are recent ones). What follows is sometimes better and sometimes worse for the community.

The tools used by repressive societies to inhibit free-thinking and creative expression are religion and authoritarian government. No government lasts forever. But the current historical trend for repressive regimes seems to be a relatively short life span and then revolution or devolution. The tools of religious orthodoxy and tyranny were more effective in previous ages. They are losing their effectiveness in the modern age.

Constitutional democracies which protect civil rights and have relatively free but reasonably regulated economies are demonstrating more staying power than despotic regimes or rigidly-ideological single-party governments (whether communist, fascist, or Islamic). Eccentric and innovative thinkers that question conventional wisdom and traditions are valued in open-democratic societies. They might or might not be universally celebrated during their own lifetimes, but the

Tom Paines, the Mark Twains, and the Kurt Vonneguts of the world eventually find receptive readers/listeners, because we learn from criticism and alternative perspectives.

It's conceivable that a benevolent dictator, like Plato's conception of the "philosopher-king", would value criticism and human rights. But do we have any recent examples; Castro's Cuba, Chavez's Venezuela? Nope; it seems that constitutional democracy is the best we've come up with so far to promote and protect the values of personal freedom and equality of opportunity. "It has been said that democracy is the worst form of government except all the others that have been tried," said Sir Winston Churchill.

We should take note that the "communist" revolutions of last century did not occur within the capitalist-liberal democracies as predicted by Karl Marx. It was the oppressive regimes of czars, kings, and emperors which were overthrown by communist insurgents. The oligarchic rule of a communist party politburo is not democratic, but it is less exclusive than a hereditary monarchy. People could join the Communist Party and move up through the ranks in Soviet Russia and "Red China". Under the Tsar and Emperor, birth was destiny.

Islamic revolts that rippled through Middle Eastern and North African countries at the end of the 20th Century were also directed at authoritarian rulers, like the Shah of Iran and military dictators, not constitutional democracies. A few years later, young people in Iran bravely challenged the iron-fisted authority of the ayatollahs in 2009 and 2010 during the failed Green Revolution (aka the Twitter Revolution). Most recently, the "Umbrella Revolution" in Hong Kong has inspired Occupy-type protests against decrees from the central Chinese government which limit democratic participation in elections. Reuters quoted an 18-year-old student protester in a September 29, 2014 report, "We are fighting for our core values of democracy and freedom."

It's too early to tell the ultimate outcome of "the Arab Spring", which began in 2011. So far the positive results are democratic rule in Tunisia and pressure on other repressive regimes in the Middle East. The corrupt despot Hosni Mubarak was toppled in Egypt, but then President Mohamed Morsi and his Muslim Brotherhood were ousted from power in a military coup after winning at the polls. The jury is still out on whether Egypt is moving toward a more open society or another military dictatorship under General and now President el-Sissi.

As described in Chapter 9, history does not progress in a steady and ever upward arc toward a world-wide Utopia. (Let's also hope the "Left Behind" vision of Tribulation and world-wide apocalypse is not around the bend). Progress is bumpy.

Two of what were considered the most advanced countries and evolved cultures, Japan and Germany, became the imperialistic-fascist aggressors in the second half of the 20th Century. So far in this young century, China has begun to open up to greater economic and personal freedoms, while Russia seems to be retreating toward repression and paranoid nationalism under Vladimir Putin. Ego-maniacal Khadafy was ousted, captured, tortured, and killed in a democratic-Libyan uprising, but the country has since devolved into chaos. The revolt against the dictator of Syria at first appeared to be a democratic movement but has spawned more Islamic militant-extremists and the indescribably despicable ISIS. Any progress toward John Lennon's vision of utopia is difficult to detect in the Middle East. So far, it's mostly aspiration.

Stability and a general respect for the laws of the land are required for open-liberal societies to survive and flourish. Freedoms and responsibilities must be balanced. We want to live in an open and vibrant community, but we have to be willing to pay the taxes that support the infrastructure and to compromise our own liberties, to some extent, for everyone else to enjoy theirs.

We thoughtful and sensitive folk want to be able to freely ponder the great and deep questions about the universe and the human condition. And we want to be able to talk openly about our philosophical speculations. We want to live where scientific discoveries are made and art is created. To do that, we have to be willing to accept some regulation of our freedoms in order to live together in relative peace and security.

All reasonable people and decent folk understand that there must be a balance of liberty, taxes, and regulation in order to achieve a just and prosperous communal life. Where the balance is out of whack and there is political oppression, economic strangulation, and religious intolerance, where the enemies of freedom, equal opportunity and progress rule, life becomes unbearable. Civility shrinks as people skulk through life with their heads down to avoid trouble from the authorities. Education becomes indoctrination. The arts and sciences atrophy. Who would want to live in the grey desolation of Soviet society, under the cruel harshness of Saudi Arabian Sharia Law, or the terrifying absurdity of a place like North Korea?

Constitutional democracy as a form of government was imagined by Enlightenment Age thinkers to promote and protect the values of individual rights and equality of opportunity. Sorry Karl Marx, but so far it's the best way to break the cycle of authoritarian rule followed by revolution or chaos and then replaced by another form of authoritarian government which fails and is followed by revolution and chaos. It's become conventional wisdom that African, Arab, and Asian countries (hmm, the nonwhite areas of the world) do not have traditions of democracy and so might be unable to develop into mature republics. But it has to start at some point in time to develop.

Maybe Islamists do not value human rights and economic opportunity. They may care far more about forcing their beliefs upon their neighbors than Enlightenment Age values. But there is currently a dialectical struggle between the democratic and Islamic movements begun in the Arab Spring. Perhaps a form of government unique to Middle Eastern Islamic culture will be born through the upheaval.

A liberal interpretation of Sharia Law may be able to accommodate a sufficient degree of freedom to create a peaceful and prosperous society. A new balance of the values of order and freedom might be in the offing in a country like Tunisia. That achievement would encourage, instead of stifle, all the aspects that we love about human community. A thriving community nourishes values like creativity, intellectuality, and romance.

~ ~ ~

Why is this lesson so hard to learn? Why did it take the Roman Church 350 years to apologize to Galileo? He observed through his telescope that the planets orbit the sun, not the earth. Galileo could show this to the Inquisitors if they had been willing to look through his telescope with their eyes open. Instead, he was accused of heresy and forced to deny the truth of his proof. Galileo understood what was at stake. In 1600, ten years before Galileo's planetary observations, Giordano Bruno was burned at the stake. The Inquisition tortured and executed Bruno because he let it be known that he held the view that the earth traveled round the Sun.

Entrenched powers fear challenges to the status quo. Those on top, understandably, like the way things are. Even enlightened rulers and elites must be pushed and prodded to risk change. Pushing and prodding, challenging and criticizing, are the duties of those willing to move beyond conventional beliefs about economics, politics, and religion.

As individuals, members of a community, nation, and the world, we should celebrate new discoveries of science and art about where we come from, where we are going, and what it means. Let's call out those who claim they know The Answer and then prescribe rules derived from their special knowledge and privileged place in society. We don't need anymore tin horn dictators or pontifical potentates. We do need more Brunos and Galileos; thinkers, tinkerers, and researchers who create new technologies and challenge conventional thinking about climate change, voter registration, marriage rights, immigration laws, minimum wage, right to life, and right to die with dignity.

~ ~ ~

Karl Marx cleverly condemned religion as the opiate of the ignorant masses. He prescribed a secular replacement drug, Marxist-Communism. But it turned out that the Marxist cure was worse than the illness in some cases.

Marx attempted to explain the origin, history, and current state of humankind through social science rather than religious mythology. Using social science, instead of religious tradition, was an advancement of sorts. But Marx went about the process backwards in developing his theory of dialectical materialism. He spent long hours in the British Museum suffering from hemorrhoids and deducing the history he needed to support his political ideology. The result was a massive body of scholarship and a finely honed intellectual weapon to be used by charismatic leaders like Lenin and Mao to attack the ancient traditions of their cultures.

The cultures of Russia and China, as well as the other Asian and African countries, Cuba and several countries in South America, where communist movements gained support from significant populations, were all authoritarian and repressive. The promises of Marxist-Communism were to overthrow tyranny and to impose a more equal distribution of wealth. It's understandable that intellectuals and poorly paid workers were attracted to communist movements.

The advocates of constitutional democracy were not as politically adept or as ruthless in the use of organized violence as the Marxist-inspired revolutionaries in the countries that became socialist dictatorships during the 20th Century. The democrats valued peaceful compromise and elections. The communists cared nada about values. They just wanted to impose their ideology on society through class warfare.

Democracy lost the battles in the countries that became socialist dictatorships, but it seems to be winning the war. Because, contrary to what Marx proclaimed, the Dictatorship of the People turned out to be just another form of tyranny.

A repressive political ideology imposed by force was not much better than an oppressive religiously-supported monarchy. Neither system allowed the creative use of freedom. Both systems stifled dissent and alternative thinking, because both religiously-supported monarchy and Marxist-Communism claimed to explain all that needs explaining. Since we have all the answers, anyone who thinks differently must be wrong and must be silenced.

A cure for the illnesses of religious intolerance and oppressive political ideologies begins with an acceptance that we do not have final answers to the most fundamental questions that pester philosophical minds. Does God exist? What is the good life? What is the ideal form of government? We might, in time, be able to reach a consensus on some of these great questions. Maybe it doesn't really matter whether there is a Supreme Being or not. Perhaps there is no single definition of the good life and maybe there is no ideal form of government for all people in all countries. We don't have answers to these fundamental questions that satisfy everyone. Unfortunately, too many people have answers they would like to impose on others.

We may be on the brink of solving some of the most profound puzzles that have baffled science since the Relativity Revolution begun by Einstein; like, will a "theory of everything" unify General Relativity and Quantum Mechanics? We are moving closer to answering that question with the confirmation of the existence of the Higgs-Boson particle and the inflationary expansion of the universe by gravitational waves. Science does not, however, answer the fundamental questions that have intrigued the philosophically minded for millennia. And that is wonderful! We don't have to stop thinking.

~ ~ ~

At whatever stage of development the human species may be, it makes sense to respond to the fact of our existence with awe and gratitude. So what if we don't have all the answers, thanks be that we find ourselves on this planet which is hospitable to human life. Let us not spoil it by trying to impose on others whatever we come up with as our own Big Answer.

The humble Socratic acceptance of ignorance, combined with a thirst to seek knowledge, is a precondition for living a valuable life beyond beliefs. So is a desire to creatively express gratitude for being alive. Agnostic gratitude will not harden into an unprovable and divisive doctrine; because, it is only closed to the possibility that the search for truth has an ending.

Those who want to close the book on the search may claim that God (Karl Marx or Adolph Hitler) gave them The Answer. But God is not really the answer offered by religion. Religious edicts are the actual gods that believers follow. God doesn't direct the lives of believers, although they might claim as much. Believers try to follow the rules and commandments of their religion. Living godless does not require you to think it is more probable that God does or does not exist. It does mean **not** believing that religious doctrines and rules are gods, which must be mindlessly followed.

Most believers describe themselves as followers of the founder of their religion. The founder probably claimed a direct connection with the divine. God gave Moses the Torah; Jesus is the Son of God (or is he the same as God?); Mohammed received the Quran from God via the angel Gabriel; Joseph Smith was directed to the golden plates by the angel Maroni; yada yada yada. And the same can be said of Marxists, Fascists, and all the other ideological "ists", who treat their political ideology as if it was handed down from on high. Poppycock! (Excuse the language, please; the author became over wrought.)

Follower-believers are told to live by directives from God received by the Founder which were eventually written down and have been revised and interpreted by the priestly classes for successive generations. Why be a follower? Is it to receive the reward of salvation, heaven, paradise, reincarnation, or to achieve communist or fascist utopia? Is it because the founder was, or a current leader is, so charismatic that followers just feel compelled to do whatever the founder/leader tells them to do?

If so, please remember my fellow Hoosier Jim Jones. He led his followers out of Indiana to the promised land of San Francisco and then Guyana. When he commanded them to drink cyanide laced Flavor-Aid, they did.

Chapter 13: Just Say "No!"

This life, not the next, should be our chief concern. The world in which we live is our responsibility, not the imagined one ruled by God. The argument that this life is temporary, while the next is eternal, is specious. Any sensible argument requires a basis in fact. The only people who have visited Heaven or Hades and come back to report their experiences are in myths or sacred scripture. Have you ever met anyone who has been to Hell or Paradise? I haven't.

Just about every Sherpa I've met trekking in Nepal knows someone who has seen the Yeti. It's always a cousin or sister's brother or Dawa over in Phakding who's seen the Yeti. No one I've met has actually seen the Yeti.

Hearsay is inadmissible evidence. The accounts of heavenly or hellish visits tend to be either ancient hearsay or by someone trying to recruit followers into a religion. Christianity was more marketable to Jews because of its promise of Heaven as opposed to the Jewish ambivalence about an after-life. Christian Heaven was certainly more attractive than living as a shade in the Greco-Roman Hades. Jannah, an Edenic garden of paradise where all desires are satisfied, awaits Muslims who have fully submitted themselves to Allah. The Muslim conception of Jannah may be even more desirable than the Christian Heaven, which can seem rather boring. The appeal of Jannah might explain, in part, why Islam quickly surpassed Christianity as the more popular religion in the Middle East after the Seventh Century CE.

A Mormon friend once confessed to me he was quite perturbed. He had come to realize that he would be spending eternity with both his first and second wife. He thought he could handle it, but he was not so sure about the wives.

Religious claims about an after-life are simply not credible. While they have obvious marketing value, there is no reliable evidence to support them; and they conflict with each other. Hindu/Buddhist reincarnation is quite different than Heaven, which is different than Islam's Paradise. And the Mormon conception of Heaven is not at all the same as the Catholic, Lutheran, Methodist, or Presbyterian. Christians can't decide among themselves whether there is a personal or general resurrection. If it's general, we could be moldering in our graves for centuries before we get our heavenly bodies. (Yikes! In case the general resurrectionists are right better change your Will if you were planning on cremation.)

~ ~ ~

The argument that the possible reward of an after-life is a logical reason for making a commitment to a religion has its origin three centuries ago in "Pascal's Wager". The seventeenth-century French philosopher Blaise Pascal posed an argument for believing in God as: "If you erroneously believe in God, you lose nothing (assuming that death is the absolute end), whereas if you correctly believe in God, you gain everything (eternal bliss). But if you correctly disbelieve in God, you gain nothing (death ends all), whereas if you erroneously disbelieve in God, you lose everything (eternal damnation)."

The argument still has popular appeal, even though it's been demolished by many theist, atheist, and agnostic logicians. One counter is the following: Which god is one supposed to believe in? If I choose all of them, then I don't really believe in any one, and if I pick the wrong one, I'm still damned. So, damn! Which religion am I supposed to pick? They all claim to be the right one.

More important than any abstract argument about an after-life is the way we live the life that we actually have. This life is real, it's not speculative. Shall I spend it trying to qualify for an after-life, or does it make better sense to live a valuable life in the here and now?

While modernity has cast away much of the wisdom of ancient cultures about how to die with dignity, we are acquiring more information about the process of dying. According to a 1992 Gallup Poll there were eight million Americans who claimed to have had a near death experience ("NDE"). Since then, near death experience has become a respectable area of psychology and neuroscience research. Researchers have attempted to identify and classify common traits of the experience. "Out of body" and "tunnel" experiences and meeting "beings of light" are often cited in accounts of NDEs. But, within the field of NDE research there is wide disagreement about what is, and whether there is, a "typical" NDE. When researchers have attempted to classify the NDEs of large populations, so many different types of experience are described that classification becomes meaningless.

There is one factor identified in the research as a predictor of certain aspects of an NDE. A subject's cultural-religious background exerts a powerful influence over the person's near death experience. *Handbook of Near-Death Experiences* (published in 2009 and authored by Janice Holden Miner) explains that there is a "connection to the cultural beliefs held by the individual, which seem to dictate the phenomena experienced in the NDE and the later interpretation." Even as the brain is shutting down, the last images and feelings reflect "cultural beliefs held by the individual." So, for example, someone from an evangelical Christian or Muslim background is more likely to experience angelic beings during an NDE than one with a Jewish or secular upbringing. The power of beliefs to affect the functioning of the brain is startling; that power still courses through the brain even as it is dying.

While beliefs color the experience from person to person, they do not change the reality of what is happening to the dying person. If you don't die and have an NDE, you may describe it in Christian terms if Christian, in Jewish terms if Jewish, and in secular terms if not religious. But most significantly, you didn't die! You're not in Heaven, Hell,

Purgatory, or Jannah. You're alive!

If you do not come back, then you can't very well describe what happened when the NDE turned into a DE; you're dead. All the evidence that will be available to the living will indicate that what was you has ceased to experience anything.

What I draw from this is that while I am alive I want to live a valuable life, because when I die it appears that I am at an end. If we can all agree to live responsibly -- caring for ourselves and each other -- we will all be better off than if we do not. By focusing our care on our world and the creatures living in it, instead of focusing on a speculative after-life, we'll all be better off. That is a better bet than Pascal's wager.

We've already considered the comfort that can come from believing in an after-life for a loved one (but remembering that the most satisfying comfort comes with loving and being loved during our grief). But does it make sense that we could take some comfort in the statistical probability of experiencing an NDE with desirable traits if we believe in a religion? Apparently not. Regardless of which religion, or lack thereof, any dying person might have an out-of-body experience and see a tunnel of light. Those comforting traits are experienced by believers and unbelievers alike. Religious believers just tend to **interpret** the NDE in the religious terms of their religious tradition. But that is how they interpret all reality! Unbelievers who have an NDE interpret it simply as "seeing a lighted tunnel" or whatever. It just was what it was without religious connotation.

I would prefer to experience death as clearly as possible, undiluted and untainted by preconceptions. How else can the final experience of this life be, if not fully understood, at least embraced with as much clarity as possible for the last lesson to be learned?

~ ~ ~

To surrender our wills to religious or political leaders

who demand, cajole, or inspire others to follow them without questioning is dangerous. Charisma is dangerous. Sure, maybe Jesus, Gandhi, and King had it, but so did Jim Jones and Charles Manson. Leaders who claim a special channel to divine knowledge are more likely to be sociopathic ego-maniacs, like Hitler and Mussolini, or Osama bin Laden, than worthy models of ethical behavior.

Washington and Lincoln were not charismatic leaders. They led with intelligence, ingenuity, reason, and moral example. When a prophetic leader asks you to "follow in faith" or "just believe", hide your children and your pocketbooks. Trouble is coming. Even better advice than Ronald Reagan's on how to deal with the Soviets -- verify before trusting.

The trouble with charismatic leaders who promise their followers a divine destiny, either in this life or the next, is that they use and abuse their followers as means to an end. Despite what they say, religious organizations pay the people at the top very well. Check out the lifestyle and income of your pope, guru, lama, or imam. They aren't living lives of poverty.

Two of the most egregious examples among Christians are the Roman Catholic Church and the evangelical mega churches. This talk of "it is more difficult for a rich man to enter heaven than for a camel to pass through the eye of a needle" is hypocritical hogwash. If that is true, then how is it that Catholic bishops, cardinals, and the Pope live in palaces. But they took a vow of poverty and they don't receive personal income! Yeah, right. Who needs personal income when you get anything you want paid for by the hard earned dollars donated by parishioners. It's brilliant! Live like princes and call it poverty.

The colossal financial sins and moral failings of Jim and Tammy Bakker and Jimmy Swaggert during the go-go 1980s were raw meat for the tattle-tale press. Journalists reveled in exposing the extent to which those televangelists had feet of clay in their financial dealings and sexual practices. Despite the humiliating publicity of the transgressions of the last generation of televangelists, the next generation of TV preachers has managed to rake in their millions.

Years ago, driving through Tennessee, I was amazed and delighted to hear Reverend Roosevelt Taylor on local AM radio. He was asking for donations of ten and twenty dollars. In exchange for which he would send donors a "money tree". Money would grow from the tree if donors prayed the right way. It was guarantied! Don't know how many dollars Reverend Roosevelt Taylor made off his money tree in Tennessee, but enough to have his own radio show. But he's small potatoes compared to good Christian preachers like Joyce Meyer, who reportedly owns five multi-million dollar mansions; Jesse Duplantis, who bought an eighteen million dollar Citation X private jet while his home city of New Orleans was underwater from Katrina; and Joel Osteen, whose published net worth is forty million dollars.

Osteen was asked in an interview by CNN's Piers Morgan whether Osteen felt guilty about having so much wealth. The handsomely blow-dried preacher replied, "I don't ever feel guilty because it comes from – it's God's blessings on my life. And for me to apologize for God's – how God has blessed you, it's almost an insult to our God." From God!? His forty million came from the paychecks of working people.

Karl Marx was right in calling religion an opiate. People must be drugged to hand over their money to these charlatans. And it's not just in the US the gullible are taken in. In New Delhi, India I witnessed a fat guru in a loincloth giving blessings to Hindus who lavished him with food and money offerings. His private temple was already filled with cartons of food, but supplicants lined up to give more. The guru looked bored as he marked the foreheads of petitioners with a tilaka after they laid gifts at his feet. The procedure was supervised by two tall and powerfully built disciples.

Poverty and starvation abound in India, but at that temple people were giving away food and cash to a man who was already obese. They believed he could offer them some divine intervention to cure a disease or make an infertile wife fertile. Real drugs, pharmaceuticals, would have served them better than that fat fraud.

A more mundane experience of hypocritical greed by a religious leader occurred when I was serving as an elder in a Presbyterian church some years ago. The church was running in the red. The Finance Committee proposed to cut the pay of all employees with one exception, the pastor's. I protested. The pastor was already paid over $100,000 plus generous benefits. Our custodian was paid less than a third of the pastor's salary with no benefits. The chairman of the Finance Committee informed the session of elders that the Presbyterian Book of Order required that we award the pastor at least a four percent cost-of-living raise. The rules made no such provision for any other employees. The system was rigged by the religious professionals to benefit only themselves. The pastor thanked us. At the next Sunday service he probably preached a sermon on Christian charity.

~ ~ ~

Every religious organization, and, for that matter, political party, separates the world into us and them. Others are judged at the very least as wrongheaded unbelievers. Zealous true-believers are likely to go even further and judge nonbelievers as sinners, apostates, heathens, or heretics. And then it starts. Can you smell the kindling being lit for some burnings at the stake?

We would be a step closer to the ideal of a cooperative community, where people are judged "by the content of their character", rather than the content of their beliefs, if we scrap the unprovable claims of religious and political truths. Each one of us Homo sapiens and all things in our universe come from the same source -- the Big Bang, if you will. Everything shares the same fundamental chemical-physical elements. If we walk the path of life in humbleness admitting that we do not know how that common source came to be, then we are more likely to judge the worth of others on how they live, create, and treat others, rather than on a set of beliefs prescribed by someone, or some organization, claiming to have The Truth.

The danger posed by religious and political True Believers (or poseurs as such) is not academic. It's real. Only one of the numerous Republican candidates in the 2012 Presidential primaries "boldly" stated that global warming is a serious problem which must be addressed with serious policies. Michelle Bachman stated in the debate on September 12, 2011 that the Earth is 6,000 years old. She knows because the Bible tells her so. In the same debate she and Rick Perry agreed that Evolution is just a theory and Intelligent Design is really how our world was created by the Creator. Many Republican heads were nodding in vigorous agreement. John Huntsman, the lone voice for scientific sanity among the Republican candidates, garnered few votes and made an early exit from the Primaries. What if one of these candidates, who claim to believe that the world is only 6,000 years old, global warming is only in Al Gore's imagination, and vaccines are the cause of autism, had been elected President of the United States and Leader of the Free World?

Let's just say, No! No, to the false prophets and charlatans telling us that their beliefs count more than provable facts, that their religious beliefs should be the law of the land, and that they speak the word of God and ultimate Truth. Don't you prefer to live in freedom from the shackles of the mind controlling drug Marx compared to opium? Released from the bondage of religious dogma and the chains of political ideology, we are free to find our own way to live a valuable life. And we can help to lead our communities in a direction that is grounded on values and facts rather than fantasies.

Chapter 14: Existential Freedom without Beliefs

Without a system of beliefs, how does one navigate the rocky shoals of life? Do you become a faithless wayfarer wandering aimlessly through life?

Guiding your life by values you have consciously chosen is a way of living faithfully. Instead of subscribing to a set of beliefs based on imagined divine edicts, why not utilize your own free will to choose positive values to help you make decisions and to guide your actions? The purpose of this book is to try to persuade readers that living faithfully to values thoughtfully and consciously chosen is the way to lead a good and valuable life. A life based on a foundation of values is more firmly grounded in reality than trying to be faithful to a metaphysical superstar whose followers made up stories about Him. It's a better way to go than trying to live by the commandments of imagined God(s) speaking through self-proclaimed prophets.

Faith based on the requirement of believing things that really don't make sense, like God delivered the Ten Commandments to Moses on stone tablets, does not satisfy thinking people. We question what does not make sense to us; don't we?

Living according to thoughtfully chosen values may very well be a way to live by the worthy lessons taught by the founders of the great religions. The values promoted by most religions are very likely consistent with values an ethically sensitive and thoughtful person would independently choose. We don't have to believe the unbelievable to respect the values stressed by Moses, Krishna, Buddha, Jesus, Muhammad, etc. You don't need to believe that it was magically written on a stone tablet on top of Mt. Sinai to value and return the love of your parents.

Trying to live according to a set of beliefs, which are based on superstition, creates in the mind what social scientists call "optimism bias". This condition has utility for people who work in sales or are entrepreneurs. They know that they will fail much more often than they will succeed, but they have to believe they will succeed to keep trying. It becomes less productive when it cannot come true and is almost guarantied to lead to disappointment.

A friend and former client of mine once told me he was very upset because he didn't make a sale he was counting on. "Ted" was an insurance agent and had prayed that he would close the sale on a particularly large commercial lines account. He'd put a lot of work into selling the policy he thought perfectly fit the business's insurance needs. Ted told me he was sure God wanted him to have that account. He couldn't understand what went wrong. Ted didn't lose his zeal for selling insurance, but he began to doubt the power of prayer.

Living according to consciously chosen values will not guaranty successful outcomes and it offers no promises of material reward. But it doesn't create false hope. Values do not demand submission of the intellect as do religious creeds and rules. Values do not promise heaven, reincarnation, paradise, or gold at the end of the rainbow. Living a values-guided life does require mindful living. Attention must be paid to care properly for yourself and to be considerate and respectful of others.

~ ~ ~

Living in the expectation that ultimate beliefs will come true has a track record of failure. There were a lot of disappointed Nazis by the end of World War II, when it became clear that the Eternal Reich was a Hitler-Goebbels pipe dream. There will be many disappointed Muslim Jihadists when the Pan-Arabic Final Caliphate is not realized. Same goes for apocalyptic-believing Christians and the still-patient Jews awaiting their Messiah. I can't say with certainty that believers who expect to meet St. Peter at the Pearly Gates will be disappointed -- but I'd place a large bet on it.

One of the most exquisitely embarrassing historical

examples of the crushing disappointment of a failed belief system is the Millerite Christian sect. Their leader, William Miller, prophesied that the Rapture of the Second Coming was to occur on October 22, 1844. He had arrived at this date through years of diligent study of the Bible and careful calculations.

Miller's followers expected to be raptured straight up to Heaven on that date. Many of them removed their clothes and climbed up on the roofs of their houses. They didn't want to smash through the ceiling on their way to Heaven. And, they expected to be given "heavenly garments" upon arrival. The neighbors must have had a good laugh at the naked Millerites the next morning. By the time Pastor Miller and his elders came up with a second and then a third revised date for the imminent Rapture all but a handful of believers had fallen away.

The Millerites are an easy target. But well educated Marxists have been just as guilty of believing in a future event based on the writings of their prophet, Karl Marx. Who still believes in the imminent coming of the benevolent rule of the Dictatorship of the People to be followed by the utopian state of Communism? Just a few decades ago plenty of student activists and professors with PhDs believed in the apocalyptic and utopian claims of Marxism with as much passion as the Millerites believed in the Rapture.

~ ~ ~

The obvious yet brilliant discovery of Jean-Paul Sartre and other existentialist philosophers was that human beings are free to choose how to live their own lives. By the 1970s existentialist philosophers had thoroughly demolished (to the extent philosophers demolish anything) the goal oriented approach to life advocated by the 1950s zeitgeist of flat-topped-football- coach sort of American boosterism as "inauthentic". "Anyone can grow up to be President. Set your goals, Son, and get out there and achieve them!" That was the post-War American Can Do optimistic attitude before the quagmire of Viet Nam and the disillusionment of the silent majority after the Watergate revelations.

We have become more sophisticated (some might argue just more cynical) in our political thinking since then. Whatever one thinks about the teleological 1950s versus the exhibitionist 1960s, let's hope the current zeitgeist of skepticism toward government and authority reflects a more mature understanding of what politicians and religious leaders are actually about. (We're counting on you, Millennials!)

We are well into the 21st Century and it ought to be clear by now that we really do not need to submit ourselves to the domination of a Great Leader or the prophecies, predictions, or doctrines of the Leader's organization. We can choose our own beliefs, or better, find and commit to a set of values we intend to use as our guides for living well.

A number of recent studies indicate that the "unaffiliated" as a demographic category is gaining in numbers at a greater rate than any religion in the US. Younger people are less religious than older people, and religiosity has declined with each successive generation since World War II. In the 2012 Pew Research Center report on religion and public life, one-fourth of eighteen to twenty nine year-olds are classified as unaffiliated, a far higher proportion than among their parents (15 percent) or grandparents (9 percent).

Why are Millennials opting out, or not opting in, to the religious affiliations of their parents? They have spent more time in formal education beginning in preschool than previous generations. According to the U.S. Department of Education, National Center for Education Statistics: "A higher percentage of 4-year-old children (57 percent) were cared for primarily in center-based programs during the day in 2005–06 than had no regular nonparental care (20 percent) or were cared for primarily in home-based settings by relatives (13

percent) or by nonrelatives (8 percent)." The United States
Bureau of Labor Statistics reports that 2.2 million high school
graduates (68.6% of all high school graduates) enrolled in
college for academic year 2008. There has been a slight down
turn in the rate of college enrollment since the 2008 Recession,
but more kids in the current generation receive at least some
formal post-secondary education than any previous
generation.

Whether they are smarter than us is open to debate, but
there is no question that the children of Baby Boomers are
more schooled. When you spend most days learning math,
science, history, literature, and social science, what is offered
in church, mosque, or temple might be hard to swallow. If
Sunday schools and Catechism classes were devoted to
teaching positive values, like Compassion demonstrated in the
story of the Good Samaritan, and dispensed with doctrinal
indoctrination, churches might stand a better chance of
survival in an age of increasing disbelief.

~ ~ ~

Now, I recognize that the claim of existential freedom
has been criticized as reflecting a Western-bourgeoisie-elitist
bias. I can see the bony index finger of my Lefty-politico
friends pointing at me accusatorily. How can a person
growing up poor in an urban ghetto, or in a traditional culture
with a rigid class structure, learn to exercise this existential
freedom? A subsistence farmer in Africa or a Dalit
(untouchable) in India is probably not reading Sartre at a
Starbucks.

Maybe, but there's a paternalistic bias in those
assumptions. Why could not a person living in poor material
circumstances, if mentally and psychologically stable, choose
to live life according to independently chosen values just like
a philosophy student at an elite university?

I know a man, first name of Tik, who lives in the
subsistence-farming village of Basa, Nepal. Tik chose to leave
the traditional religion of the Rai people of Basa to become a

Buddhist. He later converted to Christianity. He remained within his home community, but decided through reading and reflection to try out different ideas and to live by beliefs different than all of his neighbors. Tik has a curious mind and was not content to accept the status quo and traditions of his village. He questioned the conventional wisdom of village elders and consciously set out to find his own way.

I happen to think that Tik has not made the wisest decisions in leaving behind the traditional animist understandings of the Rai people to follow Buddhism and then Christianity. More on this in Part III of the book, but according to the traditional Rai religion there is spirit in every thing, whether animate or inanimate. So, every thing is valued. In this sense the spiritual, communal, and cultural traditions of Tik's people are more value based than belief oriented.

Nevertheless, Tik proves the point that a subsistence farmer in a poor village in Nepal has the capacity to step outside of his cultural heritage to think independently and construct his own understanding of reality. (When I last spoke with Tik, summer of 2013, he had developed a syncretic approach to Christianity, which included elements of Buddhism, Hinduism, and animism. He admitted that friends in the village helped persuade him to alter his initial strict and puritanical approach to Christianity. They said it was no fun to follow a religion that opposed drinking and dancing and expected weekly money offerings.)

Someone whose life is constrained by poverty does face obstacles that one born into affluence does not when it comes to challenging conventional thinking. Not having access to books or the Internet to encounter new ideas certainly makes it easier to accept whatever beliefs are dominant within the local community. Without exposure to new and different ideas a person must be uniquely curious and creative to develop views antithetical to the conventional wisdom of her local culture.

But whatever circumstances you're born into, it's difficult to challenge the dominant belief system of your society. Challenging the totems and taboos of the status quo is likely to have repercussions. The establishment has power. Unless tolerance and diversity are values of the established order, those who think unconventionally will pay a price.

Choosing to confront the normal way of viewing the world may be considered subversive by the authorities. Authority over how the masses are to understand their place in the world is the prerogative of the ruling class. Keeping people happily, or at least grudgingly, in their places insures that the power elites maintain their control. Read Dostoyevsky's story of "The Grand Inquisitor" in *The Brothers Karamazov* for a frighteningly convincing description of how the powerful maintain order at the expense of the freedom of the masses

In the story, Jesus returns and comes to Seville, which is governed by the Grand Inquisitor during the Roman Catholic Inquisition in Spain. At first, crowds of people recognize Jesus as The Christ and fall down before him. But soldiers seize Him and bring Jesus to the Grand Inquisitor. In the privacy of a jail cell the Grand Inquisitor explains to Jesus that so long as the people have sufficient bread and are kept entertained they will be compliant. If the people have too much freedom, disorder will break out. The Grand Inquisitor tells Jesus he should not have come back, because he is not needed. His image is used by the authorities to manipulate the masses. In person, Jesus will just cause trouble. The Grand Inquisitor reminds Jesus that Authority can turn a fawning crowd into a mob demanding the crucifixion of one even as pure and innocent as Jesus Christ.

The lesson of Dostoyevsky's Grand Inquisitor is not limited to the Roman Catholic Church in Medieval Spain. Note the parallels between the Grand Inquisitor's Seville and the US with our welfare system to guaranty bread for the masses and our spectacular sports and entertainment events which keep us distracted. In the primary election of May 2014 there was an eight percent turnout of eligible voters in Indianapolis. The night of the election Bankers Life Fieldhouse was sold out for the Pacers vs. Washington Wizards NBA playoff game and the sports bars were packed with enthusiastic fans.

~ ~ ~

The US is one of the most open, tolerant, and diverse societies in the history of the world. Many of us, however, are concerned about an increasing concentration of wealth and power in the hands of a few. The accumulation of greater economic and political influence of the super-rich and multi-national corporations, while the middle class shrinks, is troubling. The health of our republic is at stake. When a relatively small number of people have accumulated vast sums of wealth, it warps how the political and judicial systems of the nation work.

The rich and powerful tend to be treated differently by the law. They get "the best justice money can buy". The poor qualify for free legal services of over-worked and under-paid young and inexperienced lawyers. Working people can't afford private attorneys and don't qualify for free legal aid. They just get screwed.

The OJ Simpson murder trial of 1994 revealed to every TV viewer in America how money affects outcomes in the US judicial system. Television viewers saw evidence the jury was not allowed to see. OJ's all-star defense team bullied a wimpy-cringing judge and out performed the much less experienced prosecutors. OJ was found "not guilty" because his lawyers performed better. ("If the glove don't fit, you must acquit!") The TV audience was convinced OJ was guilty of murdering Nicole Brown Simpson and Ronald Lyle Goldman.

Middle class folks find it difficult to get the attention of their government, while the rich and large corporations employ lobbyists to wine and dine officials. We are rightly worried about the loss of democratic control over our government. The hollowing out of the middle class continues despite our concerns.

To an extent, beliefs are the culprits that are preventing effective action to address the problem of the dangerously inequitable divisions of wealth and political power. Many Americans strongly believe that everyone has the right to acquire as much wealth as possible and people should be free to do whatever they want with their money. Initiatives to diminish the wealth/power gap bump up against these beliefs. Counter-intuitively, it is not just the wealthy that hold these beliefs; so do many working people sympathetic to the Tea Party.

During every election cycle and legislative session more and more money pours into political campaigns and the coffers of political action committees to effect electoral results and legislation. "Politics is the art by which politicians obtain campaign contributions from the rich and votes from the poor on the pretext of protecting each from the other." Oscar Ameringer, union organizer and newspaper editor.

Many of our citizens who believe in the absolute right to use wealth without constraint to influence politics will be the victims of the consequent loss of their own democratic political influence. Many in the peasant and merchant classes believed in the "divine right of kings" to rule, because that was what they were taught by the Church and State authorities. Lenin opined that capitalists believe so strongly in free enterprise that, "A capitalist will sell you the rope to hang him with." The irrationality of living by beliefs rather than values often leads us to cut off the branch on which we stand.

It isn't easy to question the beliefs which support the status quo and the conventional wisdom we have been taught, so long as we have food and shelter. Middle-class folks are trained to be frightened by dissent, protest, and novelty. Conventional beliefs about the way things are supposed to be support the status quo of power relations within a community. Those beliefs will be defended by all means available to the rich and powerful.

It's not easy to step out of the typical way of understanding reality and to try to see clearly how things are and how they could be better. It's risky business.

Yet this challenge has been met by people facing the most difficult circumstances imaginable -- conditions even tougher than the shackles of material poverty. Consider the martyrs of early Christianity that were tortured and executed for their unacceptable beliefs. Who is not moved by the beautifully inspiring words of Martin Luther King, Jr., which challenged the conventional belief of "Negro inferiority"? But back in the day when he marched, protested, and gave his memorable speeches, the establishment labeled him a communist-sympathizing radical and whore hound. King expected to be martyred, and he was.

The gloriously frightening claim of the existentialist philosophers is that everyone with full human consciousness has the freedom to accept or reject society's conventional truths. The cost might be that of becoming a social outcast or worse. The reward is living the life you construct like a work of art through your own choices.

That doesn't mean getting from the world, society, or the economy what you want. We can't control the reactions of others. No matter how clearly we might see the vision of a better future, all we can do to try to make it happen is to model it and try to persuade others to our point of view.

If we commit ourselves to living according to values we have freely and consciously chosen, we are assured of living valuably. Success as the world judges it is not guarantied. But we will be living true to ourselves, because the values we have chosen to live by, if rightly chosen, truly express who we are and who we want to be.

~ ~ ~

Viktor Frankl, an Austrian Jew and psychiatrist, was a Holocaust survivor. His wife died in the Bergen-Belsen concentration camp. Dr. Frankl suffered terribly in the Nazi death camps and witnessed the horrors perpetrated within those camps. The limits on Frankl's personal freedom as a concentration camp prisoner were so narrow and constrained as to beggar the imagination. After liberation he wrote a book, *Man's Search for Meaning*. Frankl explains in the book how the camp guards tried, and the concentration camp system was designed, to strip prisoners of all personal dignity and sense of individual identity. He had to submit his body to the orders of the guards and the regimen of the camps in order to survive. He refused to submit his mind.

Frankl describes in *Man's Search for Meaning* how the concentration camp experience almost succeeded in extinguishing within him all that he thought he believed in and valued. How could God let this happen to me? How could my country do this to me? How could my neighbors let this happen?

Where this led Dr. Frankl was not to abandon all he valued. Rather, he forced himself to examine what he actually valued. His internal quest was to determine what could sustain his life as meaningful and how he could help to affirm the meaning of the lives of others. Despite the inhuman conditions of his existence as a concentration camp prisoner, his mind was free to choose his own thoughts and to continue to value his own self and others as human beings.

Viktor Frankl's is an extreme and inspiring case arguing for the human right and ability to choose who we will be. The first step is to recognize your freedom to discard conventional religious and political beliefs. The next step is to decide to guide your life by consciously chosen positive values.

Part II: Creating a Valuable Life

Chapter 15: Selfish and Unselfish, Positive vs. Negative

"Remember, if you ever need a helping hand, you'll find one at the end of each of your arms. As you grow older, you will discover that you have two hands, one for helping yourself, the other for helping others."   -Audrey Hepburn

If we are free to construct our own lives, then we must answer the question, "Who do I want to be?" The construction of our selves begins with a fundamental understanding that we need to take care of ourselves and there are other people in our lives and in our communities that will, at times, need our care. We have to figure out how to balance fulfilling our needs with the needs others have of us. There will be occasions when our need to care for ourselves is in conflict with the needs of others. We come to know our selves even more deeply when required to grow and learn by resolving conflicts with others and within our own value systems.

When my boys were young and either of them got caught doing something wrong, after I calmed down, I would say to the little offender, "Ask yourself; is this who you want to be?" We want our children to think before they act. Often, they won't. But after they get caught, we can oblige them to reflect on their actions. As our children mature, we hope they will decide how to behave based upon the values we have tried to teach them. Some kids have not been blessed with parents who taught and exemplified positive values. But whatever the degree of helpful instruction from parents and other authority figures, or lack thereof, after reaching the age of reason each of us has the ability to choose the values we use to guide our actions.

So how do you figure out what are the values that should guide your life choices? It's not that intimidating.

David Hume, the great Scottish Enlightenment philosopher and father of Empiricism, argued in his book, *A*

Treatise of Human Nature, that values are not based in facts and they do not come from divine dictates. Hume was caustic in his criticism of religious nabobs who claimed that ethics and morality were handed down from above. Neither did he accept that values are natural laws or scientific facts to be discovered by secular philosophers or scientists. Values are developed in a social context through the ways that people figure out how to live with each other.

Over time, cultures evolve normative answers to ethical questions and moral challenges. Societies develop traditional values, which are passed down from generation to generation. But traditions evolve over time as new challenges are faced and different questions are raised by the distinctive circumstances confronted by subsequent generations. For example, earlier generations of Americans didn't worry much about preservation of the natural environment. The frontier seemed endless and so did the natural resources we used for fuel. Cut down trees, dig out coal, pump out oil, release natural gas; there will always be more. Now that we know material resources are finite and use of fossil fuels harms the quality of the air we breathe, our care and concern about the environment has changed. Environmentalism has become a cherished value of many and is likely to be seen as a traditional value by post-Millennial generations.

The challenge each of us in every generation faces is to sort through the values offered by our cultural traditions, and any others we are aware of, and then consciously choose which values should guide our lives.

~ ~ ~

If you think deeply about it, the values most of us care about can be broken down into one of two categories or a combination of the two. The two categories are: 1) for self, and 2) for others. In simple terms, we make choices based on:
What does it do for me?
What does it do for someone else or others?

The philosophical father of Capitalism, Adam Smith,

explained economic-consumer decision-making in his book, *The Wealth of Nations,* as trying to get what's best for me. I want the best product at the lowest price. Materialistic thinkers have extended Smith's analysis of consumer behavior to all aspects of life. Some very bright people think that the good life is obtained by acquiring as much wealth as possible. "He who dies with the most toys wins" is the bumper sticker expression of this approach to life.

The second approach is to be sacrificial. We see this approach routinely in the way loving parents take care of their children. Parents in most cultures generally think first of their children and second of their own welfare. A loving parent will die to protect her or his child. Most all of us, to some degree, extend unselfish behavior beyond our own immediate kin. Some Christians interpret "the Great Commandment", to love God and your neighbor as yourself, to mean that followers of Jesus should always be willing to sacrifice themselves for others. All of the great religions glorify martyrs that have acted sacrificially.

To find examples of selfish and unselfish approaches (admittedly in a fairly trivial way) just peruse Facebook. Some "friends" regularly post items about themselves but rarely, if ever, "like" or comment on other user's posts = selfish. I have a friend who hasn't posted anything on his "timeline" in over a year, but every day likes and comments on other friends' posts = unselfish. Granted, this is superficial analysis, but, if you are active in social media, I'm sure you recognize the types I've described. Most of us fall somewhere in between these extremes, right? We might lean more toward being selfish or more in the direction of selflessness, but we're not at either extreme end of the spectrum.

There is an unreflective bias in some religious cultures that selfishness is bad and unselfishness is good. That view is morally pretentious rubbish. Many people say it; few live by it. If you don't take care of your self, who will? We certainly don't prefer dependency over self-reliance.

The bias in favor of selflessness within Christian communities originates with the "love your neighbor" part of the Judeo-Christian "Great Commandment". But a reasonable interpretation of the instruction recommends a synthesis of selfishness and selflessness. "**Love** your neighbor as **yourself**," in common-sense practical terms means to take good care of yourself and then help your neighbor out as you are able and when you are needed.

If you are trying to take good care of yourself and you're a reasonably giving person, then you are living according to the ethic expressed in the Great Commandment. Underlying all positive values (pick a few, say Frugality, Loyalty, Honor) is caring for the self, others, or a combination. Positive values are the ways that we care for ourselves and each other. When you're Frugal, you're taking care to save money for when you'll need it more than you do now. You can then use your savings to benefit yourself or others. When you're Loyal, you're standing up for others who need your support. When you're Honorable, you're living up to your own expectations while treating others respectfully. Guiding your life with positive values is living the Love Ethic -- loving yourself and others.

~ ~ ~

There are people, regrettably, who are outliers and do not fit within the spectrum of leaning toward selfish or unselfish. These people are not guided by positive values. They are guided by negative values. These are people who are dangerous to themselves and others.

There are charismatic leaders who lead their followers down a path of destruction. Some of the great historical conquerors, like Genghis Khan, Pizarro, and Hitler were probably sociopaths. These men treated whole populations as nothing more than wheat to cut down and harvest in their insatiable appetite for power.

On a lesser scale are mass murderers, such as Ander

Breivik, who bombed government buildings in Oslo in 2011, killing eight people, and then shot and killed sixty nine students and teachers at a youth summer camp. To Breivik, these were not human beings. They were targets to be blown up and shot to make an ideological-political point. He later explained that he was drawing attention to the "fact" that too many immigrants had been allowed into Norway.

Serial killers like Jeffrey Dahmer and the BTK Strangler torture, maim, and kill with horrifying intelligence and pleasure. They lack the normal sympathy humans have for the suffering of other creatures. Iago in Shakespeare's *Othello*, as a literary example, lies, cheats, and murders out of envy and the sheer perverse joy of destroying lives and relationships. As if that wasn't enough, he's also a racist. And then there are the con men and hustlers, like Bernie Madoff, who might never draw blood, but have no compunction about ripping off the life savings of trusting people, even close "friends".

These types of destructive personalities are a danger, obviously to others, but also to themselves. Most will die violently or in prison, but certainly not as merry old souls. They do not care for others or, in any healthy sense, for themselves. They guide their lives by negative rather than positive values.

We all start out as infantile narcissists. Babies are totally self-absorbed. They like to crap their diapers and barf on dads (moms too). They knock food off their high chair trays and don't care if it's picked up, or expect someone else to do it. And they cry, and cry some more, at the slightest provocation. But as our bodies grow we also develop psychologically and mature socially. One aspect of the maturation process is developing a conscience so that we feel remorse when we screw up and cause harm to ourselves or others. As we become self-reflective, we realize that we don't like feeling the pangs of discomfort, so we try to avoid hurting ourselves and hurting other people. That's the case with emotionally healthy folks, anyway. Most of us will want to figure out how to take good care of ourselves as well as be a good neighbor and productive member of our community.

It's also true that, unless there is a Perfect One among us, we'll sometimes give in to the temptation to be guided by negative values; to act in ways which harm ourselves and others. Sometimes we just lose it momentarily and go temporarily nuts. Yes, I confess it. I kicked my cat once when I discovered he'd peed on my new suitcase just as I was beginning to pack the car for a family vacation. If going berserk is rare and aberrant from our usual pattern, damage may be done, but it will normally be fixable. Most of the messes we make can be cleaned up. In the case of the suitcase, it couldn't be cleaned up; it got trashed. But the cat got petted and apologized to. He forgave me.

Sometimes we break things or relationships that can't be fixed. Abusing a spouse or child cannot be justified. It's just bad. A person who develops that sort of pattern of behavior leaves destruction in his wake. He's chosen to live according to negative values. Blame can be cast on bad genes or a difficult childhood, but a competent adult that has adopted a pattern of acting destructively has chosen not to be guided by positive values. There may be psychological reasons why Jack the Ripper eviscerated women. But no one held a gun to his head. He chose.

The underlying motivation of these people goes beyond selfishness. It's hatred. It's the antithesis of living a life caring for yourself and others; loving your neighbor as yourself. Acting selfishly in the sense of looking out for Number One first is qualitatively different than living a life guided by negative values.

Trying to be the center of attention by talking too loudly while waving around a cigarette, drinking a little too much and blowing a bit of money in a poker game, is unattractive and selfish. But it makes some people feel good about themselves and doesn't harm anyone else. It crosses a line when the money lost in the poker game was needed to feed the baby or pay the mortgage. That's harmful to your family and to you. Sure, the gambling addict has a psychological problem, an addictive personality. She also hates herself and her family when she gambles away the rent money and kids' college savings. When destructive actions become a regular thing, the perp is living by negative values and motivated by hatred of self and/or others.

~ ~ ~

The Roman Church created a list of vices which it called the Seven Deadly Sins: wrath, avarice, sloth, pride, lust, envy, and gluttony. I would agree that each of these "sins" can be harmful to the self or others. But I must quibble with being condemned to Hell for the occasional slippage into lusty sloth. Destructive behaviors worthy of eternal damnation do not fit neatly under seven labels. And, in some cases actions which harm others may be justified.

Unkindness ordinarily has no positive effect for the person being unkind or the victim. But, if the Navy Seals who captured Osama Bin Laden were unkind to him and those sheltering him, well, we might consider their unkindness justified despite that it was harmful to Osama and his retinue.

All forms of incarceration and punishment do harm to the accused. We can't lump cops, prosecutors, judges, and prison guards doing their jobs into the same category as those who intentionally harm other people, can we? Law enforcement officers and soldiers, to do their jobs, sometimes must act in ways which harm others, and may have harmful effects on themselves (e.g., PTSD). So long as their motives are dutiful rather than hate-inspired, we do not consider them to be guided by negative values. We want our soldiers, cops, prosecutors, judges, and jailers to be guided by positive values like Duty, Justice, and Integrity.

Reviewing the Seven Deadly Sins, we can agree that

being wrathful rather than in control of your temper may lead to regrettable behavior. But there is a time for controlled wrath, like, when your children act out, so they will know their misbehavior is taken seriously. Who is so insensitive not to feel anger, along with sadness and horror, when we heard news reports of the beheadings of journalists Daniel Pearl by Al-Qaeda member Khalid Sheikh Mohammed in Pakistan, and more recently, James Foley and Steven Sotloff by ISIS in Iraq? Americans were justified in feeling wrathful toward Al Qaeda and the Japanese military in response to 9/11 and Pearl Harbor. Most of us agree that to the extent wrath motivated America's determination to wreak destruction on Al Qaeda and the Japanese military it was a righteous anger. Americans held onto the feeling of justified wrath, as well as Duty, Patriotism, and Loyalty to buddies on their ships, in the foxhole beside them, and on the assembly line next to them to carry the nation through the war years following Pearl Harbor. It has waned after thirteen years of fighting with no end in sight to the war on terror. The revelations of torture and mistreatment of prisoners in Abu Ghraib and Gitmo and mission creep from destroying Al Qaeda to nation building in Iraq and Afghanistan has sapped the righteousness from our anger and called into question whether we are being guided by positive or negative values in the way we have been fighting "the war on terror".

Moving on down the list of Seven Deadly sins, Avariciousness is the antonym of generosity. But we have to be at least self-interested enough to take care of ourselves or we become a burden on society. Sloth is definitely a vice when it comes to college roommates. (If I step on one more piece of cold pizza left on the floor! I will become justifiably wrathful!) On the other hand, orderliness can become neat freakiness to the point of an obsessive-compulsive disorder. Pride vs. humility; lacking pride in oneself and being excessively humble is harmful when it reaches the point of obsequiousness.

Lust -- well, perhaps Jimmy Carter said more than enough when he confessed to having lust in his heart. That was embarrassing, but small potatoes compared to President Bill Clinton. Everybody except gossip columnists and voyeurs in the Congress wish President Bill had restricted his to a throbbing heart rather than, uh, you know. On the other hand, without at least a bit of lust, wouldn't the species die out? Let's not forget that the men who wrote the list of mortal sins were, supposedly, celibate priests.

The things you learned not to do in Kindergarten are as useful as lists of sinful vices in understanding negative values. Remember when you had to stand with your nose in a circle on the chalkboard, because you got caught tinkling in the potted plant and then lying by saying that mean kid Danny did it. I was -- I mean, you -- were prosecuted and found guilty by Mrs. Schenck of public exposure, destruction of class property, and lying under oath. The motive to pee on the plant might have been no more than an immediate call of nature, although inconsiderate to the potted plant, but lying and blaming it on Danny, uh huh. Even in a five year-old, that was intended to harm another kid.

It is a matter of intent, a choice to let hatred be the driving force rather than taking care of yourself, others, or a combination of caring for self and others. Rejecting the temptations of negative values requires a fundamental commitment to try not to harm yourself or others. Some desirable actions might benefit you but harm others. And, some heroic actions might help others but harm you. Making those kinds of choices reveals whether you are taking a more selfish or more unselfish approach to life. But those who act in ways which are intentionally harmful to others without regard for the ultimate consequences for themselves, or, who intentionally harm themselves with reckless abandon for how it affects others, are not just making choices to lean more toward being selfish or selfless.

The "sin" of living according to negative values goes beyond being selfish and beyond being a door mat. It's intended to be destructive of human relations and community. If there is a pattern of living by negative values, then that person is guiding his life by hatred rather than the love ethic. And he must be stopped.

~ ~ ~

There is a relationship between being guided by negative values and living according to a set of beliefs rather than positive values. Doctrines and ideologies dehumanize people and can motivate destructive behavior. Fanatical jihadists are motivated by the antithesis of the love ethic, they hate the unbeliever.

We good and decent folk living in polite society will experience momentary lapses and will rarely, but sooner or later, give in to the temptation of a negative value. I led a discussion group at a church which had members that self-identified as conservative evangelicals and others that self-identified as liberal-progressive Christians. In a discussion which had wandered into the treacherous territory of gay rights, one of the "conservative" members of the group remarked that he was opposed to gay ordination of ministers on Biblical grounds. He did not state his view in a confrontational or challenging way, but just to clarify where he stood on the issue. A "liberal" member of the group, who happened to be the pastor's wife, responded in a harsh tone of voice, "Anyone who would say that is just stupid!"

The next week the conservative members decamped to form their own discussion group. I tried to employ shuttle diplomacy to reunite the two camps, but failed. The Conservatives no longer trusted the Liberals to be respectful of the Conservatives' right to hold differing views. The last I heard, the two groups had not reunited lo these many years since their divorce.

The pastor's wife is not a bad person at all; she is a good person who generally guided her life by positive values.

But, she was momentarily blinded by her ideology. Rather than seeing a feeling person across the table from her, she momentarily saw "Bob" as representative of an opposing ideology, an opponent on the issue of gay rights. Having lost sight of Bob as another human being, even just for an instant, she gave in to the temptation to lash out hatefully.

She thinks gays are entitled to the same rights as heterosexuals. Same here, but the way she expressed it was harmful to herself and others. Her self-righteous anger (dare we say wrath) exceeded her commitment to respectful consideration when she called Bob's statement "stupid". She hurt the feelings of a man who had been her friend, broke the bond of trusting community, and damaged her own integrity as a person of caring-liberal principles.

Specific categories of vices, such as envy, greed, unkindness, etc., are helpful in giving us the language of labels to attach to motives and behaviors, which have harmful consequences for our selves or others. These are negative rather than positive values. But life is too messy to be easily categorized in a list of negative or positive values. What's more important is an understanding of your intention. Am I trying to be a person who takes good care of myself and is respectfully considerate of others? Or, have I crossed the line into acting out of hatred, though it be momentary, so that the ultimate effect is harmful to my neighbor and to me?

~ ~ ~

In Part II of the book we'll concentrate less on the negativities of religious doctrines and political ideologies and more on what it means to live a valuable life. We will consider selfish and unselfish approaches to life in the personal sphere in Chapter 16 and then in the political-social-economic spheres in 17. But the trick is to find a satisfying balance between self-interest and being a responsible member of the community, so that's the topic of Chapter 18. How to deal with conflicts which threaten the balance you've achieved follows in 19. Then, we analyze how communities are shaped by the values of members within the community. And finally, we consider how we as parents and mentors can help to guide, or mislead, those who look to us for guidance.

If we are trying to live by the Judeo-Christian-Humanistic ethic of caring for the self and others, we'll have a lifetime of challenges to face. How we overcome the temptation of negative values and find the right balance in caring for our own self and caring for others? It begins with mindful attentiveness.

Chapter 16: Mindful Attention to Your Intentions

Most of our behavior starts with a selfish motive; **I** want to do such and such. Most of our behavior as adults also has a beneficial effect for others. For example, feeding my self is selfish in motivation -- I want to satisfy my desire to eat. When I buy food my purchases benefit the farmer who grew the food, the trucker who transported it, and the grocer who sold it to me. Each of these participants in the economy earns money which allows them to buy food for themselves and their families. When they buy food, more people benefit. At the local, national, and international level, the way economies work is to extend selfish desires for products or services out from the individual into a commercial network of others.

Family life and social life also have webs of intersecting relationships. How an individual's action moves out and through a social network might not be as concretely measurable as commercial activity. But our actions do move out beyond ourselves and the persons with whom we are in immediate contact. What we do vibrates our web of family, friends, and acquaintances. Communities are created and sustained by all of the intersecting actions and communications within the complex of relationships which make up a society.

Children gradually learn that other people are real human beings, just like them. But as we become adults many of us, especially those who go into business or politics, unlearn the common humanity of others. People become objects to manipulate for personal gain and corporate profits. It is more efficient to treat fellow human beings as "markets" and statistics than to remain aware that all of us are conscious human beings that feel and think.

Consider the wonder of us! Every functional human brain has at least as many neurons as there are stars in the Milky Way. Our neurons are connected to each other through billions of spines and synapses. Our minds are the most amazing thing yet to be discovered in the entire universe. Just as wondrous as our cognitive abilities are our other capacities, the human hand to manipulate objects, our feelings to fall in love. Every single one of us is an amazing creature. If we pay attention to the wonder of us, we won't sink into this slough of temptation to objectify others.

To live in mindful practice of valuing our own self and other selves requires introspection into what motives/desires underlie our behavior, as well as "ex-trospection" about the effects of our behavior on others. There is tension within us about how willing we are to give rather than take. I think for most of us, certainly for me, taking comes more easily than giving. So, we train ourselves through conscious effort to be giving and to overcome our instinctive selfishness. I'm sure you also know people that have a tendency to be giving to the point of being taken advantage of. It also takes mindfulness to avoid the obsequious "door mat" syndrome.

Immanuel Kant, the great 18th Century German philosopher, argued that no action was truly moral unless it was motivated by a morally right intent. For Kant, means couldn't justify ends, and ends didn't justify means. One's motives, means, and goals all had to be morally correct for the person to be considered moral.

You don't have to be a neo-Kantian scholar to agree that our motives should align with our goals. It just makes good sense. I want my neighbor to like me, so peace and good cheer will prevail between our households. When Tom asks to borrow my flathead screw driver, I readily loan it to him. My motive is both selfish and unselfish. I selfishly want to live in a friendly neighborhood. So, I'm willing to share my tools unselfishly. It's an easy calculus that sharing and lending among neighbors creates goodwill. (To meet Kant's standard, I must now admit that in reality I am much more likely to borrow Tom's tools.)

I also must admit that our neighborhood has declined

in communal friendliness in the thirty years we've lived here. It has become denser in population and more demographically diverse than when we moved in. Only one family has taken the initiative to organize a block party in the last five years. We used to have one every year. There are even a few people that are down right unfriendly.

When the most recent newbies moved in near us, my wife and I invited them to dinner, which has been our custom. After three rejections we gave up on them (a fourth invitation would have qualified us for a diagnosis of the "door mat syndrome"). The newbie wife has made it clear she is uninterested in friendly relations with neighbors, or at least with us. In another instance, when requested by one of the neighbor men to slow down when driving down our street, a neighbor's boyfriend pulled his shirt up to reveal a hand gun.

The trend I'm describing for my neighborhood is typical of many urban neighborhoods. Many smaller towns and cities are challenged, not so much by fracturing of the community, but by sheer loss of numbers in the community. The population shift from rural to urban since the Industrial Revolution continues to decimate many small towns.

Either form of loss of community is distressing and depressing for those experiencing the downward trends. But there are also neighborhoods and towns which are being revitalized. Conditions could not be worse for Detroit. But hold on, there are indications that the city hit bottom and it's on the rise. Downtown office occupancy is up to ninety-five percent, unemployment has declined, population has increased, pensioners have agreed to a proposed reduction in benefits, and a plan for resolving the city's bankruptcy was moving forward when I wrote these words. If Detroit can pull itself back from the brink of anarchic dissolution, there is hope for every community and neighborhood.

Actions motivated with the best of intentions will not necessarily be reciprocated, especially in urban neighborhoods which are not bound together through shared interests and activities. Still, isn't it preferable to try to be part of the solution rather than give in to the temptation to become part of the problem? If we value Community, then we need to be motivated to act in ways which enhance our communal connections rather than detract from a sense of belonging.

It takes energy and optimism. Living busy, tiring lives, and seeing discouraging images night-after-night on television news makes the challenge pretty daunting. I often find myself daunted and pessimistic. So, remember Detroit!

~ ~ ~

First, understand your motivations. Do you want to live in a place where people smile and speak to each other and invite new folks over for dinner? Then, take action to connect with your neighbors by greeting them, inviting them into your house or apartment, and giving their kids a treat or a no-longer-used toy. If you have paid attention to how your actions affect yourself and others, then, so long as your intention was to be a responsible member of the community, you have played your part as well as can be expected.

Tom actually does readily loan me anything I've asked him for (his borrowed bike rack is in my garage at the moment). He knows I would reciprocate if he ever needed anything of mine. Our mutual willingness to share is working. Our level of friendly trust is so high that we bought a pontoon boat together. We have keys to each other's house.

We are not the only families in the neighborhood resisting the trend toward fracture and alienation. Two other households are boat sharing. Almost everyone living on the channel behind our houses has agreed to share in the cost of defoliation of an invasive water-borne weed. Seven guys in our hood joined in the effort last summer to chain saw and remove trees that had fallen into the channel. Perhaps these examples of communal participation will entice recalcitrant neighbors into more friendly relations. Perhaps not; but we won't know if we don't try.

When we realize who we want to be in relation to ourselves and others, we begin to adjust our behavior to achieve our relationship goals. It would not have occurred to me that it would be a good thing to co-own a boat with a neighbor, when I lived in an apartment. I had many fine neighbors and friendly relations in each of the apartments I lived in, but my relationship goals did not include a commitment to the sort of enduring relationship co-ownership of a boat helps to cement. Tom and I both expect to be neighbor-homeowners for many years, possibly the rest of our lives. So, a deeper neighborliness makes good sense for both of us. Trusting each other to be responsible partners with our boat has, I think, added a layer to creating the person each of us wants to be. Maybe it is rippling out into the neighborhood. Whether it has or not, it has enriched the lives of our families.

~ ~ ~

Returning to the example of food purchases; we understand, of course, that we want to eat because we are motivated by hunger. When I shop for groceries I am acting on that primal selfish desire. How that desire is to be satisfied raises multiple issues for the consciously discerning values-guided person. How much food is required and what foods will best satisfy my hunger? There is need to evaluate how much I eat, what I eat, and where the food comes from to properly care for myself in consideration of others.

I value physical fitness and good health, so attention must be paid to a well-rounded diet to provide the nutrition needed for optimal health. I need to pay attention to what experts, like Michael Poilan, say about the value in eating "real food" as opposed to processed foods.

But sometimes I just want to satisfy my sweet tooth, so can I enjoy a candy bar, calorie laden dessert, or a soft drink without compromising my value of healthy eating? Hell yes, he says while tucking into a bowl of mint chocolate chip ice cream with whipped cream and a cherry on top! It's not destructive of yourself or others to indulge in the occasional guilty pleasure. So long as I don't let my enjoyment of sweet-fattening foods become obsessive to the point it jeopardizes my health from obesity or tooth decay, these three scoops of ice cream are the embodiment of the selfish but positive value of Pleasure.

Enjoying the taste of food, watching a good movie or TV show, walking in the woods, shooting hoops, all the ways we have fun and seek pleasure are expressions of positive values. Pursuing and engaging in activities that make us laugh, smile, or just feel good inside may be primarily self-centered, or they may include others. Whichever, Fun is valuable and it doesn't require much deep consideration to know that the life lacking in pleasure is not worth much. All work and no play really does make Jill a dull girl.

It takes mindful discipline to live a valuable life, because it requires us to try to align our motivations with the values we consciously choose so that our actions express those values. It takes attention to intention.

So, spending time and money on a Himalayan trek may be the expression of the positively selfish value of enjoying hiking, camping, and majestic scenery. It would be negative, if it recklessly put my life or health at undue risk, or the money spent was needed to pay an overdue debt. So long as it's not harmful to me or others, although selfish, Himalayan trekking or eating a banana split express a positive value. When we enjoy a good meal or a camping trip with friends or family, it's even more fun. Because including others transforms the experience from a solely selfish pleasure into a shared and, to some extent, an unselfish pleasure.

We need not be stern old Kantian sticklers to align our selfish and unselfish motives with positive goals. Getting to know yourself and your neighbors should be fun.

~ ~ ~

Most of our actions intertwine selfish and unselfish

motives and effects. As you think through who is the person you really want to be and consider how to become that person, you will notice with increasing clarity that you are mixed up with all sorts of other people, both close to you and so distant you will never see them (e.g., the trucker who delivered the food to your grocery store). We live within a family, a neighborhood, a community, state, and nation, and we belong to social circles and organizations, and probably participate in social media. Our lives are incredibly tangled up with other lives in ways we might not ordinarily notice.

So take some time and pay attention to your intentions. Exercising mindfulness in this way will probably reveal that to a significant extent you are living a life guided by positive values. Most of us, regardless of our religious and political affiliations are intentionally following the "Great Commandment" to love your self and others. We do try to take good care of ourselves, and we do try to help others in need when we can.

But when it is stated as a commandment or expectation -- Love your neighbor as yourself! -- It might feel like a heavy burden too great to bear. The bar is set too high. Do we really have to **Love**, can't we just settle for getting along?

If you think of loving as just being consciously considerate, perhaps it won't seem like such a great burden to love yourself and to love your neighbor. Participating in the economy as a producer and consumer affects countless people and the natural environment. Surely we can do that considerately, being mindful of how our actions express care, or a lack of care, for ourselves and other selves. If we care enough to be conscientious in our work and as consumers, we can surely be considerate of our loved ones and friends.

A tenet of Chaos Theory in physics is that the tiny movement of a butterfly's wings may have unforeseen and tremendous consequences as the effect of that tiny movement ripples out into the physical universe. Like the butterfly's fluttering wings, the way we behave may have effects way beyond what we can foresee within the bounds of our little universe of family and friends.

Now, wait just one minute Buster! You just put the pressure back on! You said the standard should feel like it's lower, now you're saying I have to take the entire universe into consideration every time I do anything! That's an even greater burden than being expected to love my neighbor as myself!

Not really. It's just a fact, whether you pay attention to it or not, that our actions ripple out and have effects beyond what we can observe or know. I can only imagine what the grocery truck driver will do with the penny my purchases indirectly contribute to his paycheck. I am not responsible for what he does with that penny. But, I am responsible for how I spend my money. So, if I have thought through how I am going to use my money to take good care of myself and have considered the effects that I know my purchases or investments will have on others and the environment, then I have acted responsibly with my money.

We will get along better as individual selves, members of the human community, and creatures on this planet, if we live with mindful attention. If I want to be a person who values physical fitness, I will exercise regularly and not consume too many calories. If I care about clean air, when I purchase my next car it will be a model which pollutes the air less than my current one. Or, I might choose to live without a car. If I want to be a person who values public education, I should join the PTO and volunteer to work at the next fundraiser to support the arts and sports programs of our local schools. If I am motivated to care for the elderly or disabled, I could become a driver for Meals on Wheels. To be a compassionate spouse, I will help clean up the wine my wife spills instead of grumping at her.

When you know yourself, who you truly want to be, then you will be mindful of how and whether your choices reflect your own unique intentions of how to take good care of yourself. You will also be mindful of how and whether you are affecting others and the natural world in the ways you intend. "Real life" or "truly living", depending on the translation, is described in the first letter of Timothy 6:18-19 as doing good deeds and generously sharing your wealth. In other words, taking care of yourself so that you are able to help those less fortunate than you is the way to live a valuable life.

Warning: After you have consciously considered your motives and how your actions affect you and others, live expressing the values you have chosen. But please don't take all the joy and spontaneity out of life by self-consciously questioning every move you make every moment the rest of your life. You'd never get anything done. Spend some time figuring out who you want to be and reevaluate now and then; but live! It should be fun.

Chapter 17: Blindness of Political Visions

A useful way to analyze the politics of parties and politicians is to determine whether they lean more toward valuing selfishness or unselfishness. Let's consider two of the more idealistic approaches on the extremities of the current political spectrum in the US, Libertarianism to the right and Socialism to the left. The fundamental value of American Libertarians is individual freedom. The fundamental value of Socialists is an equal distribution of material resources. Each ideology has a vision of the ideal state.

Libertarians think the ideal society is one in which government does no more than enforce laws and provides for mutual defense. Libertarians have little interest in communal life. They believe that life will be better if individuals are allowed to pursue their own interests without interference from the state. In that sense their fundamental value is selfishness. Individual rights and freedoms are more important than the local community or nation.

Socialists believe in an ideal state in which, as Marx put it in his 1875 *Critique of the Gotha Program*, "From each according to his ability, to each according to his need." Socialists think society will be more just if there is an equal distribution of wealth. The fundamental value of Socialism is unselfishness in the sense that Socialists want every one of us to contribute as much as we can to the greater good, but we shouldn't expect to receive any greater benefit back from the state than somebody who was unable to contribute anything. Socialists care more about equalizing material wealth than individual rewards and economic freedom.

Libertarians are blinded by their ideology to the need for some level of distributive justice within society. They are not necessarily less generous as individuals than others, but they resent and resist any government intervention requiring them to help others in need. Libertarians think that government is inefficient and an ineffective vehicle to assist

those in need. Socialists fail to grasp the values of self-
sufficiency and ambition. "Rugged individualism" and pride
in individual accomplishment are not particularly admired by
strict Socialists.

Talking politics over lunch (often a bad way to ruin a
good meal) with three friends, I described, as I'm doing in this
chapter, how Socialists and Libertarians are blinded to some
aspects of reality because their goal is to transform society into
an ideal state. "April", a confirmed Leftist-Progressive, argued
that Socialists were realistic and Libertarianism is "the
philosophy of teenage boys, utterly selfish and unworkable".
"Joe" pointed out that all of the governments which were
Marxist-Socialist had failed or liberalized into a blend of
Socialism, Capitalism, and limited democracy. April
responded that the Scandinavian countries were Socialist and
very successful. She refused to accept that the Scandinavian
economies are actually a blend of Socialism and Capitalism
and the governments are constitutional democracies which
protect many of the individual liberties cherished by
Libertarians. She snorted at the idea that the Bill of Rights in
the US Constitution is essentially Libertarian because it
protects individual rights from governmental oppression.

I looked around the table and said, "I rest my case."
April refused to believe there is anything worthwhile in
Libertarianism, even though she thinks the Bill of Rights is a
work of genius (except for "the god damn Second
Amendment"). Libertarianism, like Capitalism, is simply bad
and wrong, because she sees reality through the tinted glasses
of her ideology.

Ideologues start with a vision of what is not real, a
utopia. They are blind to certain aspects of what is real. They
find it difficult to accept that people are different and don't
agree on what is the ideal socio-economic-political system.
Ideologues believe in the perfectibility of the individual and
the achievability of an ideal state. Perfection means agreeing

with their vision and submitting to their rules.

Violent use of force has been the mechanism used by ideologues on the far left (Communist revolutionaries) and on the far right (Fascists) to try to create an ideal state. Karl Marx believed that violence was necessary to overthrow the status quo and advocated proletarian revolution as a necessary stage in the historical movement to a communist state. Hitler had no qualms about using force to oust all opposing parties from the Reichstag in his putsch to end the Weimar Republic and establish the "Eternal Reich". Unbelievers and rebels that fail to agree with the revolutionaries' vision of the ideal state must be coerced or eliminated. The horrors visited on Shia, Christians, and Yazidis by the self-proclaimed Islamic State of Iraq and Syria is a current manifestation of the insanely inhumane zeal of idealistic revolutionaries.

Anticipating an objection, yes Counselor, I agree not all revolutions are led by crazy-ass violent extremists. The American Revolution was not. Because it was not led by men with a utopian vision. The American revolutionaries fought to throw off the monarchical tyranny of a foreign government. The process of creating a constitutional government following the Revolutionary War involved pragmatic leaders who valued individual freedom and representative government and were willing to compromise on issues to try to accommodate the reasonable concerns of all parties. A decade later the French Revolution was led by crazy-ass violent extremists.

I should note that the American versions of Libertarianism and Socialism have been a good deal less dangerous to the established order than Communism or Fascism. Because Libertarians are opposed ideologically to coercive collective action, it would be difficult for them to unite into an organized armed revolution on the scale of what Lenin did in Russia or to create a mass party movement like Hitler did in Germany. Libertarians and Socialists in the US, tend to be quite dissatisfied with the political status quo (who isn't?), but both groups of believers do have political parties which work within the legal-political framework.

Libertarians, like former presidential candidate Ron Paul, have had some influence on the Republican Party. And, there is a theme of Libertarianism within the Tea Party movement, which has had a considerable impact on the GOP. Bernie Sanders, Vermont senator, is a Socialist but caucuses with the Democrats. The welfare programs of Democrat presidents Franklin Delano Roosevelt and Lyndon Baines Johnson were significantly influenced by Socialist ideology.

"Progressive" historians interpret American history as a bumpy evolution toward Scandinavian-style socialism. Libertarianism is seen as a losing rear-guard action. Conservatives might agree with Progressives about the direction history is moving. And, because they abhor America's decline into European-socialistic-decadence, they think it's their job to resist it.

Since Socialists and Libertarians do have influence within the political system in the US, it's unlikely either would mount a serious attempt at violent revolution to effect change. Not to say there is not political violence in the US. It usually takes the form of confrontations with law enforcement. On the right, there was the standoff in April 2014 of Cliven Bundy and his armed supporters. They faced down the Feds over Bundy's refusal to pay fees assessed by the Bureau of Land Management for his cattle grazing on federal land.

On the left, violence occasionally erupted during the Occupy Wall Street protests which began in 2011 and flared up on occasion over the next few years. Windows got broken and cops cracked some heads.

The effects of Libertarianism and Socialism in the US are inconsistent and random. Our populace has not bought into either vision of their ideal state. Many Americans treasure our historic values of individual freedom and equality of opportunity. We appreciate visionaries like

Washington, Jefferson, Madison, Lincoln, the Roosevelts, and King, who pushed us toward actualizing those values for our people. We haven't much cared for utopian extremists who would impose their visions and beliefs upon us.

~ ~ ~

In my lifetime civil unrest which turns violent in the US is usually inspired by specific issues and incidents. The many riots in African-American neighborhoods, beginning in the 1960s up through those in Ferguson, Missouri in August of 2014, usually began with a perceived incident of police brutality or some kind of crackdown on local people. Well-meaning protesters respond by marching and carrying signs demanding change, respect, and dignity. The Reverends Jesse Jackson and Al Sharpton show up for the cameras and make inflammatory speeches. Dissatisfied with the response of authorities, anger mounts and the outlet is trashing cars and assaulting cops. Looters take advantage of the disorder and break into local shops. A bunch of people are arrested and several small businesses are trashed. In time, order is restored. The local police force is required to undergo a course in sensitivity training. Some sop will be thrown to local civil rights leaders, so a group of black ministers can pose for photos with white city officials. Streets are eventually cleaned and the stores which were insured reopen. Those without insurance remain shuttered. A few years later the cycle repeats, if not in Ferguson, somewhere in another US city.

Until the power structure of each city includes in meaningful ways significant numbers of those who do not feel enfranchised, we will continue to see that same cycle of images on our TV screens. Neighborhoods seething with anger over how their young men are treated by cops are not mollified for long with photo-ops by local politicians. Being included in the decision-making process which affects conditions in the hood, so that residents have voice and influence in the governance of their community, is the way out of the cycle of "ghetto" violence.

Participation in neighborhood associations, town hall meetings, and local politics is how you get to be heard. Encourage young women and men in under-represented groups to enroll in police and fire academies. Run for local office yourself, or help out with the campaign of somebody running for city council in your district. Stuff envelopes for a candidate during the campaign; if she wins the election she'll listen when you call her office. If illegal discrimination in education, housing, employment, or by City Hall is keeping you down, file a class action lawsuit.

You gotta stand up for your rights. Those with power ain't gonna just hand it over.

~ ~ ~

The world in which human beings actually live their lives is not perfectible. To be human is to be imperfect. There is no one answer to the many social-political-economic problems faced by cities, states, and nations.

We should always question the status quo. Progress in technology, human rights, economic efficiencies, and all other aspects of human affairs is dependent on recognizing that we can do things differently and better. But let's try to progress beyond using violence to effect change, unless there really is no alternative and living in accordance with our fundamental values requires it.

If government becomes so oppressive, as it is under most dictatorships, those who value freedom for themselves and others might have to fight for it. The founders of my country did. If the economic system is so unfairly rigged to benefit the few at the expense of the many and the legal-political system offers no real means to combat injustice, then to live a valuable life may require the sacrifice of nonviolence.

Seems to me that the use of defensive violence was justified by the brave young people who occupied Tiananmen Square in 1989 and who took to the streets in the rippling protests and riots of the Arab Spring. The Chinese and Arab protesters lived under governments which had their boots on the necks of citizens. The economic systems of their countries are kleptocracies designed to benefit only certain elites. Even so, the protests only became violent when government and militia forces attacked protesters.

Martin Luther King, Jr. is considered a saint by many of us, because his campaign to end racial discrimination in the US used Ghandhian-style nonviolent civil disobedience as the method of attack. (Mahatma Gandhi called it Satyagraha, "truth force".) Malcolm X advocated meeting the violence of racial discrimination with violence ("by any means necessary"). Some historians of the civil rights movement theorize that the movement would not have succeeded to the extent it did if King's nonviolent approach was not balanced by the threat of Malcolm's willingness to use violence.

When a nation is attacked it is justified in defending itself. It has a duty to try to protect its people from criminal harm and from invasion. If a person is threatened with harm she has a right to defend herself. When a government devalues its own citizens so that they are prevented from decently caring for themselves and others, then the citizens have the right and duty to revolt. Under those conditions revolution would be an expression of caring for the self and others.

People in any sizable group are not all going to agree on what is the best form of government, social organization, or economic system. If we have the freedom to pursue living decent lives as individuals and are allowed the opportunity to participate meaningfully in the management of our communities, reasonable people will work within the established order to improve it. By valuing self and others it follows that we will individually and collectively take on the challenge of pushing the boundaries of individual liberty and economic fairness a little further each generation.

Most revolutions are very costly in lives lost. Belief-driven revolutionaries are more likely interested in creating their version of utopia than improving the actual lives of real people, like you and me. Caution is an appropriate response to those calling us to the battlements for revolution. Because we might find ourselves up against the wall, if it turns out we don't agree with all the details of the revolutionaries' beliefs.

We need to ground visions of our community and nation in well-balanced attentiveness to our needs and the needs of our fellow citizens. We can do this by guiding our lives according to consciously chosen positive values. Unfettered selfishness led to the economic inequities and abuses of robber baron capitalism at the close of the 19th Century in the US. Trying to impose a vision of the ideal state in which all are equal led to mass starvations within the Union of Soviet Socialist Republics and the People's Republic of China, the Gulags under Stalin and "reeducation" camps under Mao.

So let's cease trying to create a utopian state in which we are all equal. It has the unfortunate history of killing too many of us. Let's also chuck the idea that a society which allows total freedom to the individual with no obligation to the community would be an improvement over a relatively free but regulated market. If there are no legal safeguards to protect consumers and workers, the gross injustices of the Robber-Baron era occur. Cruel exploitation of workers in the mines of Africa and the sweat shops of South-Eastern Asia is happening right now, because of a lack of humane regulation.

It's just an unfortunate fact about our species that there are people who don't give a damn about others. Some of us will lie, cheat, and steal to benefit the self at the expense of our neighbor. Laws and regulations are the tools civilization has developed to restrain those who would take advantage and abuse the uneducated, the poor, the weak, and the young.

If you live in a constitutional democracy with the right to vote and organize political parties and equal protection under the law, be content with incremental advances. That's as good as it gets. But act politically to exercise your individual rights and to effect change which reflect your values. Well balanced individuals will strive to create a society which balances the needs of individuals for freedom with the needs of the community for sacrifice. If we find a better balance of care for self and others, we will move forward toward communities and a nation which is more united and less divided.

Chapter 18: Find Your Golden Mean and which Way to Lean

Preservation of the self and our species is biologically and psychologically hard-wired into us as humans and all other species, according to Darwinian biologists. If we are conscious, functioning, and not psychologically damaged human beings, we will pursue our own interests and we will want our family, community, nation, and species to survive and prosper. That's the way we are, and it is good.

The pyramids of ancient Egypt were supposedly created to be launching pad to send pharaohs off into their next lives. The pyramids also glorified the egos of the pharaohs. What a ridiculous waste of resources! And yet, these marvelous creations still amaze us so many millennia after the passing of the last pharaoh. From a 21st Century Judeo-Christian (or most any) moral perspective we may condemn the pharaohs for their extravagance and insensitivity to their slaves and servants. Yet their incredibly selfish "edifice complex" delights everyone who sees pictures of the great pyramids, and especially those fortunate enough to stand in the sand in the shadows of these amazing monuments.

The world would be a lesser place were it not for the grandeur of self-centered human egotism. Not to say that any of us should try to become a pharaoh. If that is your life's aspiration, you might want to put the book down and check in with your therapist. Or, if you have no ego and just skulk about in the shadows always avoiding the spotlight, you too might want to check out some therapy.

A theme developed by ancient Greek, Roman, and Chinese philosophers was that the good life has a "golden mean". They hotly disputed what is the right balance, but most of the ancient philosophers of both Eastern and Western Civilization taught their students that living well required an equilibrium of virtues (ennobling actions which benefitted the community) and what some would call vices (an allowance for self indulgence). Aristotle expressed this understanding as "moderation in all things" in his *Nicomachean Ethics*. About 250 years earlier, Confucius expressed the concept more poetically: "Balance is the perfect state of still water."

Our character and the legacy we leave are reflected in the balance we establish of selfishness and selflessness. Some of us will lean more toward a selfish polarity in search of a healthy balance that works. Others will lean toward unselfishness seeking an equilibrium tilted in that direction. It's worth remembering the tiresome but (I grudgingly admit) helpful instruction of the flight attendant as your airplane readies for takeoff: "If you are seated with a child, secure your oxygen mask before you assist your child." The point being that you can't help others unless you are already secure yourself. The "good neighbor" in Jesus's parable of the Good Samaritan had the funds to pay for the robbery victim's food, lodging, and medical care. If the Samaritan had not been financially capable, he wouldn't have been much good.

Not to say that the poor cannot be giving. Since we're on a Jesus roll; remember the story of "the widow's mite". Jesus describes how a poor widow by giving two small coins gave proportionately more to the Temple than the rich with their silver. For each of us, no matter what our economic, psychological, and social circumstances, there is a balance that's right for us. While we might lean one way or the other, living a healthy balance will engage us in both self-centered and sacrificial activities.

So, what's the formula for the ideal balance of selfish/selfless? Yeah, you, Mr. Author, you're the one writing the book. Well, let's see. The Judeo-Christian tradition of tithing suggests we should each give ten percent of all we earn to the temple or church. So, maybe a 90/10 division of selfishness/unselfishness is a good balance. But that seems more than a bit heavy on the selfishness spectrum, too pharaoh-ish. Financial planners suggest that a properly balanced investment portfolio for most people is 60/40 stock funds to bond funds; which means putting sixty percent into more risky funds and keeping forty percent in more secure funds. Maybe this suggests we should be willing to take the risk of putting ourselves out for others more than we should hold back to protect ourselves.

Then again, financial advisors recommend a 40/60 stocks to bonds ratio, when you've saved enough for retirement and should be taking less risk. This suggests we might need to shift our balance and lean more toward looking to our own self-interest as life circumstances change or as a different stage of life is entered. But, if we've planned well, wouldn't we be able to be more giving in a later stage of life? But, whoa! During the child-rearing stage, or the career-building stage, aren't we constantly giving ourselves to our kids and/or our company, profession, customers, or clients? So what the hell is the golden mean for a rewarding and prosperous life?

I don't know what works best for you. I do know the balance has shifted for me during different stages in my life. I can't claim that I ever knew, or worked out, an actual percentage of 90/10, 60/40, 40/60, or any other numerical division. It's more a matter of deciding to lean somewhat more for self or for others, and then making decisions as life presents forks in your road and choices to make. Maintaining your balance as you encounter challenges and changes is what develops your character into the person you consciously choose to be.

If we don't consider to what extent we are willing to give of ourselves to others, and to what extent we need to devote to caring for ourselves, how do we know who we are? We find ourselves too easily pushed and pulled by the pressures put on us by authority figures, peers, and the internal forces of guilt and shame. Living in thrall to external pressures and subconscious forces is following a path in life chosen not by you, but by others for you. It is the way of sheep. It's not a way illuminated by your own thoughtful discernment.

~ ~ ~

Destruction and construction, tearing down and building up, entropy and synergy, -- this is the fundamental dichotomy, the yin and yang, the balance which maintains and sustains the universe and life. This is ancient wisdom. It is reflected in the Book of Ecclesiastes ("There is a season ...") and the Hindu conception of Shiva as destroyer of worlds and Vishnu as the creative life source. How we participate in building up and tearing down, of living and dying, is how we create our selves. The integrity of our character is expressed through the choices we make as we develop a career and have and raise children. And so it is as life winds down and we face our own death and leave a legacy behind us. (Aristotle proposed that a life could not be judged successful or a failure until long after death, because ultimate success depends on how well things turn out for our descendents.)

Human community is created through our participation in building up and tearing down. To acquire an estate is to build. As we tear down that estate by spending or giving away our material wealth the community is built up by others using the wealth we acquired. Like ants constructing an ant hill, our individual efforts help to create the material wealth and ethical character of the community in which we live. We do, in a sense, work ourselves to death for the benefit of our family, company, community, and the economy.

The value of your life to the greater community is a consequence of all that is built up into your character as well as your material contributions. Our communities are us. Life within a community is good or bad depending on who its members are; to what extent they are living lives well balanced in terms of taking care of themselves and giving to others.

Since the 1960s social scientists like James Q. Wilson have described life in crime-ridden inner cities in terms of behavioral pathologies. The typical prescription of political conservatives to cure "ghetto blight" has been to crack down on crime. Wilson is credited with "the broken windows theory", which was employed by the Giuliani and Blumenthal administrations with much ballyhooed success in bringing down the crime rate in New York City. Political liberals have criticized the broken windows approach for being a treatment plan that only addresses the symptoms but not the underlying causes. Liberals tend to advocate for more generous poverty alleviation programs and additional funding to try to improve inner-city schools.

Both approaches are right, and both are wrong. They are both right in recognizing that the community would be a better place to live if crime was reduced, citizens felt secure in their homes and neighborhood, standard of living increased, and education improved. Where both approaches fall short is in a failure to address the reality that the character of the community is determined by the character of the individuals that are the community. So long as many characters in the community are inclined toward criminally selfish behavior, the pathologies of the community will continue no matter how much money is poured into welfare programs and how many cops patrol the street. Creation of high character among community members, so that most folks will take good care of themselves and then help others in need, does not happen because a single mother gets a couple hundred more dollars per month in a welfare check. Nor is it created because a young man thinks he is likely to go to jail if caught breaking a window.

The character of an inner city community does change when it is gentrified. That is because hardworking twenties and thirties have different values than gang bangers, burglars, and taggers. Not to say that all people living in high crime rate neighborhoods are criminals. Most are not. And many engaged in victimless crimes, like nonviolent drug dealing, gambling, and prostitution are actually people with as high moral character as the good burghers of small towns. People whose livelihoods are based on victimless crime may be taking care of themselves, their families, and adding to the local economy in the only way they think they can. Outsiders with political power have criminalized victimless crimes out of a self-righteous imposition of their beliefs onto a community they do not understand and which has different cultural attitudes toward use of narcotics, sex, and gambling. Practitioners of these trades are more concerned with how to make a living than the "thou shalt not" rules so important to stiff-necked puritans.

The fundamental economic values of a drug dealer might be the same as a neighborhood pharmacist, to provide for herself, her family, and her customers. The pharmacist and pusher may have each made the best choices possible given the different circumstances of their lives.

Liberals may dream of turning "ghettos" into middle-class neighborhoods, if we just commit enough money. We've already seen the failure of one version of that vision in the urban planning policies in the 1960s and 70s of the Johnson and Nixon Administrations. Poor but healthy neighborhoods were destroyed. Aging single family homes were razed and people were pushed into and stacked up in high-rise poorly-constructed apartments. Women were given welfare checks for having babies, so long as the father was not living with the family. Brilliant! A generation of poor urban kids grew up in crappy housing projects without fathers in the home.

If more money in itself resolved the character issues associated with criminal pathology all rich people would be moral beacons, right? Not. The rape of the economy by investment bankers, securities traders, and mortgage brokers, which caused the economic crash and Great Recession of 2008 through 2012, should be proof enough that there's no direct link between wealth and high moral character.

A study by Princeton University's Woodrow Wilson School, involving a survey of 450,000 Americans, found that there is a link between earning around $75,000 in annual income and emotional happiness. The further below $75,000 one earns in annual income, the unhappier on a daily basis one is likely to feel. However, there is no incremental increase in happiness by earning more than $75,000. When our essential economic needs are fulfilled we generally wake up feeling okay. If we wake up worried about the ability to pay our bills, it causes anxiety, depression, or both. Making more money than is needed does not contribute to a positive mood, according to the Princeton study.

Another finding of the study was that acquiring greater wealth does offer the opportunity to feel a deeper sense of satisfaction with life. A rich person has greater freedom to make desirable life choices for himself and to share his material wealth with the community. If I'm rich, I can afford to spend $100 on a haircut, pamper myself at a spa, and still make the payments on my cigarette boat and Learjet. I can also start a foundation to improve inner-city schools, distribute mosquito netting in at-risk areas for malaria, and fund a forum for peaceful inter-faith dialogue in the Middle East.

Material wealth does make it easier to indulge in a self-centered pleasurable lifestyle and to share unselfishly with those in need. Material wealth does not mitigate the challenge of finding your own golden mean of selfishness/selflessness. Whether rich or poor we have twenty-four hours in a day to choose how we live. Rain falls on both the rich and poor alike; the only difference is the rich can afford to buy an umbrella.

Whatever our material circumstances, we decide each minute of each day how we spend the time of our lives, selfishly, unselfishly, or well adjusted. If freed from the daily concern of making sufficient money to meet one's material needs, the wealthy person should find it easier to lean more toward unselfishness than selfishness.

The philanthropic efforts of Bill and Melinda Gates through the Gates Foundation have become an inspiration and challenge to other billionaires to lean toward unselfishness. A more approachable example: a friend of mine left his private surgical practice to spend three months in the winter of 2014 in South Sudan as a volunteer for Doctors Without Borders. Had Bill not already achieved financial independence he would probably not have felt free to give three months of his life to benefit the people of a country with an under-developed healthcare system.

Wealth comes to the rich person from the community. She didn't build the companies which issued the stocks and bonds in her investment portfolio. She may have earned the money to pay for the investments, but others labored to create and operate the companies in which she invested. And the money she earned as a doctor, lawyer, banker, or whatever came from payments by patients, clients, and customers in the community. We are justified in expecting the rich to feel an obligation to give back to the community and world that has given them much.

"You built a factory out there? Good for you ... But I want to be clear; you moved your goods to market on the roads the rest of us paid for; you hired workers the rest of us paid to educate; you were safe in your factory because of police forces and fire forces that the rest of us paid for." Elizabeth Warren said that in a campaign speech when she was running for the US Senate in Massachusetts in 2011. She went on, "You built a factory and it turned into something terrific, or a great idea? God bless. Keep a big hunk of it. But part of the underlying social contract is you take a hunk of that and pay forward for the next kid who comes along."

Balance shifts. We might spend decades with a focus on building an estate and caring for family. But, at some point, the focus will shift; kids grow up and careers come to an end. For those of us who are materially wealthy, we can focus more on giving away some of what we accumulated. Or, we can choose to spend all that extra time on the golf course. Whether we've become rich or not, after childcare and retirement are in the rearview mirror, we'll have more time to volunteer for worthy causes, political activity, and to assist organizations that benefit our communities.

But it's really quite okay, if your golden mean has you out playing eighteen holes every other day; especially after you've given much of your life to benefitting your employer, customers, and kids. The balance is **yours** to find at each stage of your life. And, it's you who will leave the legacy of your choices.

Saint Martin, so the legend goes, was a Roman soldier who came across a beggar on a freezing cold winter day. He cut his cloak in halves and gave the poor man half his cloak. Bertolt Brecht finishes the story in an aside by a character in his play, *Mother Courage*: "And they both froze to death."

Finding your golden mean doesn't mean being a saintly martyr. Don't let guilt, shame, or peer pressure take that freedom from you. It's up to you to decide which way and how far you lean.

~ ~ ~

The evil spider-like Henry Potter in *It's a Wonderful Life* was not a happy person. He profited from but did not give back to Bedford Falls. George Bailey gave overly much to the community to his own detriment. He wasn't happy, because he never got out of town to live his dream of traveling the world. The two characters are paired. Potter is alone and bitter because he is too selfish. George is surrounded by loving friends and family but is frustrated and resentful because he is too sacrificial. With the help of Clarence the angel, George comes to understand that he sacrificed his own self-actualization for the greater good of the community. He also comes to realize that the life choices he made helped create a well balanced community. His selflessness balanced Mr. Potter's selfishness within the community of Bedford Falls.

George is not self-actualized, but by the end of the movie he is self-realized. He becomes conscious about the choices he's made and accepts the uncomfortable balance of his life. If *It's a Wonderful Life* had a sequel, perhaps George would be on a round-the-world trip with his family paid for by the donations of grateful depositors in the Bedford Falls Savings and Loan.

Potter is unchanged by the end of the movie, still a lonely bitter old man. He was fully realized. He consciously decided to live a life guided by selfishness. Potter found the money Uncle Billy misplaced. Potter could have saved George and the Savings & Loan; instead, he kept the money, even though he was already the richest man in Bedford Falls. Potter viewed the rest of humanity as sheep and himself as a wolf. He is a predator and he leaned entirely toward selfishness. In the beginning he was, and at the end he still is, a bitter old man with no friends.

Whose life had more meaning? He who gave too much or he who gave none at all?

There are many stories about people who leaned more toward others than toward self. We need to be inspired to give. So we tell stories about, and relate the histories of, Krishna, Moses, Buddha, Jesus, Gandhi, and King as exemplars. George Bailey might have been happier had he tempered his unselfishness with a few weeks off every year to go traveling. But Bedford Falls needed his sacrifice, and he willingly, if resentfully, gave what his community needed. He was so appreciated by the town that everyone gave money to save him from going to jail.

It's a Wonderful Life has an ambiguous ending -- neither George nor Uncle Billy goes to prison -- but justice isn't done. Potter gets away with not giving the money back that Billy lost. The townspeople had to give up their hard-earned cash

to save their previous savior. George had "saved" each
member of the community during the Great Depression
through the liberal lending and lenient collection policies of
the Savings & Loan he ran. The story includes the message
that a wonderful life might not turn out to be fair or equitable
in the material rewards received from the world.

"He makes the sun rise on both the evil and the good
and sends rain on both the righteous and the unrighteous."
Matthew 5:45. Justice often does not prevail in our world.
Results are not guaranteed by living a valuable life, only the
knowledge that you have lived and loved as you chose to do.

~ ~ ~

That last point might seem pretty obvious. But I've had
conversations with many friends and clients which revealed
they were not living a life they consciously chose. All of them
were unhappy.

I had not seen "Ralph" for several months at our regular
Sunday volleyball group. When he finally showed up for a
game, during a break in the play, he was whinging that he
had no time for himself; he'd gained twenty pounds, had
developed high blood pressure, and hadn't had a vacation in
eight years. He was over-worked and spent "all his free time"
caring for his aging parents. I asked Ralph if he could cut
back on his hours and had he considered moving his parents
into an assisted-living residence. He replied that he couldn't
cut back because his business was booming and his parents
didn't want to leave their house. I pointed out that he could
hire an assistant and a part-time home health-aid could help
look after his parents. "It's too time-consuming to train an
assistant and my parents don't want a stranger in their house."

Ralph was not living a balanced life. He was unhappy
working such long hours, but he wouldn't cut back or hire an
assistant. I suspected that he feared he'd take home less
money. He submitted to his parents' demands that he
sacrifice his time to be their caretaker rather than spending the

money to hire a home health-aid. Ralph was conscious of his
decisions to an extent. He consistently chose to give his time
to make more, or spend less, money and to remain in thrall to
his parents' demands. His own diagnosis was that he was out
of balance by working too much and sacrificing too much time
for his parents. Ralph also recognized that his health was in
jeopardy if he didn't re-balance how he spent his money and
his time.

What Ralph refused to recognize was that he is in
control of his own life. He blamed other forces, his business
and his parents, for the choices he made. He was unhappy
with his life, but he didn't want to take responsibility for
change. He was being pushed toward a cliff by these other
forces he'd let take control of his life.

~ ~ ~

At the other end of the economic spectrum from the fat
cat Mr. Potter and Ralph with their booming businesses is the
person who grows up "on the wrong side of the tracks". What
hope is there that one of life's unfortunates will consciously
create a life in healthy balance, when she was born into and
grew up in poverty and a dysfunctional family?

The examples of my friend Tik and Viktor Frankl
demonstrate that no one is so trapped by circumstances that
he can't create a valuable life. But, the statistical evidence
shows that kids growing up in economically deprived
situations without college-educated parents in a stable
marriage are probably going to repeat a cycle of poverty and
live messy-troubled lives likely leading to incarceration.

Economics historian Gregory Clark claims in his book,
The Son Also Rises: Surnames and the History of Social Mobility
(published Feb. 2014 by Princeton University Press), that
social mobility is actually a myth, if viewed historically and
statistically. Clark used public records in the UK, US, China,
Japan, and other countries to analyze socio-economic-political
status by surnames over hundreds of years. His conclusion is
that one generation tends to follow the other in social status

and economic class. The records he studied show that it
"takes ten or fifteen generations (300 - 450 years)" for most
families to move up or down significantly. Clark reluctantly
concludes that where you end up in life is largely determined
by where you start.

Two other books which generally concede Clark's point
on the inevitability of nature and nurture are Charles
Murray's *Coming Apart* and *Marriage Markets: How Inequality Is
Remaking the American Family* by June Carbone and Naomi
Cahn. But these author-scholars are not quite as pessimistic as
Gregory Clark. They argue for creating social policy supports
for stable, happy marriages, among less-educated Americans.
Their view is that supporting and encouraging two-parent
households, improving public education, and other
interventions which benefit under-privileged folks will better
the odds of socio-economic advances for future generations.

As a society we should certainly try to assist kids and
families through policies based on the values we hold dear as
a nation, like equality of opportunity in education.
Ultimately, each individual will have to choose her way of life.
We are not trapped by statistics. Our genes (nature) and the
environment in which we grow up (nurture) may be the two
most influential factors in our development. But another
factor is our free will. If we exercise it consciously and
diligently, we can transcend most any other influence in
determining who we will be.

Folks living in urban squalor in the US have more
wealth than the most successful farm families in my friend
Tik's home village of Basa, Nepal. But in Basa village divorce
is a rarity and the communal support of children is amazing to
American eyes. The entire village really does look out for the
children. The nine orphans of the village live with the school
principal. Food and clothing for the orphans are provided by
the village. There is no crime, despite the material poverty of
the village. The village even has a distributive welfare system.

Blacksmiths and tailors are allotted a set amount of the crops from each of the farm families, because the blacksmiths and tailors are unable to spend as much time tending crops due to their duties as skilled tradesmen for the village.

The village is populated by people living happy balanced lives who care about each other. That is the culture in which each succeeding generation is reared.

In the US poverty and crime are interlocked. Statistical analysis of *State and Metropolitan Area Data Book* of the Bureau of the Census reveals a consistent pattern of high crime in low income neighborhoods. Other factors do come into play, but the data is compelling that the crime rate in urban areas is highest in the poorest neighborhoods.

So-called conservatives might want to fill prisons with wrong doers, but that doesn't solve the problem of crime. It just shifts the criminal population off the streets and behind bars. The taxpayers then bear the burden of the cost of criminality instead of the potential crime victims within the neighborhood. Statistics provided by the Bureau of Justice on criminal recidivism reveal that more than two-thirds (67.8%) of released prisoners are arrested for a new crime within three years and over three-quarters (76.6%) are arrested within five years.

These are depressing statistics. How many years will it take before we learn that locking people up in pens with other criminals does not reform them? We can lock up criminals to protect the community, but the criminal personality will not change unless the offender chooses to reevaluate his values to take better care of himself and to care more for others.

Violent criminals and conniving Ponzi schemers are probably sociopaths. Other people are just victims or adversaries to these users and abusers. The unhappy person with no friends has also failed to value others sufficiently to develop mutual relationships. The resentful person who has no time for himself and is being taken advantage of by others has become a door mat for others to step on. All of these personality types are out of balance by leaning too far toward selfishness or valuing themselves too little.

The statistics on criminal recidivism are convincing that as horrible as incarceration is it does not cause reform of an unbalanced personality. The rewards of more generous welfare checks and schools with air conditioning and computers will not alone turn a crime-ridden neighborhood into a well-balanced community. Changing external-material conditions will not alone cause an unbalanced person to develop a healthy equilibrium of caring for self and others.

Counseling and therapy may help a person, who has been victimized or is a victimizer, to recognize his own value and that of others. Much of the work of the helping professions, if you think about it, is devoted to dealing with clients that have not developed a healthy attitude and habits of caring for themselves or others. Many of these clients have been harmed by someone who didn't care about others. It is a vicious cycle which repeats itself.

Physical health issues like the epidemic of diabetes and obesity are due, at least in part, to our failure to care for our bodies. Many of the disorders and syndromes listed in *The Diagnostic and Statistical Manual of Mental Disorders* can be described in terms of the sufferer as "unbalanced". The evidence of people and communities failing to find the golden mean of healthy living is manifold throughout the world.

Health professionals are only available for a certain amount of time on certain dates. What is most effective in helping to develop healthy attitudes and behaviors are long-term relationships with family members, friends, and mentors, who will be there for us throughout our lives and who model living well-balanced lives. One of the reasons Basa village is such a peaceful and cohesive community is that villagers know each other so well they can recite the genealogies of their neighbors back five generations.

People who truly care about us will make themselves

available when we need them. If we lean toward helping others in need, we will seek opportunities to befriend those in need. When we realize we are in need of help we should reach out to those willing to provide it. There are many in our communities who need a friend or mentor to model and explain how to live a balanced life guided by positive values. There are also many fine and generous people in our communities willing to give of themselves to others in need. We can find each other if we try.

So, the sermonette of this chapter is: Find an equilibrium of caring for yourself and caring for others that works for you. Thriving communities are created through the willingness to give as we are able and for those in need to receive as needed and then paying it forward.

Chapter 19: Ethically Conflicted Growth

In my ethics classes in both law school and seminary many of the academic ethicists we studied held that living according to certain ethical principles is the highest and best way to live. Others argued that following the "love ethic" is more ethically enlightened.

So that my former professors won't take me off their Christmas card lists, I should clarify that "ethical principles" is synonymous with the way "positive values" is used in this book. So, living according to ethical principles, if they were independently and consciously chosen with the intention of living a balanced life in caring for the self and others, is pretty much the same as what I've described as guiding your life with positive values. But that formulation is not completely adequate.

Life is too complex to be wholly captured in boxes of particular values/principles. Choosing to be guided by positive values (worthy principles) at one point in your life is not sufficient in itself. Neither is achieving a balance of taking care of yourself and giving of yourself to others during a particular phase of life. Different circumstances and stages of life will cause, or allow, you to shift your emphasis between self and others. Being single, getting married, having children, building a career, retirement, or being a grandparent might shift your balance from focusing on self to others and back to self. Being a student or teacher, co-worker, volunteer, teammate, club member, and member of a family, and all the other roles you play within your work and leisure time may impel you to shift your balance of leaning toward self or others several times within a single day as your roles change. The appropriate choice from the menu of values/principles you have chosen to guide your life might also change to some extent as your roles and stage of life change. You will need to be nimble in responding to current circumstances, and you will need to know yourself well to find your golden mean as you move through the different stages of your life.

Life is not static; it is dynamic, changing as a river flows. The better we come to know ourselves the more consistency there is in the values we use as guides and in the way we lean toward selfishness or unselfishness. Still, the most placid and well-grounded lives sooner or later encounter challenges which shake us up.

~ ~ ~

If you consistently lean toward the unselfish, no matter the situation or your stage of life, then it's fair to say that you are living the "love ethic" in your creation of a valuable life. The Love Ethic means seeking to care for yourself and others in a balanced way which is tilted toward the unselfishness of loving thy neighbor.

Positive values or principles serve as our guides. But sometimes even guides might take a wrong turn. Life has a way of bending and breaking the bounds of the neat boxes and formulae we articulate. You won't find in this book a list of positive values that will always in every situation reveal the right thing to do. [Sorry, no refund if that's what you expected. But, Part III does have a list of "Quaker values" to consider. The book would be thousands of pages instead of a couple hundred if we had to list and sort through all possible ethical principles/values to consider and compare. So you should be thankful we're not going to do that. Partial refund? No!]

Values, even the most deeply-passionately held at the core of your identity may be tested in ways that shift the balance you thought you'd established. In this chapter we'll explore how to maintain balance when we're tested with conflicts in our own values and with those of other people. How we resolve, or don't resolve, conflict reveals who we really are, sheep, shepherd, or wolf.

~ ~ ~

Truthfulness is a principle/value most of us would

choose as one of our guides. We rely on others to be honest with us. Our web of relationships would disintegrate if we couldn't trust that family, friends, co-workers, associates, etc. are generally truthful with each other. But, on reflection, we might have to admit that we are not as fully committed to the value of Truth as we like to claim.

Being truthful can be selfish when it is self-righteous or impulsive. It might feel good to let it out, but what comes out might be hurtful. I'd just as soon not be told, "Why, you have even more grey hair than the last time I saw you." On the other hand, we value truth-telling in certain situations so highly that perjury is a crime and you can be sued for libel or slander and held accountable for damages in civil court if you defame someone.

The eminent and ancient ethical authority Plato argued in Book II of *Republic* that rulers have a duty to lie if the lie benefits the country and the truth would harm it. Machiavelli is maligned for being, well, Machiavellian, while Plato is generally lauded, but on this point they are in agreement. So, was President Eisenhower acting unethically when he, at first, denied that the US was conducting fly-over spy missions of the USSR? Or, by lying was he being guided by values such as Curiosity to determine a foe's military capabilities, Duty to protect the US, and Security in creating appropriate defensive strategies? Advocates of "Realpolitik", like Henry Kissinger, maintain that spying and lying are useful and necessary tools in the conduct of international relations in a dangerous world.

As citizens of a democratic republic we are furious, are we not, when we learn of lies and cover-ups by our political leaders? Presidents Nixon and Clinton were both impeached for lying under oath. But Nixon was forced to resign and Clinton not only survived politically, but has become one of the most popular ex-presidents in recent history. They both lied to the press and public. ("I am not a crook!" Oh yes you were. "I did not have sex with that woman!" Did too.)

Clinton's attempted cover-up was about a private sexual indiscretion, while Nixon's was about a conspiracy to guaranty his reelection and silence political foes. The country forgave Clinton for his dishonesty but not Nixon. They both lied to us; so why such a disparity in how the country and history have treated the two?

Special Prosecutor Ken Starr and the hypocritical Speaker of the House, Newt Gingrich, being the exceptions, most people recognized that Clinton's breach of faith was on a different order than Nixon's. Monogamy is probably not among the primary values Bill has chosen to guide his life. Clinton was guided on occasion by his value for self-indulgent pleasure in sexual adventure. Yet, through most of his life he seems to have leaned toward unselfishness. As a politician and statesman, Clinton worked extraordinarily hard to win elections and then to govern well. He's given much of his time and talents to humanitarian endeavors as an ex-President. There's no doubting Bill Clinton's personal ambition for achievement and recognition, but he's channeled his innate selfishness into unselfish endeavors.

We might wonder whether he intentionally shifted his balance temporarily to selfishness, or did he just become unbalanced, when he engaged in his affairs with Monica Lewinsky and others. To the extent there was a war of conflicting motives and desires within Bill, his screw ups (sorry, couldn't help it) reveal a pattern of occasionally giving in to the temptation of acting on impulse without due regard for the consequences to himself and others. As a workaholic he didn't have the time to express his value for adventure by mountain climbing, so he let it out by doing quicker climbs, if you will.

Many of us could imagine ourselves involved in a similar conflict and not handling it any better than Bill. In a survey conducted by the Associated Press for the Journal of Marital and Family Therapy in January of 2014, it's reported that "74% of men and 68% of women responded that they would have an affair if they knew they would never get caught."

The country has largely forgiven Bill's occasional tilt toward selfishness and guiding his conduct with the negative value of untruthfulness, because he eventually came clean; and while he was President the economy boomed, the federal deficit was erased, and we didn't engage our ground troops in any wars. The country and world have benefited from the effects of Bill Clinton being guided by the values of hard work, perseverance, intellectual effort, and philanthropy.

Nixon rose to political prominence as a member of the House on Un-American Activities. He was a zealous investigative prosecutor and persecutor of witnesses accused of communist sympathies. But as President Nixon normalized relations with "Red China"! Nixon claimed in his 1968 campaign for the Presidency that he had a "secret plan" to end the war in Viet Nam and bring all US troops home. There was no plan and US forces were not withdrawn until 1973. Nixon always described himself as an advocate of free enterprise, but he ordered wage and price controls (Socialism!) as President. His actual economic policies were so bizarre they were dubbed "Nixonomics". While Nixon was President the country endured a lingering recession combined with sky high gas prices during the Arab oil embargo of 1973-74.

The most jarring contradiction about Richard Milhous Nixon was that he carefully burnished his brand as being The Man on law and order. The Watergate hearings and tapes exposed Nixon's actual contempt for the rule of law. He approved burglaries, bribery, illegal wire taps, election tampering, and character assassination.

Nixon, like Clinton, gave much of his time and talents to politics and governance. But instead of asking what he could do for the country (to paraphrase President Kennedy), it seems Nixon thought the country's duty was to him. We can only guess at "Tricky Dicky's" ethical struggles during the dark nights of the soul. He never came clean, admitting only to "mistakes". There were reports that he suffered from depression during the twenty years of disgrace and obscurity after leaving the White House and before his death in 1994.

Did Dick feel conflicted? It's hard to reconcile the image Nixon projected in public and the private Nixon surrounded by cronies you can hear on the Watergate Tapes. Despite his admirable drive, intellectual capability, and hard work, the Dickster chose to be guided by negative values. He was a crook.

~ ~ ~

Honesty/Truthfulness and every other value/principle will bump up against other values/principles in an active life. Choices between values to which you are committed will have to be made. You will have to choose which guide to follow when you come upon a fork in your road. Maintaining balance requires discernment in deciding which way we want to lean and it requires sensitivity to the people involved, the situation at hand, and where we are in life. We will find ourselves conflicted.

Stubbornly following absolutist principles/values without sensitivity to the effects on ourselves and others might earn us kudos from strict ethicists like Emmanuel Kant. To those we are in relationships with it might just make us look like insensitive dicks.

In Chapter 16 we discussed mindfully aligning motives with affects to be intentionally selfish, unselfish, or a combination; and the process should be guided by positive values we have consciously chosen. The result is living a life balanced at a golden mean of caring for the self and others. But the process doesn't just stop with an once-in-a-lifetime decision. Because circumstances and situations will arise in which different values will bump into each other, the process should work like a computer's operating system, running all the time within our minds. We sift through the relevant principles to apply to the situation at hand and select the ones that will be most effective in achieving an alignment of our motives with intended consequences. We have to be nimble enough to shift to a different value-guide as circumstances change in order to maintain our golden mean of an ethical balance.

The pattern that develops from the choices we make in trying to maintain our desired equilibrium of caring for self and others is the record which reveals to the world who we are. We might like to think of ourselves in terms of our aspirations, or ideal self, but we are known to the people we encounter in our lives through our conduct and interactions with them -- which might be a bit different than the image we'd like to project. Few people will know, or care to know, what motivates us and how hard we try (or don't try) to select the values/principles that will best express the balance of care for self and others we intend to achieve. They will only know us through what they experience of us, or hear about us. Just the tip of the ice berg that is us, our words and deeds, determine our ethical reputation (or lack thereof). Then again, how comfortable would we be if others could see below the surface to know our actual motives, especially the ones we don't act on?

So, even if I've chosen my values with conscious intent to be a highly principled fellow, or to live the Love Ethic, I may not be perceived as such, because the affect on others somehow doesn't come off that way. But surely, if we try to guide our lives with positive values which are intended to create an equilibrium of caring for ourselves and others, and we sensitively (and sensibly) adjust the values we are trying to express appropriate to our life circumstances -- most of us will have the reputation we deserve (like it or not) within our communities.

If the communities you participate in are made up of good, decent, and balanced folks, then you will more than likely be given the benefit of the doubt if, on occasion, you stray from the normal pattern you've established. We would surely forgive the moral slippage of a friend who had acted with due care and concern ninety-nine out of one hundred times. We'd still think of him as a good guy. He just messed up this once, or maybe even a couple times.

On the other hand, a, shall we say, morally lax attorney I knew described himself as "facing temptation one hundred times and only giving in ninety-nine." That seemed to be an honest assessment, and it described how "Bif" was perceived by the legal community. The pattern of behavior we experienced disclosed a person driven almost entirely by selfish motives whose "principles/values" were generally self serving. Bif was big on Loyalty; to him.

Bif was fat, wore a toupee, smoked cigars, liked to gamble and whore around, over-charged clients, and was quite successful in the legal business. He was also a cracker-jack gunslinger of a litigator. Bif's character was revealed through behavior and interactions which consistently leaned far into the selfishness spectrum. In a legal fight you'd rather have him on your side than oppose you, as long as your interests aligned with Bif's. He was a tough litigator because Winning was a dearly held value. He was also a lot of fun to go out on the town with. (Another guiding principle was Pleasure.) But you wouldn't want to find yourself in a position of depending on Bif to sacrifice his material self-interest to help you out. At least that is the tip of Bif's ice berg that I saw.

In the ordinary course of life, we might not be especially challenged to conduct ourselves consistent with the golden mean we'd like to achieve in caring for self and others. If we live very quotidian lives, establishing the ethical reputation we'd like to have might not be too difficult. The challenge ratchets up when circumstances give rise to conflicts among our principles/values and/or conflicts with the values of others with whom we are in relationship.

~ ~ ~

I'm in a bicycle riding group. Everyone in the group, except me, wears a helmet when we ride. Safety experts and serious riders seem to be in unanimous agreement that bicyclists should wear helmets to reduce the risk of head injuries. I've been riding a bike since I was four years old and I've never fallen and hit my head. I've tried wearing a helmet and find it uncomfortable. I almost never wear a hat; just don't like the feel of it on my head. I rode motorcycles for many years and usually went without a helmet (we don't have a helmet law in Indiana). I value feeling the wind in my hair and, for me, that aesthetically pleasing feeling of freedom trumps the value of an extra layer of self-protection. Paying really close attention is how I express my value in safe riding.

The way I worked out this conflict in my own values is unacceptable to some folks that value safety over aesthetics. I felt forced to resign from the Safety Committee of the Indiana Wilderness Club, because I was the only committee member that opposed rules requiring members to wear helmets on all bike rides and to wear (rather than just having in the boat) a PDF at all times on flat water (as distinguished from white water) canoe and kayaking excursions. The tradition of the club was to recommend wearing a helmet on bike rides and a life preserver on flat-water paddles, but each member was free to make her own decision. A new regime wanted and got a mandatory rule.

I respect folks who value a higher level of protection than me, and I understand their concerns. But respect for difference in value priorities was not returned by the new leadership in the Wilderness Club. Several members left the Club because they, like me, felt that our values were not respected and, in a sense, we were unacceptable to the Club. It was okay with us that other Club members had values different than ours. But the new regime decided that we would no longer be allowed to express our values in the way we chose to. The rule change told us that our values were rejected and we had to become other than who we are to remain within the community of the Club.

Reasonable people can disagree about the priority of positive values. Actuaries might suggest that issues of safety are simply a matter of risk assessment. What is the most likely scenario and what are the costs if less likely scenarios occur. But even that analysis will lead different people to different conclusions. Some will decide that, although unlikely, the terrible consequences of a head injury are clearly worth the minor inconvenience of wearing a helmet. Others will conclude that, since an accident is so statistically unlikely, I don't want the hassle of a helmet. We might have the same risk analysis results, but we might still make different choices because we weigh the value of pleasure vs. safety differently.

Negotiating ways to maintain relationships and live within a community in which there are disagreements over which principles/values should take precedence is one of the ways a culture develops and changes. The culture of the Indiana Wilderness Club became less adventure oriented and more safety conscious with the change of leadership. And that's just fine so long as that is the direction the community wants to go. There are many other outlets and clubs to join for more adventuresome souls.

It's always interesting (and often frustrating) to try to work out problems that arise from conflicting values. Tolerance of difference is a touchstone value I'd recommend when a conflict in values arises within a group. Yes, we love it when we're so convincing that everyone in the group agrees with us. But don't we learn more, and isn't it cool, when members of a diverse community with different points of view find ways to get along?

I grew up a White-Anglo-Saxon-Protestant (WASP) in an all white culturally-homogenous town and had little exposure to people of different races, ethnicities, or faiths. My first college roommates were two Mennonites in London, then an African-American kid from inner-city Indianapolis, then a

Jew from New Jersey, and I married my last roommate, an ethnic Catholic. Learning to live with students from very different backgrounds than my own created some delightful challenges.

My black roommate, Nate, eventually told me that for the first two weeks of rooming together he always made sure I was asleep before he'd let himself fall asleep. He'd heard Goshen, my hometown, was racist and since I had a World War I bayonet and a George Wallace bumper sticker on my desk, he feared I might leap out of bed and stab him in the dark.

The bayonet was a paper weight, and the sticker of the racist Alabama Governor was one of many I had in a collection, which included Shirley Chisolm, the first and only black-female-candidate for US President in either of the two major parties. Without giving it any thought, I'd put Wallace on top of the stack of bumper stickers.

Learning to become sensitive to the different perspectives these other college students brought to our relationship as roommates was a growth experience for which I am very grateful.

When intolerance of difference triumphs, communities break apart. The remaining community and the new ones that form are likely to be more cohesive. That's because the now smaller communities only include members that tend to agree with each other. But they will be less interesting and less representative of the wider community.

My current biking group agreed not to enforce any rules on helmets. They decided even if I'm weird and more feckless of my own safety than the rest of the group, they value me enough to let me do my own idiosyncratic thing.

~ ~ ~

It sounds like the theme of a high school football coach's pep talk, but resolving conflicts are growth opportunities. Skip Kappes, one of my mentors in the law, liked to quote the Chinese proverb, "The strongest steel is forged in the hottest fire." Skip is one of the rare senior statesmen in the law that has held onto his personal ethics and honor for over sixty years in the legal trenches. He always took it as a good sign if you were troubled by an ethical question. It means you have a conscience and want to do the right thing.

Sometimes ethical conflicts come as major forks in the road, while others are more like gentle curves to negotiate. I'm now mixing metaphors, but those major forks are the really hot fires through which the steel of your ethical character is forged. Over time, however, the many little ethical questions faced in daily life determine the shape, we might say, of who you are within your family and communities.

As a person who has deeply considered who you want to be and have found your golden mean of balancing your intentions of selfish/selfless, you are able to make most ethical judgments with little trouble. You know the positive values/principles which you use to guide your decision making. So, let's suppose at your class reunion you encounter a challenge which is an increasingly common experience of the middle-aged.

There she is, the Mean Girl, Sherry, who always put you down with her quick wit and sharp tongue. But, my god, Sherry's gained thirty pounds in the last ten years! Here's your chance to get even for the humiliation at her hands you suffered as a callow teenager. You'd just be exercising your value in being truthful to point out Sherry's newly developed rotundity. But, you know the snarky remark you're tempted to make would probably hurt Sherry's feelings. Deep down she's probably quite sensitive; which is why she was The Mean Girl; or, maybe she's just a natural-born bitch. Whichever, it would be unkind to mention her protuberant tummy. You resolve the dilemma by considering which action/inaction expresses your intention to live life as the person you want to be.

Truthfulness is one of your principles. And, it would satisfy an impulsively selfish desire to finally get over on Sherry-The-Mean-Girl. But, you have chosen not to live by the negative value of vengeance. You know acting vengefully hurts the victim, it damages the communal network you share, and you are likely to feel bad later. Sherry presumably knows that she's gained weight since your last class reunion, so to report your observation to her would probably not be generously sharing useful information. (Generosity is also one of your values/principles, but it doesn't seem to apply in this case.)

Now that you are Mr. (or Ms.) Successful, you knew Sherry wanted to dance with you. As she was walking toward you and the music swelled to Tommy James and the Shondells track of "Crystal Blue Persuasion", your mind did a quick calculation. Because you know yourself it only takes a millisecond to resolve the moral conundrum of whether to point out to Sherry that your arms cannot reach all the way round her in a slow dance. Taking this opportunity to satisfy a selfish desire to finally put down Sherry would not contribute to yours or Sherry's well being; it would be giving in to the negative value of hurting Sherry out of a selfish and impulsive desire to bring down She Who Was Most High, but it would be unkind. You are a person that leans toward being unselfish, so you treat even mean people (who might, as the bumper sticker says, suck) with kindness. Conflict resolved.

(No, I didn't just get even with the mean girl in my high school class by a veiled reference to her excessive lateral growth in recent years. None of the girls in my class were mean and all the women are beautiful in my hometown of Goshen, Indiana. So there!)

~ ~ ~

There are many more serious conflicts we'll face at different stages of life. Sex, booze, and drugs are the sources of lots of ethical conflicts for young people. Authority figures are likely to harp on the sinful nature of these three temptations for misbehavior. For sure, sexual abuse, violent drunkenness, and drug addiction are expressions of negative values. They are harmful to the self and others. If only the choices were so starkly simple.

What if you are young and in love, is protected sex really just wrong? Can't sex be an expression of loving affection at age sixteen, seventeen, or eighteen, just as it can be abusive and humiliating at twenty one, thirty one, or forty one? A few generations ago most everyone was married by sixteen or seventeen.

Why is moderate use of alcohol not allowed for minors? Adults can drink, and in some cultures kids grow up drinking wine or beer at meals. An eighteen-year old can vote, join the military or be drafted, but cannot legally order a mug of beer or glass of wine in most states. That just doesn't seem right, does it? The law is the law, but we're considering a deeper truth; how to make ethical choices?

Many teenagers will choose to experiment with sex, booze, and drugs. If they do so in ways which are harmful to themselves or others, then it is wrong. If they are exercising values like Curiosity, Affection, Pleasure (which is not harmful), they may very well be doing so in a balanced approach to life for their stage of development. Those who self-righteously condemn all such behavior maybe ought to take a look in the mirror and ask themselves exactly what principle is being expressed in that condemnation. And, did you really never experiment with sex, alcohol, or recreational drugs? I did.

There is need for a "however" here. If, however, the conduct is illegal, then, even if the motives align with the intended effects, consideration need be given to the possible consequence of getting busted. Is satisfying curiosity, or enjoying the taste of a brewskie in the company of friends, worth the risk of a misdemeanor arrest and possible conviction? Many of us have answered, yes, it is worth the risk, because Curiosity, Fun, Companionship, and perhaps rebelliousness have more value than living a life guided by fear and dutiful obedience to a law we do not agree with.

The real test occurs when you get caught by the law or you fall off your bike and whack your head. Living a valuable life does not guaranty the results you want. You have to realize that you might get busted, have a bad trip and end up in the hospital, or fall and bash your head open. Are those risks worth satisfying your curiosity or experiencing the temporary pleasure of getting high or sexed up? (Children of my own loins, if you are reading this book, ignore that. No sex before marriage! Just kidding; sort of.)

If the risks were assessed, the decision made to act, but it didn't work out so well, because you got hurt. Well, get up, dust yourself off, and continue to guide your life by the principles you value. If a criminal conviction ruins your plans to join the US Army, you better be willing to chart another course. If you get pregnant or your girlfriend is pregnant, now you have a whole new set of ethical questions. And, whichever way you answer the question of what to do about an unplanned pregnancy; it's going to change your life. If you can't get up, because the choice you made left you too damaged, then you best be satisfied that you have lived the life you chose yourself.

Life without any risk is not worth living. Living recklessly leaves a wake of damage and will eventually catch up to you. The good and valuable life is a matter of finding the right balance, including tolerance of risk, for you.

Those of us who value adventure, and receive cuts, bruises, slings and arrows, and maybe an untimely death might find a kindred spirit in one who was known for living an almost hermetic life. Emily Dickinson wrote: "Because I could not stop for Death -- He kindly stopped for me." He will eventually for each of us, so we best live as valuably as we can until He comes.

~ ~ ~

Shakespeare's tragedies are rife with conflict. Characters struggle with conflicting values internally and externally with other characters. Hamlet's most famous line, "To be or not to be...?" may be the most fundamental of all human conflicts. He is wracked with the indecision of youth or arrested development. (It's surprising to learn from the gravedigger that Hamlet is thirty years old. He seems much younger.) His questions are: Who am I? Should I devote myself to selfish pleasure? Must I give in to the demand of my father's ghost that I avenge his death? Shouldn't I marry Ophelia, become a responsible adult, and prepare to be king in my turn? Who am I?

Hamlet the play is described by some critics to be about a man who can't make up his mind. When he does act death and destruction follow. He impulsively and accidentally kills Polonius. He deserts Ophelia, which, combined with the reckless homicide of her father, leads to her suicide. Yes, he finally kills Claudius, but it's such a cluster fuck that it takes out his mom, his friend Laertes, and Hamlet himself.

What does Hamlet value? Is he trying to be selfish or unselfish? What does he conclude when he asks whether life is worth living? Hamlet is a man who does not know himself and can't make up his mind about the most fundamental existential question. He is conflicted. And so, he ends up with a room full of dead people, himself included.

In another Shakespearean tragedy we meet a character who knows himself well, Hubert in *King John*. Hubert is the King's man. He is loyal through thick and thin. He leans far in the direction of unselfishness. He would do anything, even sacrifice his own life, for King John. When John orders him to blind and kill the King's nephew, Arthur, who represents a threat to John's rule, of course Hubert will do so.

But there's a problem. Hubert has been put in charge of Arthur as jailer and caretaker. And he's come to feel a

paternal affection for the lad. Nevertheless, Hubert heats
irons to put out the boy's eyes and makes preparations to
execute him. Arthur, not surprisingly, protests and reminds
Hubert of their care and concern for each other. Arthur
refuses to accept that Hubert could do such a thing. Hubert
insists that he must. But Arthur knows Hubert better than
Hubert knows himself.

Hubert eventually gives in to Arthur's pleas for mercy.
He loses his balance and is momentarily lost. If he is not
wholly loyal to the King, who is he? He realizes through his
love for Arthur and his unwillingness to do such a foul deed
for John that he values Compassion. Hubert re-evaluates who
he wants to be. He is still a person who leans far toward
unselfishness. By not carrying out the King's orders he puts
his own neck in the noose, if his betrayal of the King is found
out. Hubert decides that his own life is worth risking to save
Arthur's; he will be guided by Compassion.

Hubert did know himself. He had not lived an
unexamined life. He had faithfully guided his life according
to the positive value of Loyalty to the King. But under the
circumstances of being ordered to torture and execute the lad
he'd come to care about, Hubert came to understand that to be
loyal would violate another value, Compassion. By loving
Arthur as himself, Hubert regained his balance as an unselfish
man. He added another layer of understanding to who he is.
And he nimbly changed course. He frees Arthur and reports
to King John (falsely) that the threat to John's rule has been
removed.

If only the play ended with Hubert faking Arthur's
death and the boy escaping John's grasp. But this is
Shakespeare, and so, like life, it is never so simple. Again,
living a valuable life does not guaranty success on any level
except being true to thine own self. Arthur dies a sudden and
unexpected death when he leaps off a high wall making his
escape. What happens to Hubert? We don't know.

I hate to end the chapter on such a downer. Shakespeare didn't give his audiences frothy easy answers and happy endings. He knew that some lives are tragic. He also knew that living a worthy life requires a willingness to lose your life being true to your most fundamental values.

We don't know what becomes of Hubert; we do know that, despite his death, Arthur was free at last. A monk poisons John and the King dies in pain realizing that all his scheming has left him a morally and physically shriveled man. He had leaned entirely toward self-interest. John retained the crown but had neither honor nor love.

Maybe Hubert went back to his wife, had a bunch of kids of his own and died many years later a wise and happy old man.

There! A happy ending; but now we turn the page to consider our responsibilities to the community and its responsibilities to us.

Chapter 20: Community Health Takes a Village

Sixteen year-old Ethan Couch was sentenced to ten years probation after being convicted in a Texas court of killing four people and seriously injuring two others while driving drunk. On June 15, 2013, Couch plowed his father's pickup truck into a group of pedestrians gathered around a car which had stalled. He was driving seventy miles per hour in a forty zone with blood alcohol three times the legal limit. The court bought his attorney's argument that Ethan suffered from the affliction of "affluenza". Ethan's parents had failed to teach him to live responsibly. So, instead of prison the teenager was ordered into therapy and placed on probation. Couch's father is the owner of a sheet metal company which reportedly has annual revenue of fifteen million dollars.

Ethan Couch's was the first case of a court finding that material affluence combined with parental incompetence warranted rehabilitation rather than a standard term of imprisonment. Neither Ethan nor his family made a public expression of regret at the trial. Outrage at the light sentence and the Couchs' apparent lack of concern for the victims buzzed throughout the media and blogosphere.

The extraordinary irresponsibility of the teen and his unwillingness to accept responsibility for killing four people is infuriating. So is the arrogant in-your-face double standard of the Texas judiciary. There is no way that a black kid in the inner city, or, for that matter, a white working-class kid, would have gotten off with probation and rehabilitative therapy had they committed quadruple reckless-homicide. But, at least the fury over the case did put a spotlight on the necessity of parents teaching their kids positive values.

Questions about community values should also be raised by the case. What responsibilities do communities have to their young people? What does it mean to be a responsible member of the community, state, and nation?

We noted in Chapter 18 that much attention has been paid by social scientists to the pathologies of inner-city "ghettos". We also need to recognize and admit that affluent neighborhoods of middle and upper class families in the US suffer from their own pathologies.

~ ~ ~

In the 1950s houses in the US tended to have large front porches. Folks congregated on front porches. The design of houses with large front porches signified that neighbors were welcome to come up and join in conversation and social interaction. More current home design has turned houses around. The porch is a deck in the back of the house. The edifice revealed to the street and the neighborhood might be grandly attractive for "curb appeal", but it offers no welcome for convivial social interaction.

We have privatized social interaction, so that only specific invitees are welcome to enter our homes. We live within gated communities, behind security fences and warning signs of "Protected by ...", and with multiple locks on our doors. Strangers are not welcome. We peer suspiciously through peep holes in doors reinforced with steel at those who dare to come to our homes uninvited.

"It takes a village" was a phrase popularized by then First Lady Hillary Clinton's book with that title published in 1996. Her thesis was that the whole community is responsible to make sure our kids are brought up right and given the opportunity to thrive -- like they were in Hillary's hometown, Park Ridge, Illinois. So how does the village participate in the upbringing of kids securely locked up in houses within gated communities?

When Bob Dole accepted the Republican nomination to run against President Clinton in the 1996 presidential election he threw this barb at his opponent's wife: "... with all due respect, I am here to tell you, it does not take a village to raise a child. It takes a family to raise a child." He was singing the family values tune. It didn't work. Many of the families Bob

Dole pitched his campaign at were working parents who out-source a big chunk of their child care. Dole's outdated "Father Knows Best" model of middle-American family life didn't connect with parents whose children are in pre-school, daycare, school, after-school care, and extracurricular activities.

But the Dole vs. Clinton campaign did highlight contemporary ambivalence about child rearing and teaching our children morals and ethics. Public schools are constitutionally prohibited from promoting religion, but are often pressured to do so by students and parents. Then, the school corporation gets sued by anti-religionists. Yet, there's hell to pay from religious parents that accuse the public schools of teaching humanistic-secular morality. So, who's in charge of the moral upbringing of our kids, if we've outsourced it to organizations whose hands are tied and get attacked from the right and left?

When Mrs. Clinton and her cohort of Baby Boomers were growing up, children ran free in their neighborhoods to catch turtles and frogs in the local creek. Now, when we're with our kids we buzz around them like police helicopters to make sure no harm befalls our precious investments. When we're not around we put children into so many adult-supervised activities that kids now spend more time under the control of other adults than any previous generation in modern history.

God forbid they be allowed to run in neighborhood packs with the freedom to create their own fun and games. They might get dirty! We are so fearful of infection by some foreign substance we don't just require our children to wash their hands before every meal, parents and supervisors require children to wash with antibiotic soap whenever they touch anything that might be unclean. We've become as fetishistic about cleanliness as orthodox Brahmins and Levite priests.

The Centers for Disease Control (CDC) estimates that of the 235 million doses of antibiotics given each year between twenty and fifty percent are unnecessary. The overuse of antibiotics is beginning to have worrisome consequences for the health of our children. The weakest bacteria strains are killed when washing hands with antibacterial soap. The strongest survive. Antibiotics are becoming increasingly ineffective, because bacterial strains have evolved which are immune to all antibiotics on the market. Pharmaceutical companies are falling behind in the race to develop new antibiotics which kill the new strains of infectious bacteria. Yet parents still rush their child to the doctor if she has the sniffles, because we've been herded into believing that's the right thing to do.

Our neurotic devotion to cleanliness and excessive prescriptions of antibiotics are endangering our health and the health of the next generation. "Antibiotic resistance can cause serious disease and is an important public health problem. It can be prevented by minimizing unnecessary prescribing and overprescribing of antibiotics, the correct use of prescribed antibiotics, and good hygiene and infection control. ... Some bacteria have developed resistance to antibiotics that were once commonly used to treat them. For example, Staphylococcus aureus ('golden staph' or MRSA) and Neisseria gonorrhoeae (the cause of gonorrhea) are now almost always resistant to benzyl penicillin. In the past, these infections were usually controlled by penicillin. The most serious concern with antibiotic resistance is that some bacteria have become resistant to almost all of the easily available antibiotics. These bacteria are able to cause serious disease and this is a major public health problem." (The Better Health Channel, "Antibiotic Resistant Bacteria", approved by Australia State Government Victoria Department of Health, Feb 2015)

Exposure to bacteria up to a point is good for your health, because it strengthens your immune system. Living in a sterile environment makes people more prone to infections when they do have contact with germs. There has been a dramatic increase in the rate of allergies over the last twenty years. CDC researchers have found a link between allergies and the use of antibacterial soaps. These soaps inhibit the strengthening of the immune system, so we are less able to fight off allergies and infections. Germ phobia is driving us over the cliff like lemmings.

Research by child psychologists reveals that children spending twenty hours or more per week in extracurricular activities or participating in five or more adult-supervised activities has an adverse effect on their development. The temptation to over-schedule our children is greater than ever. There is an incredibly attractive buffet of activities for urban/suburban kids. Parents feel guilty if they don't give their children the positive experience of sports, scouting, church group, summer camp, arts and crafts, dance, etc. (The kids would probably just prefer to play their video games.)

My wife and I fell prey to this temptation in raising our boys. When they were about eight and ten we sort of slapped ourselves on the proverbial forehead realizing that the boys had scheduled activities almost everyday with multiple sports teams, Tae Kwon Do, Scouts, church group, and music lessons in addition to school and homework. We had prided ourselves on being wise parents that made sure our kids had free time with their friends and down time to chill. We had become hypocrites. We unconsciously kept signing our kids up for "just one more enriching activity", until the boys were as busy as Fortune 500 CEOs. (They needed scheduling secretaries and drivers for god's sake!) When asked, the boys each cheerfully gave up activities to an agreed limit of no more than two extracurriculars.

We are raising children who are more technologically proficient than all previous generations, but how much time are they given to develop their creative talents and their moral character? Indications are that Millennials and Post-Millennials are rather unrebellious kids. They are being trained into compliance with all their supervised activities. One of the happiest summers our boys had was when a bunch of kids in the neighborhood formed their own sandlot football league, created their own schedule, and kept their own stat book. They did it on their own, it was fun, and they were proud of it. We need to let the kids outside to get dirty playing with friends in games they create on their own. They really will be happier and healthier.

~ ~ ~

According to FBI and U.S. Department of Justice reports, the rate of violent crime in the U.S. is at the lowest level in forty years. So why are American parents now more protective of their children than any previous generation in the history of the world? It must be the pathological fixation our news media has for reporting violence. We are inundated with stories of death, destruction, and decay; and then on the back page or last five minutes of nightly news there's a cute little piece about an uplifting human interest story. Parents are terrified of child abduction and molestation, even though we now have much better law enforcement systems in place, like Amber Alerts and sex offender registries. The rate of crimes against children peaked in the 1990s and has been declining since then.

We have become so protective of our children we slather them in sun screen before letting them out to play in the backyard on a summer day. Our fear of skin cancer and the desire to protect ourselves and our children from it has stampeded us to a place where many in the US population are now suffering from Vitamin D deficiency. Responsible healthcare professionals will tell you that the "sunshine vitamin" helps to protect us from osteoporosis, heart disease, and cancers of the breast, prostate, and colon. Exposure to sunlight also correlates to reductions in depression and insomnia and a stronger immune system. The *International*

Journal of Epidemiology has published articles concluding that far more lives are lost to diseases caused by a lack of sunlight than to those caused by too much. Would God have created, or natural selection evolved, a creature which hunted, farmed, and gathered its nourishment under the Sun, but could not bear being in the sunlight? Nonsense!

It's a matter of balance. We need the Vitamin D we receive from exposure to sunlight, just not too much. That's why we get sun burns. Our own skin tells us when we've received too much. We are designed, or evolved, to live in the natural world and our own systems will usually tell us when we are out of balance. Value good health and pay attention to what your body is telling you. Running to the doctor whenever a fart gets stuck in cross-wise, and swallowing unnatural foreign substances (drugs) to try to avoid the slightest pains and discomforts, is not the way to vigorous health for us or our kids. It might very well be the fast track to pain pill addiction (Exhibit A: look what happened to Michael Jackson).

~ ~ ~

Professionals like doctors, lawyers, tax accountants, and financial planners benefit by creating dependence on their services. By giving in to the temptation to let others take care of us in exchange for our hard-earned savings we are letting go of the American cultural value of independence and self-sufficiency. Letting others care for us when it's really unnecessary devalues the self, is a waste of money, and has social costs.

Excessive pill popping facilitated by the medical profession has rendered many antibiotics ineffective and left many people addicted to pain meds. Lawyers scare clients into paying for complicated estate plans. Middle class folks, and most anyone with an estate under the IRS exemption amount ($5,340,000 in 2014), are served perfectly well by owning everything jointly with their spouse and a simple

Will. Why use a tax accountant unless you are wealthy and have multiple complicated investments? For god's sake, Turbo Tax does the heavy-lifting math in completing an income tax return. There is strong evidence that financial planners and investment brokers cost far more than they are worth. Most of us are better off putting our savings into no-load index funds or broad-based stock and bond funds than paying fees on loaded or actively managed funds. (There is plenty of research indicating "the market is smarter than any individual trader." Check out Vanguard Research's April 2014 white paper, "The Case for Index Fund Investing".) Save every spare dollar, put it into a relatively low risk diversified fund, arrange to have all dividends and interest reinvested, then sit back and watch it grow. That's the best estate plan for most of us.

Yup, there's a sucker born every minute, and it's us for paying people to do for us what we are capable of doing ourselves. If you can stay out of entanglements with the medical and legal systems, you are probably living a pretty good life. When you get sucked into a relationship which depletes your life savings rather than increases it, whether it's with a Nigerian Internet scammer or a professional parasite, you will lose more than money. You lose self respect and control over your life.

Sure, some people have chronic conditions that require regular medical interventions. And yes, lawyers are necessary to help us navigate through legal issues and processes. Of course, tax and financial advice is needed in some cases and for people with large or complicated estates. The admonition to try to stay away from doctors and other professionals doesn't apply to folks whose well being really does depend on a particular medical regimen or other necessary professional assistance. I'm well acquainted with the wonders of modern science-based medicine, the skills and devotion to patient care of most health professionals, and the amazing technologies utilized by hospitals.

My beloved daughter-in-law is alive today with fully functioning kidneys. She spent the better part of her sophomore year in high school as an in-patient at Riley Children's Hospital in Indianapolis. She was in a coma and close to death with internal bleeding and kidney failure. Her family, which included her boyfriend (my son), were informed that they needed to prepare for the worst, but there was one last medication and procedure to try to save her life. It worked, and my son spent much of his junior year in high school sitting by her bedside holding her hand. They were married nine years later the week before he left for Basic Training at Fort Benning.

For those of us lucky enough only to be plagued with ordinary infections and injuries, a condition we really need to guard against is sitting on our butts too much. Our modern sedentary life is very comfy, but too much comfort is associated with all sorts of health issues, including obesity, metabolic syndrome, cardiovascular disease, and diabetes. An article in the *American Journal of Preventive Medicine*, "Sedentary Behavior and Mortality in Older Women," concludes that women's lives are shortened by spending too much time sitting on their asses. I'm sure the same applies to men, but the study only included women as subjects. The *Journal of the National Cancer Institute* has published articles linking sitting too much to colon and endometrial (uterine) cancer.

We need to remember the mantra of "moderation in all things". A sedentary lifestyle with physical comfort the major pursuit is unbalanced. Excessively valuing higher and higher levels of physical comfort has created a culture of obese couch potatoes. (See the movie *Wall-E*? It's a very cute animated dystopia. Humans have become beached whales barely able to move and totally dependent on machines.) Our bodies evolved, or were designed if you will, to live in nomadic bands in the African savannah. Spending most of the day on our posterior is unnatural for the homo sapien musculoskeletal structure. Since we're not going to return to being nomadic rovers (I hope not!), we need to value eating a balanced diet and exercising regularly. If we do that, we're probably living as close as possible in the modern world to the way our bodies were designed to function.

~ ~ ~

We affluent folks living in the comfort culture must guard against becoming weak and fearful. We are scared into believing an inaccurate description of our world. We are deluded in thinking that we cannot let our children out of our sight. Loving parents care for their children and they try to create a safe and secure home for them. Caring about the health of our children includes the recognition that kids need free time outdoors. Our neighborhoods are safer now than when this generation of parents were children. Let the kids out to run with their friends, get a natural sun tan, and develop their innate creativity and social skills through unsupervised associations with other kids.

Perhaps most important of all that we do for our children is not to have them until we are ready, and optimally, with two parents to partner and share in child rearing. In May 2014 the Centers for Disease Control and Prevention's National Center for Health Statistics issued a study which indicates children in families with two biological parents have the best chance (statistically) of avoiding a whole raft of harmful social, psychological, and health problems. The survey was based on data from almost 100,000 US households with children. It determined that there is an inverse relationship between biological parents in the household and "adverse family experiences". It should be noted that children with stepparents and adoptive parents were excluded from the study, and its comparisons were for children with two biological parents in the home vs. single biological parenting vs. no biological parents with descending outcomes in that order. Kids in foster care were exposed to the most detrimental experiences.

Again, statistics don't determine outcomes for individuals. No matter their circumstances some kids will overcome adversity and grow up to be extraordinary human beings. Whether there are two, one or no biological parents in the home, a child that is properly cared for has a good chance to thrive. Even without that, a strong will and commitment to live responsibly can overcome most any obstacle.

A friend of mine never knew who his father was, and his mother wasn't much of a mother. He grew up poor in very rough circumstances. He got into a lot of fights at school and usually lost. He was small, skinny, and probably undernourished. After high school he joined the US Navy, then went to college on the GI bill. He became such a popular figure on campus he was elected president of the student body. He went to Harvard Law School and became a very successful lawyer in a big city as well as a husband, and father.

Having known "Pete" since we were kids, what always set him off from more privileged peers was his extraordinary determination and willingness to pick himself up after a set back and press on. Pete gives much credit to a high school teacher and mentors in the Navy. These men accepted and encouraged him. But I think he would have created a valuable life even without their support. Even though he was bullied and victimized by other kids, he was empathetic and returned kindness to those who were kind to him. Few of his hometown school mates would have predicted it, but Pete committed himself to a course of responsibility and achieved the "American dream".

For those of us who are parents, caregivers, and/or mentors, what is most needed from us is to provide secure but encouraging environments in which children experience well-balanced adult models. A secure and loving home base is what we want for all kids in our communities. With that spring board, chances are our children will grow up healthy and strong to become responsible members of the community when it is their time. Adults filling the roles of teacher, minister, athletic coach, choir, orchestra and band leader may not be able to give their charges that base, but they can certainly offer the hand of support.

Fear mongering of politicians and the news media has led Americans to distrust those we do not know and to consider the natural world germ-ridden and dangerous. This is living life motivated by the negativity of fear, shame, and guilt, rather than the positivity of embracing the natural world as a place of life-giving wonder and our fellow human beings as those with whom we share our common humanity. For ourselves and future generations, let's embrace life and live robustly by taking good care of ourselves and setting positive examples for others.

As parents, guardians, and mentors we might not be perfect. But we can be pretty damn good for the kids and future of our communities. If not us, who?

Chapter 21: The Valuable Life

At the opening dedication of the National September 11 Memorial Museum, President Obama reminded us of the "man in the red bandana". Welles Crowther was twenty-four years old and was working on the South Tower's 104th floor on September 11, 2001. Media coverage of the events captured the image of a man who "emerged from the smoke, and over his nose and his mouth, he wore a red handkerchief." The President explained that Welles Crowther always carried a red handkerchief. It was his thing. "He called for fire extinguishers to fight back the flames. He attended to the wounded. He led those survivors down the stairs to safety, and carried a woman on his shoulders down 17 flights. Then, he went back, back up all those flights, then back down again, bringing more wounded to safety, until that moment when the tower fell. ... And today ... one of his red handkerchiefs is on display in this museum. And from this day forward, all those who come here will have a chance to know the sacrifice of a young man who, like so many, gave his life so others might live."

Heroes and extraordinary personalities inspire us by demonstrating what human beings can be at their very best. Most of us will never be tested the way Welles Crowther was; or, like the brave members of the New York Fire Department were who ran into the burning building. I think I'd much prefer to run away from bullets or fire than run toward them.

We are also unlikely to qualify to join the pantheon of the great religious and secular saints. Historic personalities like Gandhi and King have come to personify positive values and the Love Ethic *in extremis*. While we ordinary mortals are not going to make it into the history books, we do have roles to play. Heroes and historical figures serve as silent directors in the theater of life. They point us in the right direction.

But in terms of concrete impacts on our lives we are

more influenced by those who played roles in our lives as we grew to maturity, parents, siblings, friends, co-workers, teachers, pastors, etc. We learn from the people we're connected with as we see how they cope with struggles and challenges. We are personally affected by the way our family and friends handle personal issues, big ones and trivial ones. We gain a deeper appreciation of loyal commitment when our spouse forgives and continues to love us despite our screw ups. We are hurt and repelled when an older sister beats us and takes the dollar grandma gave us for Easter. All of our experiences with other people are opportunities to learn who we want to be like and who we don't want to be like. We give back to our family and friends as they experience us and learn who they want to be by modeling or rejecting our examples to them. The web of interconnected experience and relationships grows as our contributions are added.

We don't like malingerers, because they are lazy and selfish. They tear down without building up. They take but they do not give. Another type that repels is a person who is so tight fisted with his money and jealous of his time that generosity never comes to mind when we think of him. We like being around people who are friendly, open, interested in us, and interesting to be with.

Those who care only for themselves, like Ebenezer Scrooge, never experience the joy of mutual love, care, and respect that comes from sharing with others. Being generous with your wealth, time, and talents is how we connect with others to create meaningful relationships. Friends care for each other. That is the essence of friendship. In Charles Dickens's *Christmas Carol* what was Scrooge's life like, when his relationship with Bob Cratchit was just that of employer and his relationship with Fred was just that of uncle? There was no meat or meaning to the relationships. They were merely functional; Bob and Fred were used by Scrooge but they could have been robots rather than fellow human beings.

In giving our care and concern we add meat to the bone

of our roles as spouses, parents, friends, and participants in communities. And the world is a better place because of us. The quality of our communities is determined by the richness of intertwining relationships. In relationships as casual as clerk to customer, community is enhanced with a warm smile and a thank you. It is diminished by unsmiling coldness.

~ ~ ~

Living a life in a balanced equilibrium of caring for your self and for others will be expressed by choosing to guide your life by values which most cultures and societies have recognized as traditional virtues. The tried and trusted values have been tested generation after generation and have proved to be competent guides. It's our job to apply them correctly to our own unique situations. If we do that tilting toward caring for others as we take good care of ourselves, we are living the Love Ethic, loving our neighbors as we love ourselves.

Sorry if it's become repetitive, but the take away from Part II of the book may be summed up as: We find our golden mean of valuing self and others by expressing the positive values we have consciously chosen by the way we act in specific situations, and over time in relationships, which enhances our own well being and that of our family and communities. Living according to negative values causes disequilibrium for our selves and our communities. Setting a positive example shows others who are searching for the right path a way forward which builds up rather than tears down.

Your parents, teachers, guidance counselors, Scout masters, athletic coaches, rabbis, imams, Zen masters, gurus, or pastors probably tried to give you moral instruction both positively and negatively; do this, don't do that. Negative moral instructions create walls. Negative moral instruction is not encouraging negative values. If issued sensitively, they set appropriate boundaries, telling us how to avoid hurting ourselves and others. But they do limit us. Care must be taken not to use negative moral instructions to promote living in fear.

Children need to learn limits; don't touch that fire! Don't pull your pants down in public. Physical, social, and psychological safety require that we learn these sorts of limits. But a child shielded from danger and not encouraged to experiment and experience the world will probably grow into a very limited person. That's not who we want our children to grow up to be. We hope our children will grow into their best selves, responsible grownups who love and live with zest.

~ ~ ~

There really is a qualitative difference between living life by trying to follow rules that require absolute obedience and approaching ethical issues with flexibility and nimbleness in choosing which positive values should guide your actions. Victor Hugo painfully and exquisitely illustrates in his titanic *Les Miserables* the terrible injustice that may result from strict application of negative commands. While most of us agree that most of the time it is wrong to steal, most of us also agree that, if there was no alternative to starvation, we would steal bread to feed our family.

You can't read *Les Miserables* (or see the movie, play, or opera) without feeling the injustice of what happened to Jean Valjean after he broke the window pane of a bakery and stole a loaf of bread to feed his starving sister and her seven children. It's true that Jean violated the religious commandment of "thou shall not steal" as well as the criminal code. Instead of obeying the law, Jean acted out of love and compassion for his sister's children. What followed was nineteen years in prison. His initial sentence of five years was multiplied because of failed escape attempts. All for a loaf of bread! But, his punishment was deserved under the laws of the State and Church.

The judge could have responded by being guided by the positive value of Mercy. If the baker whose bread was taken was guided by the positive value of Generosity or

Compassion, he would have refused to prosecute. The baker, the prosecutor, and judge were justified by religious commandments and the legal code. But our minds and emotions tell us they acted unjustly and Jean Valjean acted correctly.

"Sirdar" is the Nepali term for chief guide on a Himalayan trek or mountaineering expedition. The sirdar knows the terrain and local culture from years of experience of traveling through the territory. Still, new and unexpected situations will occur on every expedition. So the sirdar will draw on past experience to try to make the best decisions possible under each unique set of circumstances. There is no guaranty that the sirdar's decisions will bring about the desired results. But expedition members trust the sirdar's wisdom because they know his experience is superior to their own. The sirdar's decisions usually turn out well for the members of the team as the expedition progresses.

The same is generally true for tried and tested values. They have lasted because using them as life guides has usually, though not always, brought about desirable results. Had the judicial system followed the values of Mercy and Compassion in the Valjean case, instead of the strict application of rules, much misery would have been avoided. The people in charge of the legal system operated it inflexibly and without any care or concern for Jean and his family. If the authorities had any wisdom, it didn't show. The scales of justice were not balanced, because mercy was not weighed against the State's need of order and the baker's desire for revenge.

Using positive values to guide you as you find your way through life is like clicking on a headlamp when night falls as you hike down a darkened trail. They light the way. Not that we will necessarily be able to see every possible outcome of the choices we make. We cannot see every detail no matter how bright our headlamp. Neither can we see into the future. We can only rely on the wisdom of the past along with our own judgment.

Perhaps Jean would have turned into a kleptomaniac if the law hadn't come down so hard on him. We can't know. We do know that the men with power over him were not guided by the way we understand the positive value of Justice.

For mature adults (like you good reader), constructing a moral self out of positive values is a more enlightened way to go than fencing yourself in with negative commandments. We can take control of our lives rather than follow the herd, which is driven unreflectively by "thou shall nots". Too often, negative commandments are used by hucksters to manipulate political fear mongering or religious superstition to divide and conquer us. So let's think clearly about what examples we want to set for our children and our children's children. If we model healthy living and communal participation, the next generation will probably pay it forward.

Finding a satisfactory equilibrium in giving to the world and taking from it is a life-long challenge. But it's an enjoyable one when we love life and live it engaged positively with others in our communities. We need to be nimble enough to recognize which values are the best guides through whatever challenges arise. That's how we become the persons we truly want to be. And that's how we help to create loving relationships and strong communities.

Part III: Values Unite Us

Chapter 22: The Rai, the Quaker, and the American Way

The Rai

I have come to know a little village called Basa in the mountains of eastern Nepal. Most of the villagers are of the "Rai" (pronounced like rye bread) ethnic group. The villagers are all subsistence farmers. There is only one significant seasonal employer for the villagers, Adventure GeoTreks, which is the expedition company I have used since 2006 to staff trekking and mountaineering expeditions I have organized. Hiking, camping, and climbing in the extreme conditions of the highest mountains in the world either creates bonds among the participants or it breaks them.

You don't come away feeling neutral about someone you've bathed in mountain streams with, crapped outdoors beside each other, and been roped to while climbing a rock face. I became very fond of the men from Basa who guided, cooked, and carried the gear during my first experience with Adventure GeoTreks on an expedition to Lobuche Mountain in northern Nepal in 2006.

The bond established with the men from Basa made it easy for me to agree to lead a fundraising project for the village school at the request of the owner of Adventure GeoTreks, Niru Rai. (All members of the Rai tribal-ethnic group have the last name of "Rai".)

Niru told me that when he was a child he went to school one day. He had to walk two hours on steep mountainous trails from his home village of Basa to the nearest school. What he learned from his one day of school was that he would rather get paid for walking long distances than walk to school. He left his village to find work as a porter with an expedition company and never returned to school. He worked his way up from porter to kitchen boy to cook to sirdar to company owner.

Niru moved to Katmandu after his business began to take off, but his heart remained in Basa. He married a village girl, built a home in the village, and began hiring men from Basa to staff his growing expedition company. He didn't forget that the children growing up in Basa still had to walk two hours to the nearest school. He convinced a French NGO to establish a school in Basa on land Niru donated. The school only had three grades.

In 2007 Niru asked, and I agreed, to raise $5,000 for the purposes of adding two classrooms to the school building and paying the salaries of two additional teachers. The expanded building and additional teachers would allow the school to grow from three-grades to five grades. That project evolved into the Basa Village Foundations.

In the US we have a nonprofit corporation, Basa Village Foundation USA Inc., which is charged with fundraising and providing technical expertise for development projects. Our sister organization is the Basa Village Foundation NGO (nongovernmental organization), which works directly with local villagers to provide supervision for the projects the villagers choose to take on. Niru is chairman of the NGO and I am president of the US corporation.

The two organizations have been working together to develop the infrastructure of Basa village while trying not to harm its traditional culture. Niru and I agreed that our joint mission is to create a model of culturally sensitive development in Basa. We hope that other villages in eastern Nepal might be able to replicate the Basa model.

Our initial goal is nearly complete. The last project the village has requested will probably be constructed in 2015, which are latrines throughout the village. The villagers do not have toilets. They do have a school, a nearby medical clinic, hydroelectric power, smokeless stoves, water delivery system, computers and supplies for the school. The US Corporation raised the money and provided technical expertise for these projects. The Nepal NGO developed the budgets, supervised construction, and disbursed funds to purchase needed building materials and supplies. The villagers built and operate each of the projects through committees chosen by the village.

The efforts by the Basa Village Foundations have all been voluntary without monetary compensation for any officers or staff. No one in Niru's organization or mine was paid for their contributions of time and talents. The villagers were not paid to provide the labor for the improvements to the village. All of the resources and work have been given by people who value Community and have leaned toward unselfishness out of love for Basa.

~ ~ ~

The traditional religion of the Basa Rai is animist, meaning that everything is infused with spirit. Whether it's a person, animal, plant, rock, or chair, every thing has its own spirit; everything is alive. This attitude instills the Rai people with a highly developed sense of respect for the natural world and other people. A traditionalist Rai would not disrespectfully kick a rock out of the way on a mountain trail. She would move it aside. Wood is the fuel used for cooking and heat in Basa. But trees are not felled. Only sticks are burned. Branches are cut as necessary but not to the point of killing a tree.

The men of Basa village are the strongest and kindest men I know. They are small in stature by American standards, most are five feet four to five feet six inches and weigh between one hundred twenty and one hundred forty pounds. These small men carry loads of expedition supplies typically weighing between sixty and eighty pounds all day long on the highest trails in the world. The porters on Himalayan mountaineering and trekking expeditions do not use modern backpacks. They carry their loads in wicker baskets with a rope looped around their foreheads. Everything that is brought to villages in the high Himalayas is carried on the back of porters including heavy rocks and timber for homebuilding and all the machinery and materials for hydroelectric and water systems.

When I receive a letter or email from one of these tough and rugged men, it always opens with this charming greeting, "Namaste Dear Jeff dhai" (I see god in you dear elder brother).

The women of Basa village are the kindest and strongest women I know. I have visited the village with different trekking or mountaineering groups five times. Each time our trekking group nears the village we are greeted on the trail by village musicians. The band members thump and toot on their homemade instruments as they lead us off the main trail down into the village. The villagers have erected a welcome banner beside the school. All 250 or so villagers await our arrival with flower garlands to place around our necks. The mothers and grandmothers in the village insist that we come to their homes, so they can offer my friends and me food and drink they have prepared for us. These women have worked all day in their rice, millet, wheat, or corn fields. But they are so delighted to welcome guests they will host us late into the night until are stomachs are bloated with rice, lentils, roti (bread), and chang (homemade beer). We sleep in the next morning, but the women of Basa are up at sunrise to care for their children and work their fields.

The villagers work hard to sustain their way of life. It is rare that crops are bountiful enough to sell at the larger market village of Sombare. The families of Basa essentially produce enough to feed the mouths in the village. Still, they love to gather to sing, dance, and drink. Every home has a flower garden, and making art out of flowers is a favorite pastime of the women and children. Villagers mark special occasions like births and marriages with week-long celebratory feasting. The whole community gathers for extended partying. The host family provides much of the food and drink, but every family contributes by bringing some provisions to the celebration. When a villager's pig, goat, or water buffalo is about to die, it is killed and its meat is distributed in equal portions to all the families in the village.

Private property is respected. Each family has its own farm land, and many, but not all, have a couple animals. Traditional customs of sharing and caring developed along side respect for individual ownership of property. For example, the tailors and blacksmiths in the village are allotted portions of other farmers' crops so the craftsmen have sufficient time away from their own farming to render their skilled services to all other members of the community. There is no charge when a shirt needs mending or a tool fixed. The tailors and blacksmiths perform their work for the other villagers, because they have been provided food through the allotment system.

If a villager is sick or injured, the shaman ("purket" in the local language) performs healing rituals. The purket is compensated only by being fed and given drink by the family he is serving. A few years ago a medical clinic was opened in Sombare, the largest village in the Basa area. Neighbors will carry an ailing villager to the medical clinic, which is a two-hour walk from Basa, if the purket's ministrations are not effective. Neighbors work the fields and handle chores for a sick or injured villager until he or she recovers.

The village does not operate like a commune. Private ownership of land and personal property is valued. It operates as a community of independent families and individuals who care for each other in times of need and who thoroughly enjoy getting together with each other to sing, dance, eat, and drink.

While the tradition of the Rai people is to value every thing as it is, they do not value pain and suffering per se. They accept it as an inevitable aspect of their lives. The most extreme examples I've seen are expedition porters carrying loads in their doko baskets weighing in excess of eighty pounds on snow-covered trails as high as 18,000 feet wearing sandals and flimsy cloth coats. I've seen porters from other expedition companies drop their doko baskets and quit, because the terrain was too difficult and dangerous. I have never heard a porter from Basa working for Adventure GeoTreks complain about anything.

On our 2007 expedition to Yala Peak, we had to ascend and descend a 16,000 feet high pass called the Ganja La. The descent was very steep and tricky down an icy snow-covered mountain ridge. Ganesh Rai, our sirdar on that expedition, fixed ropes to secure our descent. The ropes did not reach to the bottom of the ridge. We had to slide the last fifty yards down the icy slope on our butts. The porters had to do it grasping their loaded doko baskets against their chests. By the time we found a campsite, it was so cold my hiking boots were frozen into concrete blocks. Our crew members laughed and sang while they brewed tea, cooked soup, and set up tents for their shivering clients.

Although the people of Basa village are willing to accept incredibly harsh conditions without complaint, they have taken the initiative to make changes in the village for what they perceive as improvements in the life of the village. When offered help to finance building a village school, they took the opportunity to expand the education of their children beyond learning farming. When they saw that other villages across their great valley had lights twinkling at night, they sought help to build a hydroelectric system. When the villagers came to understand that smokeless stoves would reduce the incidents of cataracts and pulmonary disease, they developed a plan with the Basa Foundations to build and install stoves in every home. Some of the men have seen toilets in larger villages through their expedition work with Adventure GeoTreks. Talk has begun in Basa about whether toilets would improve sanitation and enhance life in the village.

The traditional ways of life are valued in Basa. But its value system does not prohibit changes which ameliorate hardships, decrease diseases, reduce unnecessary deaths, or improve the education of its children. Valuing all things does not mean that pain and suffering are valued. Sickness, injuries, cataracts, infant mortality, etc., are not *things* in the natural world. They are conditions. The Rai's ancient understanding of reality differentiates things, plants, animals, and people, all of which have spirit and are therefore respected, from conditions.

Ganesh Rai once explained to me, when I was suffering nausea and diarrhea, that an evil spirit had attacked my stomach. Adverse conditions which are painful or harmful to the well being of individuals or the village are the result of spirits. Sickness, pain, and injury are the symptoms and evidence of the presence of an evil spirit. The condition is not the spirit. The evil spirit is the cause; the harmful condition is the result.

Ganesh's understanding of an evil spirit is similar to how modern medicine understands a virus. The flu virus is not the headache, runny nose, and stomach ache you experience. But the virus's entry into your body causes the symptoms of the condition of having the flu. The traditional Rai understanding of harmful spirits is that they enter the body and then cause pain, suffering, or injury.

Evil spirits must be propitiated by the purket or dealt with by modern medicine and better sanitary practices. A harmful spirit is respected, but the way to respect it is to encourage it to leave.

Visitors with good intentions receive a warm and friendly welcome to Basa. During my visit in 2010 two peddlers arrived in the village. They had walked up from the border with India selling goods they carried from village to village. The peddlers were provided food and shelter by villagers in Basa for two weeks without any charge. It was simply a matter of being gracious hosts to the peddlers.

The welcome our trekking groups have received during

each of my five visits to Basa has been described by many members of the groups as one of the coolest experiences of their lives. We have been literally covered in flowers by smiling and laughing villagers each time I've entered the village. When we depart, some of the men, women, and children cry, hold onto our hands, and kiss our cheeks or hands. They are always sorry to see us leave.

As the modern world penetrates further into village life, survival of the community's values will depend on the ability of the local people to recognize who and what are of good spirit. I hope they will be able to discern who does not have good intentions and will kindly encourage any scoundrels with bad spirit to leave Basa.

Society of Friends

When I finally had the courage to leave my hereditary denomination to find a church which was not doctrinaire and belief-driven, after a few years of wandering, I found the Quakers. An element of my attraction was a similarity with the Rai. Quakers are not animists, but the founder of the seventeenth century movement in England, George Fox, taught that all people have a "divine spark" or "inner light" which is the spirit of God. The recognition of spirit in all other people leads Quakers to what they call a "peace testimony". It's based on respect for our shared humanity with people of other cultures and nations. And it calls Quakers to social justice activism.

Local congregations are not churches. They are "meetings". Instead of saying, "I'll see you in church," a Quaker would say, "See ya at the meeting."

Instead of compiling a book full of doctrines members are supposed to believe in, like the Presbyterians of my heritage, Quakers suggest that members ask themselves questions. Some, but not all Quaker meetings, publish a brochure of "Queries". These are questions that particular Quaker meetings consider important for people to consider in deciding who they want to be. An example mentioned earlier in the book proposed by First Friends is: Whether and to what extent you should consume alcoholic beverages? An interesting one I recently came across from Australian Quakers is: "How can we listen deeply to what seems strange?"

No answers are suggested. The individual Quaker may or may not consider the question. No ecclesiastical authority requires a response. It is left up to you to decide what, if anything, to do with the query.

Will Rogers famously said, "I am not a member of any organized political party, I am a Democrat." I no longer belong to any organized church; I joined the Quakers.

The formal name is Society of Friends. Members are "Friends". "Quaker" is a nickname. I've heard and read different stories of how the name originated; most are derogatory. (Folks from Indiana can relate; the origin of "Hoosiers" is disputed and not all the folk tales are complimentary.) Two major lines of oral traditions are 1) Early Friends quaked before persecuting English legal authorities, and 2) Friends quake before the Lord with fear and trembling.

The BBC Website on Religions informs us that there are only 210,000 Quakers worldwide with the largest concentration in the US. There is no single international or national ruling body for the Society of Friends. There are regional groupings of Friends called "yearly meetings", but local meetings are not compelled to join. The regional organizations have no real authority over local meetings. The largest one I've identified is Friends General Conference, which has an office and staff in Philadelphia. It has a website and sponsors an annual gathering of Quakers from the US and Canada.

I have no interest in involvement with another religious bureaucracy or ruling body, even one as loosely structured as the Society of Friends. So, I have nothing to do with any Quaker body other than Indianapolis First Friends, and I intend to keep it that way. Not long after I joined First Friends I was asked to serve on "Ministry and Counsel", which is the executive committee in charge of worship and routine administration of the meeting. It was a mistake and I resigned after a few months. I'm glad someone is willing to handle these matters, but I no longer have the stomach for debating to which magazines the meeting should subscribe and how much should we pay a guest preacher.

I am very happy to be in the community of Indy First Friends. I lead a weekly discussion class called "Coffee Circle & Wired Word". We drink coffee and have lively discussions about current topics in the news. It's quite enjoyable to share coffee and conversation with a group of thoughtful folks. Leading the discussion is not at all taxing. It's like riding a horse that is raring to go. Discussion takes off as soon as the topic is introduced.

My unwillingness to participate in the organizational structure of the Society of Friends seems to be understood and accepted by Indy First Friends. Unlike the major Protestant denominations, such as Presbyterians, Lutherans, Methodists, and Episcopalians, Quakers have retained a commitment to being more like a Christian movement than a bureaucratically structured denomination. It's been said that Quakers follow Jesus rather than Paul.

Many of he Quakers I have come to know since joining First Friends in 2009 have an anti-authoritarian streak. They are proud of their independence, tolerance, and looseness of organization.

Now I recognize that it's a gross generalization to claim all Quakers, or even all Indy First Friends members, are accurately described by the terms I'm using. There are exceptions. It's also true that not every member of Basa village perfectly fits the delightful profile I've sketched. Every group of humans has some diversity, and every bushel has some bad apples. I don't want to present a romanticized portrait of these two communities, but my generalized experience of them is reflected in the positive terms I'm using.

The theological perspectives within Indy First Friends are about as diverse as the entire spectrum of religious attitudes of the wider community of Indianapolis. A friend who was formerly a member of The Nation of Islam ("Black Muslims")) recently joined the meeting. In the class I lead there is an atheist and a conservative Christian evangelical and just about every point of view between those extremes. The majority of the group leans toward "progressive-liberal" points of view.

When there is an issue that needs to be decided by a Friends meeting, it is discussed at a "business meeting" open to all members and anyone else who cares to attend. Decisions are not made by majority vote. Whether a new pastor needs to be hired or the roof replaced, the decision is made by consensus of those attending the meeting. The clerk leading the business meeting will ask attendees to take time to meditate in silent contemplation to seek spiritual and intellectual discernment on any significant issue. Those who feel spiritually led to speak may do so. Then, discussion will be had and a decision will be made if consensus is reached. If not, the roof will continue to leak and the pastor will not be replaced.

Consider what a brilliant and problematic form of governance is rule by consensus. There is no fear of tyranny by the majority, because the majority does not rule. Minority groups need not appeal for protection from the majority, because the majority cannot make any decision without consent of the minorities. It's also unlikely that a charismatic charlatan will control a meeting by force of personality. In most any group there will probably be one or more maverick members that won't be swayed by a powerful personality.

To work effectively governance by consensus requires

trust and goodwill among the members of the meeting. Any obstreperous member can derail needed or worthy initiatives. For the system to work, the personalities within the community must be mature and willing to respect differing views. I'm sure that is not the case in every Friends meeting. If decisions can't be made and leaking roofs repaired, the community is probably going to break apart.

I need to point out that my description of how Quaker meetings operate is not necessarily accurate as to all Friends meetings. Remember, there is no authority within the Society of Friends to enforce any particular rules of order on local meetings. The content and order of Quaker worship services also varies from meeting to meeting. There are meetings which follow a tradition begun by some of the first meetings in seventeenth century England, called "unprogrammed worship". The tradition is to sit silently open to being led by the Spirit of God. Anyone led to speak is welcome to do so. Other meetings, like First Friends Indy, usually include a time for unprogrammed worship within the service (ordinarily ten to fifteen minutes), but it is not required.

Our worship service is pretty similar to what I grew up with in the Presbyterian Church -- worshipful music with a choir and organ, some contemporary music, children's message, Bible readings, a sermon -- except the Lord's Prayer and Apostle's Creed are not recited. Unprogrammed worship might be ten to fifteen minutes of silence, but the quiet is usually broken by two or three people speaking for a minute about an experience or concern that is meaningful to the speaker. Statements vary from praying for an end to the civil war and suffering in Syria to joy for a college graduation. A friend and neighbor of mine, who came to a few services, remarked to me that sometimes our unprogrammed worship felt more like group therapy than the spiritual séance she expected. Our pastor, Ruthie, calls the period of waiting in silence "Communion after the manner of Friends".

Quakers don't perform sacraments, per se. Marriages

and memorial services are performed and celebrated and babies are recognized by being introduced the first time they are brought to a service. New members are also recognized by name when they join a meeting. But there is no formal or required ritual to mark these events as especially sacred. The previous pastor of First Friends, Stan, explained that all moments of life are sacred to Quakers, so there is no need to call any particular event a sacrament.

~ ~ ~

The first time I attended a First Friends service was at the invitation of my friend Tim Meyer in 2009. Tim was a member of our 2007 trekking/mountaineering expedition to Yala Peak with Adventure GeoTreks. He was also the first contributor to the fundraising project for the Basa village school.

I wanted to find a sponsoring organization for the hydroelectric project, because the Basa Village Project had not yet evolved into a nonprofit corporation. Tim suggested I come with him to meeting at First Friends. His plan was to introduce me and ask around to see if the Meeting would be interested in being the sponsor. It was, and the Project was successful in raising the capital needed to purchase all the material components of a hydroelectric system. (The villagers built a hydroelectric power station on the nearest mountain stream. They strung cables up a sheer one hundred foot cliff and then another mile over boulders, a rocky ridge, scree, and brush to the village. Enough power is generated for each of the sixty-two households to have a few lights and an electric outlet. The next time I visited in 2011 there was light in Basa at night.)

The welcome I received at First Friends on my first visit was not nearly as boisterous as the one I received in Basa. There was no band to greet me. I was not showered with flowers and there wasn't any dancing and drinking. There was coffee and tea after the service. Nevertheless, I found

Tim's Quaker friends to be quietly enthusiastic and warmly welcoming. I thought First Friends might be what I was looking for in a worshipful community.

The openness to diverse views, the sincerity in worship, the communal method of decision making, and the emphasis on positive values rather than doctrinal beliefs, meshed with my own conception of a worship community. But I must admit that none of that was of particular importance to me when Tim invited me to check out First Friends Indy. I had the ulterior motive of just wanting to find an organization willing to sponsor the fundraiser for the hydroelectric project in Basa.

What sealed the deal for me was my first experience of unprogrammed worship. After Pastor Stan asked for silence it felt like one hundred sets of lungs were breathing together. In the quiet of the sanctuary I felt the awesomeness of the universe and was grateful to be alive in it and sharing it with the other spirits in the Meeting. It was a wonderfully pragmatic and spiritually moving worship experience. It allowed busy people living in urban America time to relax and meditate. It also allowed the opportunity for anyone who felt the need to speak from their heart. It made me glad to be there at First Friends Indy.

I became a regular attender and submitted my request to become a pledging member after about eighteen months. The Meeting has continued to support the Basa Village Foundation, even though we are now a separate nonprofit corporation. Several members of First Friends are also members of the Foundation and many have contributed to each of our fundraising projects. Tim's fortuitous invitation was the pebble dropped into the pond which has rippled out to connect Friends in Indianapolis with friends in Basa, Nepal.

American Pragmatism
The Stanford Encyclopedia of Philosophy ("SEP") describes Pragmatism as "a philosophical tradition that

originated in the United States around 1870." It is the only distinctively American philosophy. The founders of "classical Pragmatism" were Charles Sanders Peirce (1839–1914), William James (1842–1910), and John Dewey (1859–1952), per the SEP. Pragmatism is concerned with practical consequences. These giants of nineteenth and twentieth century American intellectuals, unlike many of their philosophical contemporaries, wanted to solve problems rather than spend their intellectual energy on airy-fairy abstractions. They were, well, pragmatic.

William James criticized ivory tower academics for dividing into two camps. In *Pragmatism: A New Name for an Old way of Thinking*, published in 1907, James described the two philosophical camps as having their underlying fault lines determined more by personal inclination, or personality, than rigorous analysis. On one side were those more comfortable with science and empiricism; on the other side were scholars who were of a more religious and spiritual bent. The SEP summarizes James's distinction thusly: "... a certain clash of human 'temperaments', between the 'tough minded' and the 'tender minded'. The tough minded have an empiricist commitment to experience and going by 'the facts', while the tender-minded have more of a taste for a priori principles which appeal to the mind. The tender minded tend to be idealistic, optimistic and religious, while the tough minded are normally materialist, pessimistic and irreligious."

James thought the American temperament inclines more toward the tough minded empirical-scientific-materialistic-pessimistic-irreligious and Europeans more toward the tender minded idealistic-optimistic-religious. If he were alive today, I'm not sure he would think his dichotomy between the American way and European way still holds. The SEP informs us that American academics lost interest in Pragmatism by the middle of the 20th Century, but interest has been rekindled since the 1970s.

Alexis de Tocqueville in his seminal two-volume book on the America of the early 19th Century, *On Democracy in America* (the first volume published 1835 and the second in 1840), related the explosive growth and dynamism of the US in the early 19th Century to a number of factors. He found our forefathers' to be incredibly industrious, fiercely democratic, materialistic, skeptical, and religious.

"The Protestant work ethic" is a term coined by the German father of political science, Max Weber, in his book, *The Protestant Ethic and the Spirit of Capitalism*, published in 1905. Weber's analysis of American democracy and capitalism was that it's supported by a national character which emphasizes hard work and frugality combined with a belief that a man can pull himself up by his boot straps to be successful. He related this to roots in Scottish and northern European Protestantism, with its obsession on personal salvation as opposed to Roman Catholicism with its tradition of priestly authority and mystical sacramentalism.

Nineteenth and early twentieth century intellectuals and social scientists were impressed with the vastness of the United States in its actuality and potential. The country was huge, spanning a continent from ocean to ocean. Its growth in agricultural and industrial output was staggering. To the eyes and analytical minds of European academics, the forces energizing the young giant were democracy, capitalism, and Protestantism.

The early Pragmatist philosophers were thoroughly American in their roots and approach to philosophy. But, the US had begun to change by the end of the 19th Century. Waves of Irish-Catholics and other immigrants had reached our shores. The US could no longer be accurately called a Protestant country. We were becoming the greatest "melting pot" in the history of the world. Classical Pragmatism was an effort to make sense of a rapidly changing human landscape in the US. It was an attempt to synthesize the disparate parts that America had become. The US was no longer so totally dominated by the Protestant ethos described by de Tocqueville and Weber. Catholic and other immigrant influences had to be taken into consideration. So, pragmatists focused on solving problems rather than advocating a particular religion, theology, or political ideology.

American Pragmatism held onto the characteristic American skeptical-scientific-empirical approach to problem solving and applied it to the human psyche and social relations. Pragmatism is not antithetical to religion. It just demands that it make sense. It demands political participation, but encourages a healthy skepticism toward utopian ideals.

William James was actually quite interested in spirituality and made a particular study of a famous spiritualist medium, Leonora Piper. He determined that she didn't have the psychic powers she claimed, but she was very clever at reading people.

James thought the human spirit is most profoundly understood through psychology. He admired the Society of Friends, because "it was a religion of veracity rooted in spiritual inwardness, and a return to something more like the original gospel truth ..." (*First among Friends, George Fox and the Creation of Quakerism*, H. Larry Ingle Oxford University Press, 1996). I suspect the Pragmatists would have also admired the Rai's pragmatic spirituality, if they had known of it.

Actual links, historical or otherwise, among Pragmatists, Quakers, and Rai are pretty tenuous. I did find that complimentary quote by William James about the Society of Friends in Ingle's book. But the book also states that James thought George Fox, the Quaker founder, was a religious nut case. I doubt anywhere other than in the book you are presently reading will you find American Pragmatism, Quakers, and the Rai people of Nepal associated. Possibly only in my mind and life are they woven together.

My family roots are Colonial Puritanism. Pragmatism

grew out of those philosophical roots but as an effort to transcend them as the US became a more complex national community. Focus on solving problems! That is the pragmatic way to bind a disparate community together. Forget the ideal state, utopian dreams, and decrees about how to live handed down thousands of years ago by a God that ceased speaking to us.

The Quakers of First Friends Indy and the Rai of Basa, Nepal are two communities I have found that try to live pragmatically in community. Both communities encourage their members to live lives in a healthy balance of taking care of self and offering assistance to others, rather than relying on religious doctrines or political ideologies. They both have a profound appreciation for the spiritual dimension of the individual person while reveling in their own unique forms of communal participation. The Basa Rai and Indianapolis Friends are quite different in appearance and how they live their daily lives, but their fundamental values are charmingly similar.

In the coming age of unbelief our political and religious organizations will need to find means and methods other than doctrines and ideologies to bind communities together. Promoting positive values can replace requiring orthodox beliefs as the means of communal bonding. Communities that take a pragmatic, rather than ideological or doctrinaire, approach to resolving issues will be more attractive to newcomers.

I'm sure there are many other communities that live by pragmatic values, but the Basa Rai and Indy Friends are the two I know. I hope you will find value in learning a little bit more about how the Basa Rai and Indy Friends operate. Lessons offered by these two communities can be adopted by other religious or political organizations interested in using positive values and pragmatism to move forward into a sustainable future.

Chapter 23: Rai Values; Tradition and Change in Basa Village

In 2008, Nepal ended a ten-year long civil war. It started as an insurrection of poor farmers led by Maoist-inspired Western-educated intellectuals. Seventeen thousand Nepalese died in the war. King Gyanendra was deposed and The Shah dynasty, which ruled Nepal from 1768 as a Hindu monarchy, was replaced by an elected national assembly.

Seven years before the civil war ended, on June 1, 2001 Crown Prince Dipendra shot and killed his father, King Birendra, his mother Queen Aishwarya, and other members of the royal family during a party at their palace in Katmandu. The Prince shot himself, but was proclaimed king while in a coma. He died after a three-day reign. His uncle, Gyanendra, ascended the throne. Many Nepalese suspected King Gyanendra of somehow instigating the murders of the royal family. His older brother, Birendra, had been a relatively popular and benevolent ruler. Gyanendra was unpopular with the Nepalese people from the beginning of his rule.

The Maoist revolutionaries gained support and began winning pitched battles against the regular army. In February 2005 after sporadic fighting reached Katmandu, Gyanendra declared a state of emergency, dismissed Parliament, suspended the Constitution, and declared martial law with his royal self in charge of the military. He even shut down the telephone system and Internet within Nepal for a few days. Instead of reversing the course of the revolution, the King's authoritarian crackdown on civil rights and personal freedoms inflamed increasing discontent with the monarchy.

The ranks of the Maoist revolutionaries swelled. Two more years of fighting finally brought the warring parties into United Nations mediated negotiations. King Gyanendra agreed to step down and the Maoists agreed to put down their weapons and let the UN supervise national elections. In 2008 the Unified Communist Party of Nepal (the Maoists' political wing) won the most votes of the multiple parties competing in the parliamentary elections.

The Maoists became the dominant party in the Constituent Assembly of Nepal, the first post-monarchy parliament in Nepal's history. Pushpa Kamal Dahal, who went by the nom de guerre "Prachanda" during the civil war, was the military leader of the Maoists. He was chosen Prime Minister by the newly elected parliament. But Prachanda only served one year. Once in power, the Unified Communist Party split in two. The "old guard" of liberal democrats, the Congress Party, which had been the dominant party during many years of the parliamentary monarchy, succeeded the Maoists.

Since the inception of parliamentary rule, Nepal's politics have resembled Italy's. Confused by multiple parties and frustrating to many citizens, because it seems paralyzed by political squabbling (sound familiar). But it is limping along.

The revolution and the political turmoil in Katmandu had little impact on life in Basa village. I was told by my friend Ganesh Rai that Maoist guerillas once came to Basa and pointed their rifles at people. They demanded money from the villagers. But, since the village economy was primarily barter, there wasn't any money to steal. The Maoists settled for being fed and drinking rakshi (the local distilled liquor). The Maoists never came back. Ganesh figured they decided it was too difficult to find Basa and they weren't going to be able to recruit any of the villagers to their cause anyway. There is no road to Basa. To hike from the nearest road required crossing several high mountain passes with altitudes between ten and twelve thousand feet.

The National Assembly has been debating and dithering over a new constitution for several years. One of the proposed articles would require villages like Basa to elect a mayor. When I asked several of the Basa guys staffing our trekking group in 2011 what they thought about that, they were amused and irritated. They thought a mayoral election would be an utter waste of time. Buddi Rai explained that, "Everyone in the village knows all our best men and we have the elder leader if there is a dispute to settle."

When there is an issue that affects the whole village, all the villagers gather beside the school house to discuss it. Just like the Quakers, decisions are not made by majority rule, but by village-wide consensus. Committees are chosen to run projects, like the school, hydroelectric system, and water system. I've attended village meetings, as an observer only, and they are very spirited affairs. The Basa Rai do not use the Quaker method of sitting in silence awaiting spiritual guidance. Villagers get very animated and shout out questions and demand answers from the speaker who is proposing how to handle a project. The spirits the Basa Rai enjoy during their business meetings are chang (beer) and rakshi (moonshine).

The decisions on how to work out the hydroelectric project -- how to pay for the upkeep, who would work on which details, how would food be provided to those working, who would be on the committee to maintain the system, etc. -- required two village-wide meetings which lasted two of the afternoons I spent in Basa at the end of November 2010. But it was all worked out and the village has successfully run its own electricity system for over three years now.

If a dispute arises between two villagers that doesn't get resolved any other way, then the oldest man in the village is asked to arbitrate the disagreement. Pungse Rai was the "elder leader" until he died in 2013 at the age of eighty-nine. The last time I saw Pungse was in 2010. He lived in a little shed about fifteen yards down a narrow dirt path behind his family's house. (Buddi acted as my interpreter, because the older people in Basa only speak their local Rai language. The national language, Nepali, and English are both taught in all schools in Nepal, but few people over forty in the mountain villages have any schooling.) Pungse explained that he preferred living alone to being in a house with his daughter, grandchildren, and great grandchildren. He said his daughter, who is over sixty, irritated him. "She is always trying to do things for me." She was standing there with us while he was telling us this and seemed unfazed. In fact, she brought her father a plate of food while we were standing outside his shed. Pungse waved her away without so much as a thank you.

Pungse said he had everything he needed in his little shed and that he liked being alone. He proudly showed us the garden beside his shelter. Pungse said he liked working it and he also "liked to spend time remembering."

Is Pungse Rai qualified to be a competent arbitrator? He has neither legal training nor a degree in counseling. His sole qualification is he's the oldest man in the village; by tradition that makes him the elder-leader. The resentful reaction of the Basa guys to the requirement of electing a village mayor reveals that they value the tradition and trusted Pungse to handle the job. Because the village is pragmatic about solving problems, it might have changed the tradition if Pungse made bad decisions. But none of the men in our crew indicated any concern about or desire to change the way the village settles disputes among residents.

It's contrary to our modern Western value system that only a man may serve as "elder leader". Our values are not at issue. Basa is not our community. Neither is it the politician's in Katmandu. The community has a pragmatic system for dispute resolution, which has been working as far back as the village's collective memory goes. It might be forced to change because city folks believe Anglo-American-style democracy should be imposed on "backward" villages. Which is the more enlightened approach, to respect a traditional way which is working or to impose a new way from the outside based on a foreign ideology? So, "W", how has nation-building worked so far in Iraq and Afghanistan?

~ ~ ~

Pungse's and Basa's commitment to self reliance are quite striking to us modern folk. Americans trumpet the value of independence and self reliance as fundamental to our national character. Yet, how many of us could live as independently at the age of eighty-six as Pungse Rai did? Basa villagers are far more capable of taking care of themselves than modern Americans, including me. They have no stores to buy food, clothing, or their farm implements. How long would any of us last if we had to raise our own food, let alone provide ourselves with all the other things we think are necessary in life?

Counter-intuitively, the value the villagers trumpet is not self reliance or independence, it is Community. Another Adventure GeoTreks guide, Sanga Rai, proudly described to me how the village takes care of all its orphan children. Nine of them live with Sanga and his wife Nanda, who is the principal of the village school, but the whole village helps to provide food and clothing for the orphans.

When the village first decided it wanted electricity, a petition was prepared and submitted to the local government office, the Village Development Committee. The petition requested the government to provide support to electrify the village.

Way across the huge river valley from Basa there are lights that twinkle at night from other villages which have electricity. Ganesh told me that the villagers saw those lights increasing in number over the years, and so they were hopeful the government would help bring light to Basa. He said, "We thought we had a good chance, because we had never requested anything from the government." After waiting a few months for a reply that did not come, it was decided instead to appeal to Niru and me for help through the foundations we were in the process of creating. I agreed to seek funding on the US side and Niru agreed to develop a technical plan and budget in Katmandu. The villagers assured us they would provide all the labor to build their own power station.

The approach the village took to creating its hydroelectric power station is a wonderful synthesis of the values of self reliance and communal engagement. The villagers knew they lacked the capital to purchase the necessary component parts for the system and the technical expertise to put it all together. They made the pragmatic decision to request outside assistance for money and expertise. But they organized themselves into work details to build the system and management committees to run it. The two men who live closest to the power station were chosen to receive the technical training necessary to operate the turbines in the little power station.

The village has been an independent community organically functioning with few outside influences for many generations. Just within the last few years life has begun to change with access to a medical clinic, the opening of the school, electricity, a water delivery system, and other modern amenities that are being integrated into village life. In 2013 sporadic cell phone coverage reached Basa. A road is eking its way through the mountains toward Basa. Its furthest eastern spur, a rutted, muddy pathetic excuse for a road, is now a two-day hike from the village.

I can't help but wonder whether and how in a generation or two the pragmatic-independent-cooperative-communal character of Basa will change. As it obtains more of the amenities common in the outside world, will its communal and spiritual way of life be lost?

So far, the "improvements" to its infrastructure don't seem to have affected its culture. Villagers still farm their crops, create flower art, gather to sing, dance, and drink, and make decisions by consensus. The future will tell whether Basa is a delicate flower or a solid tree.

~ ~ ~

The Rai people do not have a written language. They do have their own language with multiple dialects. Since there are no written records or sacred books, all of their cultural heritage and traditions are passed down by oral tradition and practice. Friends in Basa tell me they think the village has existed for hundreds of years, maybe five hundred years. "That is what the old people say," Ganesh told me sitting by a campfire in 2010.

It was our last night in the mountains on a trek through the Middle Himalayas in the Solu region of Nepal. The main purpose of the trek was to get Mike Miller, the head of the hydroelectric project on the US side, to Basa to meet with the villagers and the local supervising engineer. Niru's team had hired an electrical engineer named Chandra Nepali to oversee construction of the power station. Over the course of four days in Basa, Mike, Chandra, and I held meetings in the village to finalize plans for construction. It all went swimmingly. All that was left for us was to trek out of Basa and over a couple of high mountain passes, camp two more nights, and then hike to the airstrip in Phaplu, where we would fly a Twin-Otter back to Katmandu.

It was the first of December when we set up our campsite on the ten thousand feet high ridge of the Ratnagi Danda. After all our trekking mates and the staff were asleep in tents, Ganesh, Buddi, and I sat by the campfire. Burning sticks crackled as smoke and sparks wafted up from the fire past the great white peaks of the Himalayas to join the vast array of millions of stars blinking above us. Ganesh and Buddi told me stories about their traditions and homeland.

Earlier that evening I had obtained Kumar's permission to write down, and possibly publish, information shared by the guys in our crew about the oral traditions and practices of the Basa Rai. Kumar was the senior member of our staff and son of a purket (shaman), so it fell to him to decide whether it was okay for me to record "the old ways". Kumar told me that no white man knows about the religious rituals and festivals of Basa.

~ ~ ~

Basa ("resting place") is one of many villages predominantly inhabited by the Rai people on the slopes of the Himalayas in eastern Nepal. There are over 635,000 Rai in Nepal, according to Nepal's 2003 Central Bureau of Statistics. It is difficult to find information about the Rai, but a Nepalese demographer, D.R. Dahal, in his *Social Composition of the Population: Caste / Ethnicity and Religion in Nepal* (2003) reports that the Rai had their own kingdom, which lasted 1,225 years into the 19th Century, and that the Rai are "one of the most ancient indigenous ethno-linguistic groups of Nepal". They make up less than three percent of the population of Nepal.

Because the hills and mountains are so high and the river valleys so deep in the Himalayan region where the Rai live, the Rai do not speak one common language. Ganesh told me there are ten distinct Rai languages in Nepal. None are written languages. Etymologists place the Rai languages within the family of Tibeto-Burman languages, which would indicate their ancestors came over the Himalayas south from Tibet or north up into the Himalayas from Burma. Hmm, not very helpful.

One story Ganesh and Buddi related to me as we sat by the campfire was about a man five generations ago who felt trembling by a huge boulder. It must have been an earthquake. The man scratched at the rock to see what would happen. Someone appeared and poured milk on the rock. A cave opened up through the boulder. It became a sacred place for the villagers. The story was told that the Hindu goddess Kali Devi had used the cave. The tradition developed that a man from the first man's family who felt the rock trembling must take care of the cave. Purification rituals developed that are required before the caretaker may enter the cave. He must perform these rituals twice each year. Buddi's father is an old man and he is the Kali Devi Cave priest. Buddi should be the next Kali Devi priest.

The ancient Rai were supposedly purely animistic nature worshippers. Certain trees, mountains, caves, and animals were especially respected, but the spirit of nature was all around suffusing all things with life. The Rai religion is described as "liberal and embracing" in one of the few articles I found about it. As the Rai had increasing contact with Hindus and Buddhists, especially after the loss of their ancient kingdom, the purity of Rai nature worship began to be diluted. Whether wise or unwise, the Rai embraced, or at least accepted, change in their religious practices.

It appears to me that Basa has incorporated Hindu mythology and Buddhist practices too. Kali Devi, a powerful Hindu goddess and consort of Shiva, and milk, associated with the Hindu goddess of love, Laxmi, were woven into the local legend of the sacred cave. Hindu Brahmins engage in purification rituals for their holy occasions. The purification rituals associated with entering the sacred cave are probably an imitation of Brahmin rituals. The shamanic chanting and symbols used by the local purket resemble the Tibetan-Buddhist ceremonies I've witnessed at Sherpa gompas (monasteries).

The religious syncretism of Basa is evidence that the community embraced changes in its way of life during previous generations. Incorporating attractive aspects of Hinduism and Buddhism may have resulted from cooperation, contact, or competition with more powerful Himalayan neighbors. Whatever the reason, Basa successfully adapted new ways in the past while preserving its essential character and communal values.

~ ~ ~

I didn't question Ganesh and Buddi about why they believed in Kali Devi. I did ask Buddi whether he intended to continue the line of Kali Devi Cave priests in his family.

Buddi told me that his wife Soni is in college studying "polytechnical". She might look for a position in Katmandu or try to get a job teaching in one of the larger villages in the Basa area. Buddi said he'll be able to fulfill his duties as Kali Devi priest when he's home during the off-seasons of guiding. But, if Soni finds employment in Katmandu, it might become difficult to come back to Basa two times every year. Soni and Buddi have a little daughter, Samjhana.

Buddi said he wants his family to live in Basa. But Soni wants to see what opportunities are available in Katmandu. Looking up at the magnificent star-filled sky by the campfire, Buddi said he wants Samjhana to be raised in the village, but he thinks she would receive a better education in Katmandu.

Buddi has ambition. He's begun trying to develop clientele for Adventure GeoTreks through social media. Buddi has a Facebook page which he checks when he is in Katmandu. He tried to get a visa to visit clients in the US who have become friends of his. The visa request was denied. Nepalese are not welcome in the US, because our Immigration and Naturalization Services fear they will not leave.

Buddi is smart and energetic. He is among the best and the brightest of Basa. He loves the village. But he feels the pull of the city. He is conflicted about and uncertain of his family's future, because there are no employment opportunities to use Soni's education in Basa. Ganesh moved his family to Katmandu because he wanted his son to get a "city education".

~ ~ ~

In the late nineties a medical clinic opened in the market village of Sombare, a two hour hike from Basa. It was the first major outside influence that changed Basa village. Access to modern medicines dramatically reduced the village's infant mortality rate and increased life expectancy of the elderly. So there's been a baby boom in Basa at the same time that grandparents are living longer.

Family farms in Basa are divided among the sons.

Daughters marry and move into the homes of their husbands. If a daughter doesn't marry, she'll continue to live in her parents' home. Due to the declining rate of infant mortality the terraced farm land has been further and further divided among sons making it difficult to support the next generation. Many of the current generation of boys and girls will be forced to leave Basa. There is not enough tillable soil to grow food sufficient to feed all the children this Basa baby boom has produced. This is a consequence of the introduction of modern science-based medicine into the village.

Tourism, specifically Niru's company, opened up seasonal employment opportunities for some of the villagers. The ability to make money and purchase food in Sombare on market day helps, but it hasn't completely solved the problem of too many mouths to feed.

The village decided it needed a school. If the kids got an education, they would have some prospect of finding jobs in cities. So, with Niru's donation of the land and the financial backing of a French foundation called Sol Himal, the village school was established.

The population increase upset the equilibrium of the village. The cost of the population bulge will be the loss of many kids to the city. The village is adjusting and trying to reestablish a new equilibrium. Education was introduced to help the children that leave for the city. Family planning has begun to re-balance the population to sustainable levels. But the smokeless stoves, electricity, water system, new school building and computers for the school have all changed life in the village in various ways.

Each of the projects the Basa Village Foundations have supported, even though requested by the village, challenges the traditional ways of doing things. The village women and children used to gather by the river bank in the morning to fill water buckets. It was a time for socializing and for the kids to play in the water under the watchful eye of mothers and aunts.   Now that water is brought to each home (there is an outdoor spigot at each house), that custom has ended.

It saddens me to imagine kids and their moms frolicking by a mountain stream and that it will no longer be a part of village life. It's a little easier to take because of a question my friend Ganesh asked me when we were talking about how the water system would change life in the village. "If you had to walk an hour every time you needed water and had to carry it in a bucket up and down a mountain ridge, and one day you were asked whether you would like to have water piped right to your house, what would you say?"

When the villagers have learned that life can be made easier, or the risk of disease can be reduced, or village elders can live longer, they have elected to try new things that will change traditional ways. The village has not descended into bitter strife politically or religiously over these issues. They have debated and discussed each proposed project at village-wide meetings; argued it out, and then decided by consensus how to go forward together.

I have listened in on discussions among the teachers about how the school can best serve the children of Basa. There is not unanimity of opinion. The older teachers argued that the fundamental purpose of the school should be education of the kids to become better farmers and future leaders of the village. The younger teachers expressed the view that the school should do its best to prepare students to get jobs in the city. The teachers pursue their passion to educate kids with zeal. They work for little pay (forty dollars per month) with rudimentary materials. Their disagreements about the school's mission hasn't dampened the teachers' enthusiasm to change the lives of village kids by opening minds to concepts, skills, and ideas unknown to parents, grandparents, or any earlier generation of Basa village.

In a Rai home cooking is a sacred act. It is done on the family fire pit which has three sacred stones on the perimeter of the circle around the fire. The stones indicate where people are supposed to sit around the fire pit. The family sits by "the woman/wife stone", extended family and regular visitors by the "man/husband stone", and special guests by "the god stone".

Inhaling carbon smoke from cooking and eating around an open fire every day causes pulmonary diseases and cataracts. After we developed the plan for the hydroelectric system, the village asked the Basa Foundations for help with a smokeless stove project.

But where to put the stoves and how would this affect the custom and tradition of the three sacred stones? As mentioned above, one of the principles Niru and I agreed on when we organized the sister foundations was that we would try to be culturally sensitive and do our best not to affect the local culture from the outside. But, if the villagers decided they wanted to implement a project which would change their customary way of life, then that would be their choice (not ours). I wondered, worried, and hassled Niru with emails about whether the new stoves would damage the traditions associated with cooking and eating around the family fire pit with the three sacred stones.

When I visited the village in 2011 after all the stoves were built and installed in the sixty-two homes of Basa, I discovered that different households handled the issue I had worried about in one of two ways. In some homes the new stove was placed in a corner of the room. Some of the cooking was done on the stove and some still in the fire pit. Meals were eaten as before around the fire pit with the family sitting by the woman stone. Other villagers had placed the stove in the fire pit on top of the sacred stones. When I asked with anxious concern, "But, what about the sacred stones?" Dibi Rai explained, "We know where the stones are." (He didn't preface his response with "you idiot", because he values Kindness.)

The issue was resolved pragmatically. Some villagers

decided it was important to maintain the tradition more formally than others. They put the new thing to the side, but made use of it and will benefit by burning fewer sticks and inhaling less smoke. Others decided they should receive the optimal benefit of the smokeless stove and use it for all their cooking and heating. But they know where the sacred stones are and they still follow the old ways.

The village did not divide, like our US Congress or competing Christian denominations, into ideological or religious warring camps over stones versus stoves. (I wondered whether the village scholar -- remember Tik -- had read *Gulliver's Travels* and might have told the village Swift's satirical story of the war between Lilliput and Blefuscu. It was over whether eggs should be cracked on the big end or the little end.)

In Basa individual choices and differences were respected. What was important to the villagers, after they realized inhaling so much smoke was harmful to their health, was to solve the problem. The villagers still value the custom and meaning of the three stones. They also value their health. They found ways to accommodate both values.

The conflict in values between the stones and stoves that I feared was resolved by each family in its own way and without interference by a higher authority. One of the strengths of the Basa community is that individual differences are respected. What was most important was to install the stoves so that health in the village is improved. Each family had the freedom to decide how it would integrate the stove and the stones. The village maintained its cohesion as a community by respecting differences rather than trying to impose an orthodox religious commandment on its people.

Traditional customs of the village help to bind its people together. So long as there is no reason to change, it doesn't. Individuals and families are deciding how to balance traditions with new opportunities as the outside world intrudes further into their lives. But the changes are being made within the context of a community of caring friends and neighbors.

~ ~ ~

Karen, a member of my first trekking group to visit Basa in 2008, like the rest of us, fell in love with the village, especially the kids that flocked around her. None of us wanted to leave when it was time, but we all had flights to catch back in Katmandu. As we were hiking out, Karen began suffering a strange malady. She felt like her weight had doubled. She struggled mightily to make it up the ridges we had to ascend to reach the nearest airstrip. When she finally straggled up the last high pass, she fell to her knees totally exhausted. Over dinner in a lodge late that night, Karen explained that the spirit of Basa was like a powerful magnet that didn't want her to leave. She said it felt like she was being pulled back to the village all day as we were hiking away from it. "It finally released me when I promised to return."

What I find so powerfully attractive about Basa is grounded, in part, in the ancient animistic understanding that all things have value. I think that's the foundation of the sweetly contented outlook of the villagers. They understand that everything in our universe is connected. Every thing, and all people, have spirit and share in the great common Spirit.

My friends from Basa approach religion (if you want to call it that) as a source of enjoyment -- special occasions are for partying. And it's a practical method for healing -- the purket (shaman) enters into a spiritual state to heal and protect villagers. They don't have doctrines and they don't have regular worship services or financial requirements to support an institution or a priestly class. They are even more loosely organized than the barely organized Quakers. Yet, they live a deeply simple spiritual life and they are the most winsome people I have come to know.

Jesus taught that we are all neighbors. I'm sorry, but an

awful lot of us who call ourselves Christians don't really act like it. We modern-sophisticated-urban people can learn a great deal from the kindest and strongest people I know.

Chapter 24: Quaker Values; Challenge to Communal Identity

The Society of Friends has no Central Authority which promulgates or publishes a list of Quaker values. Quakers don't have a pope or even a ruling body. As mentioned above, they do have regional groupings called "yearly meetings". These organizations are called yearly meetings because they typically have an annual get-together for members of the participating local meetings.

I've not attended a yearly meeting, but I've reviewed a few agendas and I'm told that attendees typically worship, study and discuss issues which are of concern to the member meetings. Yearly meetings provide financial support of Friends schools, summer camps, and mission work. Some advocate for social justice issues through the Friends Committee on National Legislation (FCNL), which lobbies state legislatures and Congress. Some support the American Friends Service Committee (AFSC), which offers material aid to communities struck by natural disasters as well as "peace building" mediation services and educational programs to strife-torn communities around the world.

Some yearly meetings get involved with theological issues and "recording" of pastors. Indy First Friends belongs to Western Yearly Meeting with other meetings from Indiana and Ohio. Western nearly broke up over a theological disagreement during the 2009 annual meeting a few months before I began attending First Friends.

Phil Gulley is a popular Quaker pastor and author, whose meeting is in an Indianapolis suburb. Phil's theology is God-centered and sees "the light within" all people. But he doesn't describe Jesus as singularly divine and the sole portal to connect with God. Phil became controversial within Western Yearly Meeting after publication of his book *If Grace Is True*. He was accused of espousing "a universal theology", because in the book Phil expresses the view that there are ways to God other than through Jesus Christ. This was anathema to some "conservative" Christian Quakers. Several rural meetings that lean more toward a Christ and Bible centered theology demanded that he be "unrecorded", i.e., defrocked as a Quaker minister. The larger more urban meetings refused to go along with the demand. Several of the more fundamentalist-leaning meetings departed Western Yearly Meeting with plans to form a "new evangelical Midwestern yearly meeting".

I played no part in this dust-up among Midwestern Quakers, but it was still having reverberations within First Friends when I began attending the meeting. The members who participated in Western Yearly Meeting were quite upset by the inability of the various local meetings to reach consensus on whether the theological views expressed in Phil Gulley's book should disqualify him from being a Quaker pastor. Many discussions were had over coffee during "fellowship time" after services, and the topic came up on several occasions in the class I began to lead during 2010. My friends within First Friends felt like the Quaker way of decision-by-consensus had failed. Quakers are supposed to be tolerant and accepting of differing points of view. "Why couldn't we find a way to stay bonded, despite the theological differences between the 'liberals' and 'conservatives'?", was the sentiment voiced in these conversations.

It's a conundrum why people who claim to have the same faith so often divide over theological issues. From the outside of the dispute, but the inside of one of the "liberal" meetings, it looked like the anti-Gulley forces cared more about their beliefs than about practicing the values of caring for others and tolerance. Phil's own meeting was supportive of him and it is one of the few Quaker meetings in Indiana which has been growing. So why take his livelihood away and take away from a congregation its very popular pastor? Because, given the evangelicals' strict belief in Jesus as God and that the Bible contains inerrant truth, they could not tolerate being in community with a heretic.

Each of the members of First Friends who talked to me about the division of Western Yearly Meeting told me they wanted the "evangelical Quakers" to remain within the yearly meeting. But they could not condone kicking Pastor Gulley out to keep the dissenters in. I was glad I had no dog in the fight. After my own experience with the Presbytery and being accused of being more Buddhist than Calvinist, I might have screamed and run away from the Quakers.

Instead, learning the reaction to the fall-out increased my respect for the members of Indy Friends. No one in our meeting, including those who identify themselves as evangelical Christians, has told me they think Phil Gulley's ordination should be revoked. His latest book is being used as the text for one of the other adult education classes in our meeting. The class includes members who identify themselves as conservative evangelicals.

I think my Rai friends would have reluctantly taken the same action as my Quaker friends on the Phil Gulley issue. While they would have wanted to respect the beliefs and satisfy the desires of the dissidents, they would not have agreed to make a change which would have caused pain and suffering to Phil and the members of his meeting. They would have accepted the pain that came with separation from their former friends, if that was the choice of the evangelical dissenters.

Indy Friends members involved in the Phil Gulley controversy sought compromise and reconciliation. But, it would have violated the integrity of their own community to have acceded to the demand to un-record Pastor Gulley. My friends didn't make demands of their own or stake out a rigid unbending position. They tried to find a middle way to satisfy all parties. Pragmatic efforts at compromise failed and the "conservative" meetings broke the bond of the yearly meeting.

    This is another instance where being guided by the values you choose does not guaranty the outcome you desire. It might even cost you friends. It does guaranty that you are living true to the self you have chosen to be. The identity of Western Yearly Meeting and Indianapolis First Friends was challenged by the Gulley controversy. The two communities were ultimately guided by their values of Tolerance, Sensitivity, and Kindness. They did not accede to the demands for theological rigidity nor were they insensitive to the members of Phil's meeting or unkind to him.

~ ~ ~

    A number of yearly meetings and Friends schools publish a list of particular values they recommend to their members and others. Over the last few decades agreement among many Quaker organizations has coalesced around six positive values. The values are represented by the acronym SPICES, which stands for Simplicity, Peace, Integrity, Community, Equality, and Stewardship.

    The origin of SPICES is unclear. A treatise presented at South Central Yearly Meeting in 2012 by Quaker historian Paul Buckley indicates it has evolved from the practices of Colonial-era Quakers, like William Penn, up through modern Quaker "testimonies". Early followers of George Fox in seventeenth century England advocated versions of these values and tried to guide their "outward lives" by their understanding of these sorts of values.

    It seems that since the beginning of the Quaker movement thoughtful Friends have been grappling with how to translate the "inner light" of God into outward behavior. SPICES is currently the most popular expression of that attempt. But, as with most everything about Quakers, the list is not universally or uniformly accepted by all meetings or individual Friends. What is meant by SPICES varies from meeting to meeting and school to school. (If I were chosen Grand Poobah of the Society of Friends, I would add several more items, like Kindness, Adventure, Wisdom, Courage, Curiosity, Creativity, Endurance, Strength and a few more. But SPICES does have the advantage of being easier to remember than SPICESKAWCCCES.)

Trying to write about or talk about particular values can become a descent into platitudinous blather. Try to describe one of my additions, Courage say, in a way which is universally comprehensive. You could just look up the word in the dictionary, but that is only superficially helpful. We understand the general concept of Courage, but how to live by that value in real life, that's a tougher nut. Courage has different meanings and different applications under different situations. So, I'm not going to try to define and explain in universal terms the elements of SPICES.

Another approach would be to try to describe each of the SPICES with illustrations. But there are bazillion examples. The book *Unbroken* chronicles the life of Louis Zamperini and it is filled with examples of his personal courage. But then, how does what Zamperini overcame apply to you and me? We have challenges to face, but being shot down and crashing a bomber into the Pacific during World War II, adrift in a raft for forty-seven days, and surviving torture as a prisoner of war, are probably not challenges we will face.

So, instead of taking the platitudinous blathering route, or the inspiring illustrative route, the following chapter discusses the six Quaker values using the descriptions provided by two Friends schools as starting points. (Please note that I am only quoting portions of each School's statements. The entire statements are on the Schools' websites.) The two schools have come up with somewhat similar understandings but different emphases in their descriptions of what it means to be guided by Peace, Integrity, Community, Equality, and Stewardship. And my interpretation adds a third layer of meaning (let's hope not confusion) to SPICES.

So, here's what you've been waiting for with unabated breath, examples of specific positive values that can be adopted by individuals, organizations, and communities.

Chapter 25: Valuing SPICES

- Simplicity

Connecticut Friends School proposes practical ways to live by the value of Simplicity: "We make use of our existing rich offerings such as public libraries, museums, nature centers, and historical sites.... We celebrate acts of kindness and generosity instead of bringing toys or electronics for show and tell."

The San Francisco Friends School adds a spiritual dimension to its version: "Through the simplicity testimony, Friends encourage one another to look beyond the outward and to the inward. In contemporary terms, Friends try to live lives in which activities and possessions do not get in the way of open communication with others and with one's own spirituality. By clearing away the clutter, Friends are able to more readily hear the 'still small voice' within… At San Francisco Friends School, the simplicity testimony guides students and teachers to live out the idea that 'less is more.'"

The schools are challenging the consumer culture in which most American kids live. The value Madison Avenue promotes is "too much is never enough, so buy more stuff!" The San Francisco School poses the following Queries to ponder: "What is truly important to me? How can I clear the way to focus on what I value?"

These two Friends schools are asking students, parents, and faculty to engage in introspection to reach a deeper understanding of what motivates them regarding material acquisitions. The hope is that those connected with the schools will make a commitment to living a life guided by the value of Simplicity. The effect will be a less cluttered life which leaves a less detrimental foot print on the planet.

- Peace

Connecticut Friends School suggests a practical

approach for students to promote Peace: "Build conflict resolution skills. Foster effective communication and alternatives to violence." The school recognizes conflict is part of life and will not be eradicated, even in a Quaker school: "See conflict as a springboard to moral growth. Use the conflict at hand as part of curriculum, asking each person involved to take responsibility for his or her part in escalating tension. Seek elegant, simple solutions to problems or disagreements."

The San Francisco statement follows a historical tradition of Quakers in its description of Peace as a guiding principle: "Quakers have long been known for their opposition to war and violence of any kind, whether political, social, or personal. This quest for peace comes from their belief that there is 'that of God' in every person in the world, regardless of their background or social status -- every person deserves our respect and kindness. Striving for peace is a daily endeavor, whether interacting with family or community members or working to eliminate the broader causes of war, such as ignorance, racism, and poverty."

Neither school describes Peace as a state of mind, as certain Buddhist and Hindu traditions do. Peace is a matter of human relations. It takes work. It arises out of the fundamental value of caring for others. It comes about through effective action which reflects respect for all other people.

Many but not all Quakers are pacifists. I've learned from talking to older members of Indy First Friends that most of its members supported the entry of the US into World War II and most of the men served in the Armed Forces during the war.

One of the most active members of First Friends Indy is a Bronze Star and Medal of Valor award winner for his combat service as an artillery officer in the Viet Nam War. He joined First Friends after his discharge from military service. When I asked Duffy in an email why he enlisted, this was his reply: "I was 21 years old; my reason was our country had signed the South East Asia Treaty; which said we would come to the aid of any country that asked us to help them if they were fighting Communism. I signed up because my country made a commitment to defend these countries and needed solders to honor their commitments."

Duffy also stated that he tries to live by the values of "Duty, Honor, and Country", which he thinks is consistent with his commitment to the Quaker value of Peace. In a follow- up conversation Duffy explained that war is not the way to solve problems and a peaceful world is an ideal to strive for. But he also knows that there are people who do not agree and will use force to try to dominate and harm other people. "I saw what evils men can inflict on each other in Viet Nam, like mutilated bodies nailed to a wall. We need the military to protect people that just want to live in peaceful communities."

Friends are not all of one mind on how to live out their "peace testimony". It's pretty easy to claim adherence to a principle from the easy-chair in your living room. Not so easy in challenging circumstances like living in Germany during the Third Reich under Hitler's rule.

The Quaker historian Larry Ingle describes in an article, "Living the Truth, Speaking to Power," how the 216 German Quakers coped with the Nazi domination of their country during the war years. For the most part it seems that they tried to live the peace testimony by engaging in service to Jews and German soldiers. At least one was sent to Buchenwald concentration camp for providing aid to Jews. However, another "embraced Nazism", because her inner light revealed to her that Hitler was a redemptive figure for the German people.

Ingle's article indicates that the primary lesson Quakers learned from the Holocaust is to "speak truth to power". This phrase, which has become a motto of Leftie-Progressive types, was first used, according to Ingle, in a Quaker pamphlet published by American Friends Service Committee in 1955.

Like many of the members of Indy First Friends, I'm sure I would have joined the fight to stop Nazism and Japanese Imperialism in World War II. I agonized over whether I could request "conscientious objector" status when I registered for the Draft near the end of the war in Viet Nam. I concluded that I could not, because I didn't oppose all wars (as my Mennonite neighbors did), although I was opposed to that particular war. I think the Quakers have it fundamentally right. The response to the abuse of power is to confront it; peacefully when possible, but to allow the individual conscience to choose when responding with force may be the best of only bad options. No matter that Hitler has a spark of God in him. Rational people take protective measures against natural disasters. So we ought also to protect ourselves and others from the violence of criminals and tyrants. Indeed, we need to speak truth to power. Sometimes, valuing Peace might require Quakers to do more than just speak truth to power.

- Integrity

Connecticut's statement on Integrity connects the spiritual, psychological, and behavioral: "Let your life speak: your outer life reflects your inner life. Nurture each student's inner moral compass, cultivating inner motivation not driven by externals such as grades. Treat others with respect and honesty. Set a tone of high expectations of students' work and behavior, guiding students in the process of self-assessment. Acknowledge interconnectedness and essential oneness."

Note how the author moves through the different realms of human being, from the inner spirit to psychological concerns to behavior to the effects of behavior (e.g., grades on school report cards). Integrity requires alignment of the inner with the outer person. Striving to live with Integrity on each of these inner and outer levels requires respect for the self and respectful relations with others.

San Francisco has a more straight forward take on Integrity. It begins with an admonition from the Gospel of Mathew reiterated in the Epistle of James, "Let your yea be yea and your nay be nay." The rest of the statement equates integrity to being honest with yourself and others:

"At the foundation of Quaker behavior is the belief that your words should match your deeds and your deeds should be an honest reflection of your words. In dealings with others, Quakers affirm to tell the truth and speak the truth with kindness and respect. Having integrity also means being true to oneself -- having one's outer self be the same as one's inner self ... At San Francisco Friends School, students are challenged to live with integrity in two ways: within themselves and within our community. We ask each child to look within him or herself to understand his or her emotional, intellectual, spiritual, and physical dimensions. Then we ask them to be true to their classmates and their community, to speak the truth when necessary, and to do the right thing even when no one is looking."

Here again, the understanding is that the inner and outer selves must be integrated and not alienated or in conflict. In order to have Integrity within the community, the student must follow the Socratic way of coming to know the self in one's own "emotional, intellectual, spiritual, and physical dimensions". The self-realized person is better able to become the self-actualized person. To be truthful with others requires being honest with yourself about yourself. It requires a deep understanding of your motivations and how you affect yourself and others with what you say and how you act.

Both Friends schools reject the adage that, "Sticks and stones can break my bones, but words can never hurt me." Words can wound deeply. Dishonesty hurts the inner self (unless you are a sociopath or narcissist). When mean and nasty words or gossipy lies are aimed at a target, everyone involved is reduced.

To guide ourselves by the value of Integrity, honesty is usually the best way to engage with others. But we've already agreed there are occasions when a truth might cause harm and the cost of remaining silent is minimal. Remember our encounter with Mean Girl Sherry at the Class Reunion; we decided silence about her weight gain was golden (maintaining the balance of our golden mean required that we keep our trap shut). And there's the ethical dilemma posed in Philosophy 101 Class about the man with a gun at the door demanding to know whether your friend Joe is inside. Students almost always decide against telling the truth. So, absolutely always telling the truth is not the way to live by the value of Integrity. That is the way to become an anally constricted dick.

Medical ethics require physicians to disclose their diagnosis and prognosis to patients. But we can imagine a situation in which a Doc might phrase a prognosis in more optimistic terms because she knows hope might improve her patient's chances of recovery. A number of studies have shown that stress can weaken the immune system and that a positive-optimistic attitude can help speed recovery from illness and injuries. So, isn't a physician doing the right thing by putting a positive spin on a prognosis to help the patient maintain an optimistic outlook?

Every one of us has or will face grey areas in life, when we have to balance strict honesty with the harm/help it might cause. The Quaker solution is always to lean toward truth-telling. But, if you have engaged in authentic soul searching and conclude that silence or a "white lie" is the most beneficial response to the situation, all other relevant values considered, then you are still guiding your life with Integrity.

- Community
Connecticut's statement about the value of Community

expresses the understanding that psychologically healthy individuals are necessary for a community to be vibrant and thriving. The school recognizes the challenge of balancing the individual's needs for receiving from the community with the community's need that each member gives to the community by active participation. "Be our authentic selves. Create a safe, nurturing atmosphere in which children can share all sides of themselves, such as asking questions or making mistakes. Balance needs of the individual with needs of the group."

If popular television shows tell us something about the concerns of our contemporary culture, a major threat (that's an understatement) is near apocalyptic annihilation of community followed by anarchy. The September 1, 2014 issue of *Time Magazine* listed nine "post-apocalypse" themed TV shows in "The Culture" column. I've seen episodes of a few of the shows on the list, *The Walking Dead, Falling Skies*, and *The Last Ship*. One of the points made in the *Time* article is that the fear of being wiped out by nukes subsided after the end of the Cold War, but it's rising again. If not nuclear warheads, maybe an Ebola-type plague, zombies, or even the Rapture. Each of these nine shows is set in a world where there are survivors, but community has broken down and trusting other people is both dangerous and necessary. A major challenge of the survivors is how to create pockets of decent livable environments in a world that's fallen apart.

One tool Connecticut recommends to build Community is, "Gather in silent meeting for worship and listen to other people's thoughts without judgment or comment." When we open our own inner selves, our inner spirit, we are most vulnerable. We are also most open to truly hear and accept others. This inner/outer emphasis of the Quaker value system reflects a yearning not to be in isolation but to live engaged within community. It's a bit paradoxical, but Quakers find the communal connection is made most poignantly by sitting in silence with each other.

Think about that! If you can sit comfortably in silence beside another person, you and that person have to trust each other. If only one person at-a-time can break the silence with speech, there must be trust within the community that anyone who does so will be heard. It's a very pragmatic psychological and spiritual way to build community – creating a sense of shared security by being together in respectful silence.

Unprogrammed worship might not save the world from nuclear annihilation, zombies, or any other impending apocalypse. What will? It's a damn good tool for building trust within a community. It would be interesting to see what would happen if Congressional Democrats and Republicans engaged in regular unprogrammed worship.

It's also an antidote to the degeneration of Community from living too much of our lives on-line. Yes I agree that the Internet is wonderful and it's opened up new ways to connect with others. The danger is that we spend too much time on-line rather than in-line-of-sight with other folks. We can get everything from the weather in Nigeria to the latest research on Drosophila (fruit flies; okay it's a weird example, but a college roommate was fascinated with experiments on them) through a smart phone. Kids don't need to ask parents or go to the library with friends; everything they need to know is right there in the magic of their handheld device. It's marvelous, but care need be taken that we don't lose our direct human connection with family and friends.

If we learn how to participate positively in community, affirmation ripples out through multiple levels of communal relationships from immediate family to the international community of humankind. When you're riding public transportation, a subway coach or metro bus, don't you generally try to avoid eye contact with other passengers? There is the random crazy person or threatening gangsta dude that might try to terrorize or intimidate. But most of us generally try to engage with other riders as little as possible.

Have you ever had the delightful experience of making eye contact with a stranger on a bus, plane, or train, who returns an open and genuinely friendly look? Has it led to an enjoyable conversation, and maybe even an exchange of contact information? It's not a common experience, at least for me, but when it happens, it radically changes the qualitative feel of travel. The experience is transformed from being something to bear, to just live through it, into a memorable shared event neither of you want to end.

When you walk away from that little jewel of sharing with a stranger, your step has a bounce to it. You're attitude toward the community of humankind is improved. It affirms your value of Community.

"San Francisco Friends School strives to build community at every level in a series of concentric circles: in the classroom; in the school as a whole; among the families; in our neighborhood and city; and as world citizens. Students engage with their 'buddies' in various grades, engage with adults at school through classroom extensions, and engage with neighborhood members through community projects. Family events are designed with community-building at their heart, inviting all to join in the warmth of fellowship, the comfort of inclusion, and the dialogue of kindness."

Kids growing up in this environment are likely to become the person you meet on a bus in a foreign country that you have such an engaging conversation you end it with the exchange of email addresses and the promise to stay in touch.

I like the image of a series of concentric circles representing levels of community. We do feel more bonded to immediate family than to friends and more bonded to neighborhood than to the city/town and more to our state and nation than to worldwide humanity. We are more likely willing to sacrifice ourselves for family than for friends/neighborhood than for city/town than for state/nation than for generalized humanity. There is a diminishing feeling of care and concern as we move from one circle to the next. But even at the outer circle, humankind, decent people do feel some level of bonding.

If your ship sank and you washed up on a deserted island with a stranger, wouldn't you try to bond with him? Even though the stranger appeared to be very different from you, you would surely try to form a partnership rather than live in complete isolation or try to partner with a creature of a different species? (No jokes, please, about Hoosier farm boys and sheep.) We are related by genetic origin to all other humans that have ever existed. We are all members of the family of humanity. In our shrinking world it's critical to the future of our family, the nuclear one and the worldwide one, that we are committed to strengthening communal bonds at each level.

Decent-loving parents do not reject their children because the kids develop different religious or political views. We don't cut off a sister from our affection because she moves away and lives in another state or country. Neither do we reject a family member (anymore) because she marries a person of another faith, race, or political party. So why do so many of us want to break, or refuse to recognize, the family bond of humanity just because people look different or disagree with us about religion or politics?

For sure the feeling of connection with all other humans is more tenuous than at the closer levels of the circles of community, but it's just as real. We need to value Community at each level, because our own safety and security depends on others valuing it. The first time I visited Basa village, although its residents are about as different from me as any group of people on Earth, I felt safe, secure, and welcome. And, I was warmly welcomed the first time I visited Indy First Friends. The members of these communities value Community and express it at each level of the concentric circles of human relationships.

We can't avoid participating in the global society. Even

as remote as Basa village is, it is increasingly connected with "outsiders". We are all family, like it or not. We might avoid the apocalypse if we stop behaving like a dysfunctional family.

- Equality

The San Francisco School's statement about Equality begins, "In contemporary terms, equality brings to mind equal rights and social justice. For Quakers, the notion of equality begins with the belief that everyone is equal in the eyes of God and that every individual has access to their own equally valuable inner Light. In the early days of Quakerism, Friends acted on this belief in several ways ... equally valuing men and women in worship; opposing slave-owning ..."

The School's statement reminds students that Quakers were historical leaders of the anti-slavery and suffragist movements. The Colony of Pennsylvania, founded and governed by Quakers, in 1758 became the first colony in the British Empire to outlaw the slave trade within its borders. The London Yearly Meeting publicly denounced the institution of slavery in 1761. A long and hard political fight followed. Great Britain finally outlawed the slave trade in 1807 and in 1838 prohibited it throughout the British Empire. The fight lasted much longer and was much bloodier in the United States of America.

The Indiana and Ohio branches of the Underground Railroad were established by a Quaker named Levi Coffin. As a child living in North Carolina Levi helped a runaway slave escape. After his family moved north he started recruiting Quakers and other abolitionist sympathizers into an organization which became the Underground Railroad lines through Ohio and Indiana. "Passengers" were sheltered illegally in Quaker households until the outbreak of the Civil War ended the risk of the forced return of slaves to their Southern masters.

Although Quakers were leaders in the abolitionist movement, not all Friends in the South supported emancipation. Friends in the North divided over whether to fight for the Union. Many were committed pacifists. Many others joined up and put their lives on the line to fight for the final abolition of "the evil institution".

The 1956 movie *Friendly Persuasion*, starring Gary Cooper, Dorothy McGuire, and Anthony Perkins, is based on the novel (with the same title) of Quaker author Jessamyn West. It's a moving representation of the division within Quaker meetings and families over whether to fight for the Union or take a pacifist stand. Eliza (Dorothy McGuire) summarizes the argument for pacifism in trying to persuade her teenage son Joshua (Anthony Perkins) against joining the fight: "I cannot kill one man to set another man free."

Joshua was close friends with a black farm hand, Enoch (Joel Fluellen). Josh wanted to express his value of Equality for African Americans by helping to fight for their freedom. But he also valued Peace. At first, Josh agreed with his mother's argument. The scale was equally balanced between the two competing values. When their town in Southern Indiana was attacked by Morgan's Raiders, Josh decided he had to fight. The value of Community tipped the balance.

After emancipation occurred and the Civil War ended, how to welcome (or not welcome) the people who had been unwillingly transported from Africa to America as slaves into community was left to the discernment of each individual Quaker. Some Friends meetings were more welcoming than others. Recognizing the "inner light" in those who are different from us should work like a magnet pulling us to lean toward supporting a welcoming community. Unfortunately, the magnet doesn't exert its pull on everyone.

Long-time members of Indy First Friends have told me that an African-American woman's request to join the Meeting was denied. A few members considered her a trouble-making agitator during the early years of the civil rights movement.

Because consensus is required, the majority of members who wanted to welcome her were stymied by the stiff-necked few.

Although there was not uniform support for equality of treatment of African-Americans, many Quakers were out front on the issue as they were on women's rights. Some early English Quakers tried to follow a rule of gender separate but equal in worship and management of their meetings. The separate services for men were similar to those for women. Exceptionally unusual for seventeenth century Christians, women led the service for women. Governance of the meetings was also divided in ways that were intended to equalize authority of men and women. For example, some English meetings gave women control over approval/disapproval of marriages and men authority over the budget. Eventually it was recognized that separate was not truly equal and gender-separate meetings ended.

Female Quaker pastors were common among the earliest gender-integrated meetings in the 17th Century. This was a time when it was anathema throughout most of Christendom for a woman to enter a church with her head uncovered and certainly never to speak or be heard. Samuel Johnson's quip about women preachers was recorded by James Boswell after Johnson heard a female Quaker preaching: "Sir, a woman's preaching is like a dog walking on his hind legs. It is not done well; but you are surprised to find it done at all." Strange as it was for the times, Quaker women did it.

The Women's Rights Convention held in Seneca Falls, New York in 1848 is considered by historians to be the commencement of the women's liberation movement in the US. Four of the five organizers of the convention were Quaker women. The suffragist leaders agreed to employ tactics learned from the abolitionist movement and made parallel moral arguments. Black men are human beings and so are women. We should all have equal protection under the law.

The men governing the country disagreed. They were willing to free the slaves and even give African-American men the vote, but not women.

In 1916 Alice Paul led protests demanding the vote for women. She picketed Woodrow Wilson's White House with other Quaker suffragists. The protesters were called the "silent sentinels" because they stood stock still with their signs and placards. Ms. Paul was eventually arrested on charges of "obstructing traffic". She was sentenced to time in the Occoquan Workhouse in Virginia. Not one to suffer (I was about to write "in silence", but as a Quaker, she probably did) without drawing attention to a cause, Alice went on a hunger strike to protest the miserable conditions of the workhouse. In retaliation the prison authorities committed her to the psychiatric ward and force fed her. (Imagine that! Less than one hundred years ago, the government treated suffragists the way the government now treats prisoners at Gitmo.)

Reporters in the news media of her day were fascinated by Alice Paul's stoic courage and commitment to the suffragist cause. She was good copy and press coverage finally forced President Wilson's hand. He came out in support of full enfranchisement of women. The Nineteenth Amendment was passed by Congress in 1919 and ratified by the States in 1920.

The San Francisco School completes its statement on Equality with a Query: "How do I speak up when I see someone being treated poorly?" The answer to that question should not be an intellectual abstraction. For the last 350 years Quakers have been in the vanguard of answering that question with actions. Some Christian denominations accept injustice as the status quo, and are unwilling to challenge conventions, because they value order and their privileged position within the established order. Quakers should rightly take pride in the historical and present willingness of so many Friends to walk the talk and push back against the powerful for fair and equal treatment for all people – to speak truth to power.

The Connecticut Friends School approaches Equality from a different angle. It presents a list of "politically correct" challenges.
"Respect different people and different ideas.
Encourage families of diverse race, socioeconomic status, family structure, and faith backgrounds to apply.
Honor all faiths.
Do not try to convert students to Quakerism.
Celebrate a rich community made up of many cultures.
Invite members of various nationalities to share their stories in the classroom.
Reflect a broad, inclusive spectrum of the global family."

I don't mean to disparage the sentiments expressed by calling them (tongue firmly in cheek) "politically correct". Valuing diversity and inclusion in community are critical ways of being guided by the value of Equality. The trumpeting of "diversity and inclusion" by "Progressive-Liberals" as the end all and be all can get a bit tiresome. But openness to others who are different from the majority and welcoming people of different faiths, race, ethnicity, culture, and sexual orientation is necessary to create effectively functioning communities in a melting pot society. People of similar backgrounds can cluster together into communities. But dealing with people of widely diverse demographic characteristics is an unavoidable aspect of urban life in the modern world. (Remember the point made by the Pragmatist Philosophers that the US could no longer be dominated by white Anglo-Saxon Protestants, and that the nation's demographic diversity had to be taken into account in developing solutions to national issues.)

Countries like South Sudan, Syria, and Iraq are wracked with civil war and threatened with national disintegration. Whether the geographic area of these nations should have been cobbled together by colonial powers into nations is a valid question. But, it is what it is.

Since the fall of Saddam Hussein in Iraq, some community leaders and outside instigators with ulterior motives have sought to create division among Sunnis, Shiites, and Kurds rather than unity. If the endgame of the insurrectionist and separatists is a more stable, secure, and peaceful existence for the people of Iraq, then more power to them. But it's quite clear that the leaders of ISIS, and other Jihadis, despise diversity and fear an inclusive community.

The Jihadist hatred of "the other" is a perfect example of being guided by negative values. They value strict orthodoxy in religion and are intolerant of difference. The effects on others of their negative values are murder, bloody chaos, and a form of Islamic rule which suppresses dissent and criminalizes creative self-expression by women and young people. The goal is similar to that of Nazism; purify the State by driving out or killing those who are impure in race, faith, or sexual orientation.

The Quaker answer to the voices of intolerance and hatred is to respect others as equal in value no matter that they are different from us or do not agree with our beliefs or even with our values. Friends respect the basic humanity of all others because of the tradition of "seeing the light of God" in every living person. Every human being, no matter that he might be a murderous Jihadist, has value.

So Quakers risk life and limb in conflict zones within Central America, Africa, and Palestine administering schools, medical clinics, and offering conflict resolution services and training. An off-shoot of the American Friends Service Committee (AFSC) even went so far as to violate federal law during the Viet Nam War to send humanitarian aid to the North. At the same time, a Quaker couple, David and Mary Stickney, at great personal risk, operated a medical clinic in South Viet Nam which specialized in making prosthetic limbs for war victims.

So long as there is a minimum level of mutual respect within a community (or between nations), people can find ways to get along. The AFSC sends its members to dangerous places offering to teach conflicting parties how to mediate disputes. One of the first lessons of conflict resolution is to value Equality by respecting differences rather than abhorring them. Next, while we recognize that we have disagreements, compromises can be negotiated among equals, and then we can live together in community despite our differences and disagreements.

Valuing Equality is also a way to join the battle against the rampant narcissism afflicting contemporary life. The front line of the battle, some would argue, is the selfie-taking youth culture. Students that learn to treat others with respect also learn that their trivial whims of the moment are not the most important thing in the world. You can't be a narcissist if you've developed empathy for those less fortunate than you and you understand that there are human realities other than your own.

I was disappointed to learn that at the last gathering of Western Yearly Meeting (of which Indy First Friends is a member) representatives of "conservative-evangelical meetings" were pressing an "anti-gay agenda". Their goal was to issue a directive that local meetings within Western Yearly Meeting should not perform same-sex weddings or record (ordain) gay pastors. I was happy to learn that the First Friends representatives opposed the initiative. (These reports reaffirmed my view that religious organizations above the local parish are usually more trouble than they are worth. Religious hierarchies tend to attract the ambitious and zealous; a wicked combination. These organizations are too prone to give in to the temptation to impose from above rules, directives, or doctrines on local congregations.)

History shows that valuing Equality doesn't always lead Quakers to the same place at the same time. It baffles me, however, that a Friend, or any fully conscious adult living in our Internet-connected world, can fail to recognize that discrimination against people for their sexual orientation is contrary to being guided by the value of Equality. No matter that I might find someone's sexual preference icky or disturbing, because it's different from mine. Gays and lesbians are my equal and my brothers and sisters in the family of humanity.

Justification for denying gay people the full rights and privileges of membership in the religious organization of their choice relies on particular passages in ancient sacred-texts like *Leviticus*. Being guided by a belief in the absolute truth of *Leviticus* is a classic example of how religious doctrines divide us and supports bigotry against those labeled "unclean ".

Leviticus condemns eating fat, touching the carcass of an unclean animal, letting your hair become unkempt, tearing your clothes, mixing fabrics in clothing, trimming your beard, cutting your hair at the sides, not standing in the presence of the elderly, and selling land permanently, as well as a man having sex with another man and about seventy other acts. (It doesn't condemn lesbianism; probably an indication that the pious old farts that wrote *Leviticus* got off on lesbian sex.) What would you guess is the likelihood that those who support anti-LGBT measures haven't ever eaten fat, cut their sideburns, or torn their clothes? I think their Lord and Savior would chastise these Christians for the hypocrisy of picking and choosing among Bible verses to support their own prejudices.

The principle of Equality under the law and equitable economic opportunities applies to everyone, not just to those whose beliefs, race, gender, and sexual orientation we approve of.

- Stewardship

The San Francisco School opens its statement on Stewardship with a quote attributed to Chief Seattle of the Suquamish people: "All things are connected. We did not weave the web of life. We are but a strand in it. Whatever befalls the earth befalls the people of the earth." (Snopes.com reports that an American screenwriter actually wrote this speech.) The school ends its statement with this Query: "How can we maintain in ourselves and encourage in others a responsibility for the natural world based on a reverence for life and a sense of splendor of our surroundings?"

The author of the school's statement on Stewardship, and other new agey romantic-environmentalists, look back wistfully on the way of life of Native Americans. According to tree hugger history, European-Americans despoiled the paradise in which the "Indians" lived. Native Americans were in tune with Nature. White people are an invasive species which has been destroying Nature by treating it as matter for consumption, rather than a living thing with soul. And, this view is pretty much right on. But--

The US has produced great and sensitive advocates for Nature, like Henry David Thoreau, John Muir, Rachel Carson, and Bill McKibben. A national awareness of the necessity of caring for the environment has been growing since Lady Bird Johnson's anti-litter campaign of the 1960s. From Teddy Roosevelt to Barack Obama US presidents have considered National Parks an administrative priority and have expanded protected wilderness areas. The understanding that humans have a duty to care for Nature and not just exploit it is spreading around the world.

A country as poor as Nepal has made great strides in the twenty years I've been visiting regularly. Rangers at the mountain parks now require trekking and mountaineering groups, when they exit the parks, to bring out kilograms of trash commensurate with the number of members in the group. Local people are paid for the trash they collect within the parks. The media has made a big deal about the trashing of Mt. Everest, but it's actually less littered now than ten years ago. The government began fining mountaineering companies that fail to carry their oxygen tanks and other waste off the mountain. (They haven't yet calculated the appropriate amount of fine for leaving behind the body of a climber.)

The Scottish town planner and social activist Patrick Geddes introduced the concept of "think globally, act locally" in his 1915 book *Cities in Evolution*. The phrase has been co-opted and used tritely in commercial advertising campaigns. But, that it has so penetrated popular consciousness also indicates the wide acceptance of the concept. The realization is growing that humans have a responsibility that begins in our own homes and neighborhoods and extends to the outer atmosphere and beyond. So, we start with using more energy efficient lighting, better insulation, and lower water usage in our homes. Our commitment to stewardship of the Earth ripples outward to our friends, neighbors, and the next generation. Pressure will build on governments to create international coalitions to form more agreements like the Montreal Protocol. That agreement created the framework to reduce the use of Chlorofluorocarbons (Freon) in order to protect the Ozone layer in the stratosphere.

But now for the "on the other hand". The quality of air in Nepal's capitol Katmandu has declined appallingly since my first breath of it in 1995. There are no pollution controls on motor vehicles. There is an ineffective and corrupt metropolitan garbage disposal system. Piles of garbage are often noticeable on back streets. There is a huge dump on the east outskirt of Katmandu. Instead of a landfill, it's just a mounting heap of trash. In a few decades it might rival Mt. Everest.

Katmandu is typical of "third world" under-developed cities. What are they to do? Their populations don't have enough food to eat. Pollution controls and garbage disposal are understandably not at the top of society's and the government's "to do" list.

The US is hardly a beacon of environmental enlightenment. Polls have indicated half our citizens do not believe climate change is a reality. Not sure what those folks think is happening to all the carbon material fouling the air, lakes, oceans, and ground. Oh yeah, the trees turn it back into oxygen. Except we've decimated forests around the world, and there aren't too many trees growing on the bottom of lakes and oceans.

The US refuses to sign the United Nation's Kyoto Protocols. One of our excuses is that China and India are fast on the way to surpassing us as the world's biggest polluters, and Kyoto is not as strict on developing nations as the developed nations. Duh! They want to be like us! How are the Chinese and Indians going to drive Cadillacs and live in McMansions, if they don't have their own industrial revolutions? It would be great if they could develop their industrial and consumer economies without using fossil fuels and with strict air and water pollution controls, but it ain't gonna happen. While we've successfully cut back on the rate of air and water pollution in the US, and we've cleaned up dead rivers (those old enough will remember the Cuyahoga River catching on fire in 1969, because it had such a massive oil slick), we're still doing it, just at a slower pace. We haven't even shut down our coal-fired electricity-generating plants for gods' sake!

Scientists and engineers in the developed nations have created numerous neutral, or at least less polluting than fossil fuels, energy sources. More are in the pipeline. But the transition away from fossil fuels is a slow and painful one. Jobs are lost when traditional fuels, like coal and oil, are phased out. Just when it looked like the market would help push us into alternatives to oil, because worldwide reserves were dwindling and the price was rising, shale oil was discovered and fracking developed. The "new oil" discovered in North Dakota has turned that desolate State into the fastest growing of our fifty with the boomingest (yes, damn it spell-check, boomingest is a word at least in North Dakota) economy.

Who among our courageous politicians has the balls to propose laws and regulations that will cost jobs and slow economic growth just to save some trees? So, kick the can down the road and let the Millennials deal with it when they take over. We've got big enough problems making sure there are enough workers paying into Social Security and Medicare to take care of us Baby Boomers in our dotage.

Here's a portion of the Connecticut Friends School's statement on Stewardship: "Protect and care for the Earth in a sacred trust. Walk lightly on the Earth, recycle and reuse whenever possible, and reduce the amount of energy we consume. Promote environmental, economic, and social sustainability." Yup!

We will never again live as the Lakota Sioux did or as life in Basa village still is. We are not going to throw history into reverse and live without twenty-first century comforts made possible by wood and plastic products and fossil fuels. Let's just hope that enough of us consumers, and enough governments and industries, try to live by the value of Stewardship these Friends schools recommend -- before we turn our planet into a burned out husk. The Connecticut School urges us to, "Begin in the youngest classroom to instill a sense of social responsibility and service work..." Right on!

Chapter 26: Finite

"At the heart of a Friends school education are the Quaker values, or 'testimonies', of Simplicity, Peace, Integrity, Community, Equality and Stewardship. From the daily interactions in our classrooms to our long-term partnerships with the neighborhood to our deep connections among our families, we strive to live out these testimonies as best we can. While **few of our families or staff are practicing Quakers** (emphasis added), we collectively commit ourselves to these values, each bringing our own perspective and experience."

That's the introductory paragraph of the San Francisco Friends School's statement on Quaker Values. I boldfaced the phrase indicating most of the people involved with the school are not Quakers, because it's noteworthy. These Friends are not evangelical in the sense of trying to convert others to Christianity or to join the Society of Friends. They are evangelical about promoting Quaker values. This same enlightened form of evangelism is one of the aspects of Indy First Friends which appealed to me. I need to participate in a worshipful community which does not judge people to be unworthy, because of their beliefs, lack thereof, or race, gender, sexual orientation, or any other difference. I am glad to have found a worship community which cares about values and doesn't care about doctrines and ideologies.

Living without beliefs sometimes feels like existing in a world of very intelligent zombies. Most everyone I know, including members of First Friends and Basa village, hold beliefs which color their understanding of reality. My Christian evangelical, liberal Christian, conservative Republican, progressive Democrat, etc., friends see the world through the lenses of their beliefs. My ideological friends are highly intelligent and high functioning. Yet, despite that many have higher IQs than mine, they fail to comprehend that their engagement with reality, and especially their ability to understand others, is impaired because of their beliefs.

Why do we choose to limit ourselves by circumscribing our reality with the doctrines and ideologies of labels like conservative-Republican- evangelical or liberal-Democratic-progressive? The Church, the Government, and the News Media have lost credibility because those controlling these powerful institutions use these sorts of labels to divide and conquer us. How can we make pragmatic progress to solve the problems of our community, nation, and world, if people who have disagreements can't engage in peaceful rational dialogue?

Have you ever heard somebody, or yourself, say about someone who holds contrary beliefs, "I just can't understand why he believes … (such and such)?" The inability to understand another's belief is likely due to holding a contrary belief. If you are not wedded to political or religious doctrines, you are not surprised that someone holds such and such a belief, because no belief system makes complete sense. The conceptual framework of every doctrine and ideology falls short of comprehending the capacious complexities of human being and the space-time continuum in which we exist.

Believers walk around with a model in their heads of how the world is. Their ability to perceive and respond to others and the natural world is biased by how they believe the world and people are supposed to be. They can't just take us as they find us. Living in a world mostly populated by believers can feel lonely and dangerous for us unbelievers.

The great nineteenth century German philosopher Georg Wilhelm Friedrich Hegel claimed that human consciousness evolves in stages. According to Hegel, the collective consciousness of societies advances in progressive leaps. An example: For millennia slavery was the norm in societies around the world. And then in the 19th Century, one country after another outlawed it because human consciousness had evolved to find slavery unacceptable.

Another: Most countries were ruled by hereditary kings and people accepted that kings ruled by "divine right" until more and more people began to value democracy. Monarchies with actual authority largely disappeared by the middle of the 20th Century. Women have been subservient in most cultures, but no longer (with some exceptions like fundamentalist Muslim countries). That homosexuality should be treated as a private matter rather than subject to criminal prosecution is another evolutionary change in social consciousness. Who knows; by the end of this century maybe we will evolve beyond beliefs into an age of value-based consciousness.

It's comforting to know that there are other skeptical agnostics out there. But we need not incite persecution by pointing fingers, lecturing, hectoring, and trying to throw the orthodox ideologues out of the temple or forum. We can reasonably and diplomatically advocate for living a value-based life. No need to alienate believers, especially ones that are tolerant of other beliefs. We can ally ourselves with believers in our communities who endorse using positive values as the way to move the community into a sustainable future. We need not advocate revolution but the evolution of a world less divided and more united -- a world with more SPICES.

"Finite" means limited, there is an ending. For you who have taken this journey with me, the finite hope we end this anti-sermon with is: Figure out what you truly value for yourself, the community, the nation, and world. Live in mindful consciousness of the values you choose. You're not alone.

Your friend, Jeff Rasley

If you enjoyed this book, please consider other books by Jeff Rasley such as

- *Bringing Progress to Paradise: What I Got From Giving to a Village in Nepal*
- *False Prophet, a Legal Thriller*
- *Islands in My Dreams, a Memoir*
- *Pilgrimage: Sturgis to Wounded Knee and Back Home Again, a Memoir*
- *Monsters of the Midway 1969; Sex, Drugs, Rock 'n' Roll, Viet Nam, Civil Rights, and Football*
- *Light in the Mountains -- Namaste, Rakshi, and Electricity in a Himalayan Village*
- *India - Nepal Himalayas in the Moment*

www.ingramcontent.com/pod-product-compliance
Lightning Source LLC
LaVergne TN
LVHW051623080426
835511LV00016B/2139